f **P**

RENEWABLE ADVANTAGE

CRAFTING STRATEGY THROUGH ECONOMIC TIME

JEFFREY R. WILLIAMS

THE FREE PRESS

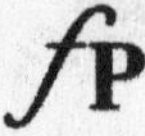

THE FREE PRESS
A Division of Simon & Schuster Inc.
1230 Avenue of the Americas
New York, NY 10020

Designed by MM Design 2000 Inc.

Manufactured in the United States of America

10 9 8 7 6 5 4 3 2 1

Library of Congress Cataloging-in-Publication Data

Williams, Jeffrey R.
Renewable advantage : crafting strategy through economic time / Jeffrey R. Williams.
p. cm.
Includes bibliographical references and index.
ISBN 13: 978-1-4165-5123-2 ISBN 10: 1-4165-5123-9
1. Time management. I. Title.
HD69. T54W5437 1998
650.1—dc21 98-11721
CIP

This book is dedicated with love to

Mom and Dad,

my history

To Rebecca,

in dynamic alignment

And to Benjamin and Stephanie,

our renewal

CONTENTS

PREFACE

This book is about crafting strategy in the new economy. There are new business creatures that behave differently from what our experience has prepared us for. Yet there are older business creatures that have changed relatively little. This work explains how these new creatures are evolving alongside their traditional counterparts. This book is for you if you want to understand whether your business model is changing.

Markets have become unpredictable. The rapid pace of technologies, deregulation, and globalization is changing the business landscape. Airlines, telecommunications, computers, entertainment, health care, industries that have grown up with the information age, are encouraging managers to redefine markets and their responsibilities. Still, other markets remain less touched by change, with companies operating along more or less traditional lines.

How do you know where you belong? Or where you are heading?

This study is based on renewal patterns observed in forty-five industries.[1] This book describes how companies succeed and fail, differently, in different markets. The study, grounded at the business unit level, spans manufacturing, service, high technology, and property-rights industries, and extends across the spectrum of business competition. We obtained evidence by examining companies for similarities and differences in patterns of growth, decline, and rebirth. The effort was guided by economic and organizational theory. Our findings were supplemented by discussions with managers and industry analysts.

Our work showed that managers can strategize renewal in terms of a concept we call *economic time*. As we came to see it, economic time distinguishes companies from one another by their opportunities for growth. It traces the history of the origin of the business. It predicts the means by which advantage evolves through the mechanisms of value creation that are distinctive for each company. In economic time, companies exist for customers. But also, customers exist for companies. Each gains meaning through the reciprocal demands put on it by the other.

The transforming feature of economic time is innovation followed by imitation. Managers pursue advantage through their own inventions or by rendering obsolete another company's innovations. Through this process, innovation has brought about what fifty years ago the economist Joseph Schumpeter predicted would become the "gale of creative destruction."

You seek and gain advantage. Value flows for a time. But then that advantage is lost and must be renewed again. Even managers in the most powerful companies find that success is temporary. Obsolescence is inevitable. Nothing lasts forever.

We will show the differences in thinking and actions that arise from moving away from traditional practice, with its emphasis on the status quo, and toward economic time, with its emphasis on competitive flows, value creation, and renewal. When you accept the fact that nothing lasts forever you expand your styles of management, your opportunities, and your responsibilities consistent with the dynamic forces at work in the new economy.

This work uncovers an order in complex, changing markets. Industries that appear unstable do, in fact, have dynamic patterns, while others that appear stable may be ripe for framebreaking change. The unifying theme is the perspective of economic time, that is, knowledge of the laws of competitive evolution.

Chapter 1 stresses the advent of economic time. This is the transforming insight that business time moves at different speeds. The growth engine of every organization has its distinguishing competitive mechanics, and its own dynamic signature that tells how value for it is created, how products age, and how advantage is potentially renewed. In the multispeed markets of the new economy, renewal comes about through convergence, alignment, and renewal. These laws make the idea that "nothing lasts forever" universal to management.

Chapter 2 reviews a style of management that is a close cousin to the traditional model, what we call scale orchestration. In standard-cycle markets, economies of scale are important, but equally important is sustaining harmony among product and process innovation and organizational learning. This balanced style of management is focused on no surprises, and zero-defects repeatability over high volume to sustain differentiated cost leadership.

Chapter 3 is about fast-cycle markets, where product half-life is short and where product managers "eat their children" to survive. The nontraditional success factors of these markets are highlighted along with some new strategies and capabilities best suited for these creatively destructive markets.

Chapter 4 completes the introduction to economic time through the viewpoint of slow-cycle, artisan-like markets. Here, advantage is like a mighty fortress, stable, long-lived, and enduring. Some slow-cycle markets can tip all the way toward one company, providing near-market ownership. The naturally arising growth constraints of these markets can be overcome through what we illustrate as staircase strategies.

Chapter 5 details the three business laws, convergence, alignment, and renewal, that we developed to understand how economic time works. The law of convergence is that nothing lasts forever. The law of alignment says that companies and customers depend on each other. The law of renewal is that 70 percent of economic value does not come from what you do today; it comes from investor guesses of what you will be capable of doing in the future.

Chapter 6 shows how to continually refocus your strategy onto what investors care about: the long-term creation of value. We suggest a few simple ideas that can move you away from an overemphasis on the short term and toward what investors—and ultimately tomorrow's customers—care about the most.

Chapter 7 is about management in multiple economic time. When customers want products and services that require a mix of possibly contrary management styles, special efforts are required to coordinate research and development, operations, marketing, pricing, distribution, and service. The basic but complicated question we respond to is, "How diverse can my business become and remain effective?"

Chapter 8 goes into managing cycle shifts in economic time. This happens when the rules of the game change so much or so fast that they demand radical changes in historical styles of management. Based on our research, we provide early warning signs as to whether your business is shifting in economic time and how to rethink your basic business model.

Chapter 9 explores the origin of renewal—innovation. We look at the different styles of innovation as they operate in economic time. But we also look at styles of innovation that are universal, applying across all cycles of economic time. This chapter has a special section on a topic of individual importance—your own, personal renewal. We suggest how you can manage your career by the same laws of renewal that apply to business.

Chapter 10 ties together our findings on economic time by summarizing the key findings of the book as a checklist for managers. We conclude with what we came to think of as the seven steps to renewable leadership.

Note that the term "renew" is used where the more traditional term "sustain" might be used. Our purpose is to emphasize that no advantage is sustainable forever. Note also that examples are denoted at the point in time that they occur, consistent with our theme that market opportunities are in a continual state of change. Throughout this shifting constellation of opportunities our goal is to show that markets can remain understandable and, most of all, manageable.

Throughout, the designation "we" is used instead of "I." Although this work has a single author, its insights have come from joint efforts among managers, students, and scholars of a similar persuasion, who see strategy as responsible for an organization's birth, inevitable obsolescence, and potential rebirth. Many of these people, notwithstanding my efforts to acknowledge them, are not mentioned in the text or in the endnotes. I trust they know who they are and that they keep my good wishes for them close as they take our message of renewal forward. I want you to know that I consider myself fortunate to share in your thinking and experiences. You are our new business leaders.

ACKNOWLEDGMENTS

Books of this kind trace their origins to the work of others. Prominent among these are the influential writings of David Aaker, Brian Arthur, Joe Bower, Robert Burgelman, Glenn Carroll, Alfred Rappaport, and Igor Scitovsky. Their work sees strategy as the search for value in increasingly complex, dynamic markets.

Work with managers provided fertile ground to test these ideas. Companies that have been influential in this regard, and that have been shaped in return, are IBM, National Semiconductor, Mellon Bank, Goodyear, Holiday Corporation, Bosch GmbH, AT&T, Bell Labs, Lockheed Martin, and Bristol-Myers Squibb. Our special thanks go to their managers who showed that the ideas in this book work.

I am thankful to David Rogers, Elizabeth Bailey, and Richard Cyert. They provided enthusiasm and support early on. There is a special and unique place in my professional experience for these extraordinary individuals. Each has been teacher, counselor, and mentor. I am thankful to Bob Kaplan and Douglas Dunn, deans of the Carnegie-Mellon University Graduate Business School, for the confidence they showed toward me, and for supporting the development of these ideas in the school's strategy courses and executive education programs.

The ideas of economic time have benefited from a strong tradition of inquiry at Carnegie-Mellon University. Although I cannot possibly thank them all, some of the outstanding students of economic time have been Gerald Abernathy, John Addis, Homura Akbari, Christine Antonio, Zilvinas Bareisis, Nancy Belz, Jennifer Binder, Ellen Bishop, Remis Bistrickas, Jason Connell, Ramkumar Dixit, Mason Douglas, Phreda Devereaux, Selim Ergoz, William Estright, Mark Friedman, Onur Genç, Craig Graham, Thomas Grimm, David Hauge, Kurt Hollasch, Jennifer Kane, Patrick Kane, Phillip Kendall, Sylvia King, Lewis Kuo, Leonard Loranger, Thornton May, Carl Trakofler, Suzanne McGann, Austin Miller, Hillol Nandi, Jeffrey Nourie, Sean O'Malley, Takashi Omote, Scott Park, Jeff Puzas, Rakesh Ramde, Jeff Repas, Perry Rice, Aurobind Satpathy, Barry

Schaeffer, Abhijeet Singh, Joe Soriano, Hsing Chuan Su, Marshall Thomas, Robert Tse, Bob Wagoner, John Walker, and Sidney Wu. Through a strong interest in the dynamics of the new economy, these individuals benefited from and contributed to the ideas of renewable advantage.

Gezinus Hidding has been a collaborator in this undertaking from the onset. His belief in the value of economic time helped sustain my enthusiasm for the work and aided me in dealing with the array of issues that came up during the research. His experience with decision making and knowledge engineering while at Andersen Consulting encouraged me to map out the initial logic of economic time. Using statistical tests, Gezinus went on to show that the methods of economic time are statistically more actionable than traditional strategy methods. My special thanks go to Bill Thomas who over the years has been my editor for the many early drafts of this work. Time and again, he edited draft after draft, providing suggestions for enhancing the readability of the book and its appeal to practicing managers. Bill's skillful editing clarified my rhetoric, minimized the jargon, and put a sharper edge on the story of economic time. Ultimately, Bob Wallace of The Free Press made the commitment to me and this work that insured its publication.

Michael Spence first motivated my thinking as to what might happen to markets when they showed different rates of learning. David Teece has written eloquently of the need to move theory and practice toward a dynamic perspective, beyond the view of the company as a black box. David's influential work includes a belief in path dependencies, appropriability regimes, and complementary assets, all central to economic time. Richard Rumelt's work prompted me to include a central term throughout this book, that of isolating mechanisms, whereby advantage is understood in terms of its ability to slow down imitation. Above all, these individuals inspired me in the development of economic time.

Think of economic time as an operating system for strategy. It is a dynamic, open system. Through it you can keep the best of your strategy thinking while upgrading your knowledge as your needs change. It is easy to adopt. It is intuitive. It is systematic. It encourages creativity. It is low risk. You can use or discard whatever part of it you wish. As we go to press we have begun work on *Renewable Advantage 2.0,* which we anticipate will have enhanced usability and more applications, consistent with the changing markets in which managers operate.

CHAPTER 1

THE ADVENT OF ECONOMIC TIME

The central idea of this book is economic time.

When we think of the effects of time on a business, we imagine that markets are speeding up and that advantage is short-lived. But business time is becoming more complex than that. Time is not what you think.

The significance of time in business goes beyond the reality that markets and companies are moving faster. There is a more interesting force at work. Business time is not only speeding up—business time is splitting markets apart, as well as the companies that compete in them.

Do we really think dynamically? Most of us don't. We are conditioned from birth to regard change with caution, even as we grow and explore the world around us. When we ask managers whether they think dynamically, we hear answers that range from a confident "of course we do!" to a perplexed "what do you mean?" Ask yourself these basic questions:

- What makes you special, different from all of your competitors?
- What is your organization ultimately capable of when stretched? What will you never be able to do, no matter how hard you try?
- What role is left for your corporate headquarters? Or should you leave your diverse businesses alone to run themselves?[1]

As simple as these questions are, they get at the heart of modern business problems. The business opportunities in the new economy are complex and dynamic. Some are different. Other time-honored rules remain little changed. Facing this complexity, failure to equip yourself to think in terms of multispeed competition—what we call *economic time*—can reduce your effectiveness to that of a horse and buggy driver facing the onset of the automobile.

But how can time move at different speeds for companies? Of course, real time cannot. Each second marks the passage of linear time along precise, equally paced intervals that have changed little over the centuries. But in the new economy, the speed and means by which advantage grows and declines are becoming increasingly diverse. This is why business leaders in the new economy need to be able to manage across different business models with the agility of a decathlon athlete.

A company that operates in fast economic time is Compaq Computer. In the personal computer hardware industry, product advantage is slippery. Compaq's ProLinea line must be replenished with new products every three to six months to sustain advantage. A delay of thirty days in a pricing decision can have ruinous effects. One decision by Compaq to reduce prices was matched by a competitor and implemented through distributors nationwide in forty-eight hours. Dell, Packard Bell, and IBM can react to Compaq's strategic moves almost daily.

But is Compaq's fast-time orientation right for you? Consider Merck, the U.S. pharmaceuticals giant whose origins date to a seventeenth century German apothecary. One Merck product, the anticholesterol drug Mevacor, took three decades to bring to market, a development schedule that would be preposterous for Compaq. But Mevacor, with a product life of a decade or more, is effectively shielded from the ravages of economic time. First-mover advantage is inherently sustainable. Business advantage is sticky. The Merck organization, even as its managers work to renew advantage, travels over its business terrain in slow economic time.

Compaq—fast time. Merck—slow time. Traditional, single-speed business thinking is not equipped to capitalize on these differences. Why not? Companies like Compaq and Merck are well managed. Additionally, traditional thinking about industry rivalry, while important, does not provide the answer. The reason is that traditional business thinking treats change as *unusual* rather than as *normal*.

The pathway to renewing advantage for Compaq is like a high-speed raceway, filled with vehicles that enter fast but burn out quickly. No single product, no matter how successful, sustains its advantage for long. Sony's portable electronics business is similar to Compaq's. Sony managers have been required to introduce hundreds of Walkman variations to renew the Sony Walkman brand. Managers at fashion companies like Liz Claiborne and Benetton, and Wall Street securities innovators like Salomon Brothers, face the same high speed of product growth, quick competitive entry, and fast product decline.

For managers at Merck, in contrast, the competitive cycles by which one product displaces another are drawn out, over a decade or more. One product in five thousand makes it through the barriers of clinical development, testing, and approval. Pharmaceutical companies find it difficult and time consuming to displace one another. For Merck, the pathway to competitive renewal is like a rugged trail through a thick forest, narrow and tough to traverse.

Consider the evolution of Merck's Mevacor. Marketing efforts for Mevacor began eight years before commercialization with the process of educating physicians. For four years during Merck's long, winding regulatory process, development was slowed because of a rumor, proven false, that competitors were having side-effect problems with a similar drug. As Mevacor neared FDA approval, 120 regulatory specialists at Merck met six thousand individual target dates by dividing each task into small responsibilities. Merck's research laboratory took a delegation of fifty employees to Washington for a last run-through, supported by a van loaded with 104 volumes of documentation, each 400 pages long. When FDA approval for Mevacor was granted, the company's reaction was "like when your team wins the World Series," according to one Merck manager. Six years later Mevacor's revenue passed $1 billion and continued to grow with little competition.

In today's fast-paced markets is Merck's product sustainability an exception? The world's most studied company at the onset of the new economy is Microsoft, a company that wrote the book on how to build long-lived advantage in the software industry. Or consider Disney Corporation: Disney managers recently issued one-hundred-year bonds, a reflection of the expected duration of Disney assets such as *The Lion King*, the first cartoon to gross $1 billion in revenues and related sales worldwide. Thirty years from now, when our grandchildren are bored on a rainy day and sit to watch high-definition television on flat-screen displays the size of a wall, they will watch the same *Lion King* movie that we have seen, and they will pay Disney for the privilege. With products like Mevacor, Windows95, and *The Lion King*, managers at Merck, Microsoft, and Disney are creating long-lived advantages.

Consider: Does the three-billion-dollar Space Shuttle use higher technology than a three-dollar electronic wristwatch? In terms of newness, a throwaway wristwatch made from parts designed recently, scores higher. IBM designed the shuttle's on-board computers in the 1970s. Twenty-five years later, NASA managers upgraded to Intel 386-based computers, machines that had been commercially obsolete for a decade. The shuttle's ceramic tiles are fitted by hand, one after another. Processes used to make the Space Shuttle recall styles of management used to craft fine furniture for European royalty centuries ago.

Compaq, Sony, and Intel operating in one part of economic time; Merck, Disney, and NASA operating in another part of economic time. The styles of leadership in these companies are being pulled apart as they shape the new economy. Yet, at a time when multispeed business opportunities are unprecedented, management ideas remain grounded in the modern-day equivalent of the Iron Age: freeze-frame thinking that treats change as temporary rather than the rule.

As the director of a major electronics company put it to us, "It's not that things are moving faster. We know that they are. But for us some things remain stable. We have a whole constellation of stuff swirling around us with rules that we do not understand. Our challenge is to know constancy from change and to manage across both."

WHAT IS ECONOMIC TIME?

Although markets operate at different rates of competitive speed, you can't see this by looking at whether people in these companies run faster or slower to the coffee machine or whether they work longer or shorter hours. While these differences are real, traditional ideas about speed don't tell us enough about the economy's expanding competitive styles.

The growth engine of every company has distinguishing competitive mechanics, its own dynamic signature that gives clues as to how value for it is created, destroyed, and potentially renewed. The reality is that customers *don't* come first—neither do companies. Each gains its meaning from its relationship with the other. Through economic time we see the dynamic forces rooted in these processes of value creation: how managers perceive environmental threats, learn and meet customer needs, and react to one another.[2]

In physical systems there is a law: For every action there is an equal but opposite reaction. In a like manner, laws of action and reaction shape company growth and rebirth. In fighter pilot competition there is the OODA loop. This stands for observe, orient, decide, and act. Rivals observe an action of strategic significance, orient themselves to it, decide what action should be taken, and finally act.[3]

At first glance, action-reaction cycles seem similar to product life cycles, which measure the rise and fall of a product's revenues. But action-reaction cycles go deeper, down to a company's growth engine, the underlying processes that create, sustain, and renew value. Action-reaction cycles, from initial information gathering to the final actions taken, dictate the management styles and organizational processes needed to serve customers. They also provide clues about the various options available for dealing with suppliers and competitors. Action-reaction cycles align a company dynamically with the key success factors in its markets.

Action-reaction cycles can differ greatly among companies, even when companies make similar products. Microsoft and Netscape provide an example. Microsoft brings out new versions of its popular Web browser software, Explorer, at a fast pace. So does Netscape, which pioneered the Internet browser software called Navigator. Yet, how economic time operates within Microsoft and Netscape is different. Advantage for Explorer is sticky. Like Merck, Microsoft operates in slow competitive time. For Netscape, however, economic time moves fast, like that of Compaq Computer. We don't see this by looking at product life cycles.

No single approach captures all of the forces at work in a market. An economic time zone is a segment of a market where the styles of management needed to renew advantage are similar. Within an economic time zone, managers learn customer needs, see threats, build control systems, and leverage capabilities with similar competitive logic. Economic time zones are the dynamic analogy to the traditional idea of strategic groups, regions of a market where competitors behave similarly toward each other. In similar economic time the growth engines of companies have similar dynamic mechanics at work to sustain growth.

Consider how things work in real time. If you were in Eastern Standard Time and tried to operate on European Standard Time, you would be out of sync with the activities taking place in your region. The clocks in your multispeed company would be mismatched with one another. Your activities would proceed at the wrong pace or be out of sync with one another for creating value. So it is for managers operating in different zones of economic time.

Another way to think about economic time is that it keeps everything from having the same time dependency; it creates priorities. It predicts how your actions are likely to produce moves and countermoves by competitors, where you are strongest in terms of your growth opportunities, and where you are most vulnerable. Economic time identifies customers that are important to you in the long run and which competitors pose the greatest threat to you over time.

It can be risky to ignore the multiple forces of economic time. Most value-creating relationships that companies have with their suppliers, customers, and competitors are grounded, in some way, somewhere, in economic time. As one CEO put it, "We had to find out how economic time operated for us . . . or we would have found out later the hard way."

HOW DO I KNOW WHERE I AM IN ECONOMIC TIME?

We conducted a ten-year study of birth, decline, and renewal in forty-five industries. The companies spanned a range of industries, including service, manufacturing, high technology, and knowledge-based markets. A range of dynamic forces were catalogued and compared, from markets where economic time moves slowly to markets where economic time moves quickly. The study was guided by insights from economic and organizational theory. The findings were supplemented by discussions with managers and industry analysts.

Dynamic groupings became apparent. Some companies, such as Microsoft, Disney, and Merck, block competition through barriers, or as Richard Rumelt puts it, strong *isolating mechanisms*.[4] These are based on one-of-a-kind advantages such as geography, copyrights, patents, or ownership of an information resource. At the opposite end of the spectrum of economic time, companies such as Compaq, Sony, and Benetton rely on new ideas, novelty, and innovation, products that are quickly copied. In the middle, between the extremes of fast- and slow-cycle markets, we find traditional, economies-of-scale-driven companies. With no preexisting method to account for dynamic diversity, we classified these competitive patterns into three broad groupings of economic time; slow-cycle, standard-cycle, and fast-cycle.

Slow-Cycle Economic Time. Companies operating in this first renewal class, like Microsoft with its Windows operating system, pursue renewal opportunities that are shielded from traditional competitive pressures. The key to renewal lies in gaining an advantage that is proprietary, slowly changing, and essential to the functioning of a market.

As a unique point of supply and demand, slow-cycle renewal efforts more or less automatically resist competitors' attempts to duplicate them. Product advantage is secured within the company and confined to it. Competitors cannot effectively gain a foothold with the company's customers, even where they find the company's advantage attractive.

As we will see, slow-cycle markets can be subject to a competitive effect we call *tipping,* whereby a market flips all the way toward dominance by one competitor. These winner-take-all markets are the focus of some of the economy's most profitable companies. In contrast to the idea that markets are becoming unstable, slow-cycle companies like Merck, Microsoft, and Disney, through the use of staircase strategies, gain enduring advantage.

Standard-Cycle Economic Time. Companies in this second renewal class are found midway on the spectrum of economic time. They are typically mass-market companies, market share oriented, and process focused. What distinguishes their success is their ability to replicate the same usage experience for customers with no surprises. Standard-cycle management styles are a descendant of traditional business thinking.

Toyota, McDonald's, and IKEA routinely make large investments, yet their isolating mechanisms are less effective than those of companies in slower-cycle economic time. To see why renewal pressures can be greater for companies that are viewed traditionally as dominant, we looked at these companies' internal processes, their investment patterns, and their management styles.

Standard-cycle companies are oriented toward serving large numbers of customers in competitive markets. Demand patterns are repetitive and relatively stable. Still, economic time moves faster for these companies because their capabilities are less specialized. Competitors have greater ability and incentive to duplicate them, improve upon them, or render them obsolete. In this way their isolating mechanisms are less powerful than those in slower-cycle time. Still, extended dominance is possible if a range of technical and organizational elements are harmonized with economies of scale. After careful study, we came to describe the management style needed to renew standard-cycle companies as one of scale orchestration.

Fast-Cycle Economic Time. The questions we asked over and over again in the study were these: Why are some products and services copied so quickly?

Why does first-mover status for some products and services, such as cellular phones and DRAM computer chips, yield such short-lived advantage? Companies producing these products, like Compaq, Motorola, Sony, and Toshiba, are well managed. Also, industry structure is not notably different from that of companies operating in slower economic time.

One clue to the dynamics of fast-cycle companies is that, once commercialized, fast-cycle products do not require complex organizations to support them. The Compaq ProLinea, for example, originated at a Comdex trade show in Las Vegas, only nine months before the ProLinea's launch. Two managers, sent from Compaq to check up on the competition, visited booths and talked with component vendors. They found that they could buy components on the open market faster and at lower prices than Compaq was getting through its purchasing department. By shopping around and asking questions, these two engineers were able to build a prototype ProLinea computer in their hotel room in three days.

Products like ProLinea have, at most, a few hundred parts, most of which can be easily purchased on the open market. Like most fast-cycle products, ProLinea is largely a nonproprietary collection of ideas, which can be readily pieced together by Compaq as well as by Compaq's rivals.

Ask yourself, "How is a 64-megabyte DRAM chip like a Cabbage Patch doll?" Remember the Cabbage Patch doll? It originally sold for $850. A few years later you could buy one at Kmart for $39.95. While worlds apart in technology and capital investment, their similarity is that DRAM chips and Cabbage Patch dolls both gain their value from their information content, which can be readily copied. Freestanding ideas are the engines of growth. With the forces of value creation and destruction operating at high speed, the pursuit of advantage takes place in its fastest, most unrestrained form. This is why managers find their journey in fast-cycle markets to be marked by a continuous gale of creative destruction, as the economist Joseph Schumpeter emphasized.[5]

How can you know where you are operating in economic time? Or whether economic time is changing for you? Or whether you are facing a two- or three-front market that demands a mix of management styles?

Begin by looking inward, to the mechanics of your company's past growth. If your products are like front-line troops, your internal core competencies or your capabilities provide your supporting logistics. But you should also understand the field of combat, or your market's critical suc-

Table 1.1. The Extent of Economic Time

MARKETS	STRATEGIES	CAPABILITIES
Fast cycle		
Schumpeterian: dynamic	Innovate and "eat your children"	Entrepreneurial, risk-seeking culture
Temporary scale economies	Ramp up—ramp down volume	Fast learning, fast forgetting
Gale of creative destruction	Access distribution quickly	Rapidly changing relationships
Dynamic and unstable barriers	Be disloyal to products	Capabilities renewed frequently
Competitors enter/exit at stage of market evolution	Reduce price rapidly	Precise timing, entry & exit
		Selection efficiency
Standard cycle		
Oligopolistic: extended rivalry	Gain and hold market share	No surprises, zero-defects culture
Scale-driven barriers to entry, mobility and exit	Standardize product & process	Command & control orientation
	Segment markets	Teamwork, improvement oriented
A few companies dominate	Emphasize brand loyalty	Process focused, mass market oriented
Competitors' segment based on cost and differentiation	Discipline competitors	Uniform systems & measures
	Price near costs to hold share	
Slow cycle		
Monopolistic: isolated rivalry	Embrace and extend market lock-in	Superstar, artisan-like culture
Non-scale barriers to entry	Pursue ownership of market factors	Specialization valued
High mobility barriers	Use staircase strategies	Scale economies limited
Market ownership common	Stable long-run pricing	Stable product support reqm'ts
Subject to tipping		Organization flexible, informal
Winner-take-all outcomes		Gardener-type leadership

cess factors, as well as the tactics and strategies available in each economic time zone. The spectrum of economic time is shown in Table 1.1.

The diversity of forces in this chart helps to understand contemporary business phenomena. Consider the Internet-based competition between Netscape's Navigator and Microsoft's Explorer. Both companies introduce improved Internet products at a fast pace to win customers. This is fast-paced competition, to be sure, but look deeper, in economic time. The reality is that fast-cycle competition is a fact of life only for Netscape. For Microsoft the competitive clock operates more slowly.

Netscape managers, capable and hardworking, have had little time to build what David Teece calls complementary assets.[6] Netscape's Navigator is based on extensions of the HTML programming language, a freely available standard in the industry. Netscape has no proprietary technology or other supporting strengths that can shield its products from fast imitation. Netscape has a lot at stake with each new product introduction. The pace of innovation must be fast and unceasing.

For Microsoft, Explorer is only one of many interconnected applications built upon extensions of Microsoft's original MS-DOS Windows operating system. The Windows95 growth engine, because it has created dynamic lock-in with customers, runs in slow-cycle economic time. Thus, Microsoft has competitive options not available to Netscape. At the same time, facing different renewal pathways, Netscape can do things that are difficult for Microsoft. Similar products—different competitive options.

In our work we developed what we call the *80% rule.* In this book you will be exposed to a range of economic time descriptors, factors that can help you to decide where you operate in economic time. Conservatively, each of these factors is accurate, that is, correctly distinguishes economic time, in about 85 percent of the cases. Thus, to know where you operate in economic time you will want to ask a number of questions about your business. Each can be thought of as offering a proposition, a hypothesis, about how your business renews itself. If three or four economic time descriptors point in the same direction, you can be relatively sure that you have correctly assessed how economic time operates for you.

In this regard, a useful way to begin a journey in economic time is to look at products in terms of their long-run pricing patterns. Pricing patterns across the economic time cycles are shown in Table 1.2.

The data in Table 1.2, drawn from a range of industries, show the range of dynamic pricing patterns possible in economic time. The stronger and

Table 1.2. Pricing in Economic Time

INDUSTRY	PERIOD	PRICE CHANGE (Ann. avg.)
Slow-cycle markets		
Hospital room per day	1987–97	+4.1%
College tuition	1987–97	+3.8%
Funeral expenses	1987–97	+3.7%
Medical care services	1987–97	+2.5%
Cable television	1987–97	+2.2%
Prescription drugs	1987–97	+1.9%
Movie admissions	1987–97	+0.7%
Standard-cycle markets		
Paper products	1985–95	+0.7%
Fresh whole chicken	1987–97	+0.5%
Beer	1987–97	–0.4%
Agricultural machinery	1985–95	–0.7%
Passenger cars	1987–97	–1.2%
Electric lamps	1987–97	–1.5%
Household refrigerators	1987–97	–1.9%
Power tools	1987–97	–2.2%
Fast-cycle markets		
Home electronic equipment	1987–97	–3.5%
Personal computers	1991–95	–4.3%
Microwave ovens	1982–89	–4.6%
Analog integrated circuits	1981–89	–4.8%
Digital PBXs	1985–89	–4.9%
Memory chips	1991–97	–7.0%
Antilock braking systems	1987–97	–8.6%
Electronic wristwatches (LED/LCD)	1973–83	–10.0%
Fully suspended bicycles	1992–93	–17.0%
Early personal computers	1980–83	–29.9%

more vigorous your company's isolating mechanisms are, the more prices stabilize or even rise. As the isolating power of your capabilities weakens, the amount of time that you have to recoup profits from innovation declines. Prices fall more rapidly. Product advantage becomes more temporary. Economic time speeds up.

In terms of theory, slow-cycle markets are a grouping of different types of mostly "natural" monopolistic advantages. Standard-cycle markets map most closely onto extended oligopolistic rivalry, or "life with the four-hundred-pound gorillas." Fast-cycle markets can be thought of as most like Schumpeterian competition, "the chase after the innovator." So in this sense economic time is a simple organizing device with which to compare a range of possible renewal opportunities and to know whether they are changing.

Renewal opportunities do not always fall neatly into one economic time zone or another. Within any company fine-grained patterns may be found and mixed economic time opportunities may arise. Success also results from the effects of industry structure, chance and uncertainty, and leadership. Any complete understanding of long-term renewal opportunities needs to account for these important forces as well. But before we lay out a framework for renewal through economic time, a little history.

THE LAWS OF RENEWAL

Evolution is central to our experience. We know this is true in physical systems, biology, chemistry, and human affairs. Although our lives center on the here and now, our experiences from the beginning have been defined by changing relationships. Death and rebirth are necessary to clear the way for newer forms. The temporary nature of things is also apparent in the birth, growth, and decline of organizations.

Still, over the past twenty-five years managers have operated by a different way of thinking: the idea that advantage, once achieved, is inherently sustainable. As success is gained, advantage is long-lived *unless* managers make mistakes. We refer to this collection of ideas as the traditional view of business. Many of us were taught that the drivers of success have more or less the same mechanics; achieve and maintain market share through economies of scale. Extended rivalry, as it is termed, has indeed played an essential role in business. Examples include the rivalry between General Motors and Ford in the 1970s, or Coke and Pepsi in the 1980s, to name but two.

Through the stake-and-hold perspective of traditional thinking the dynamic nature of your company and your markets can be difficult to see. You know that change is central to success and failure. Companies and their customers are temporary. Even where companies retain the same corporate name for decades, how managers operate within them changes so much that if company founders came back they would not recognize their organizations.

Traditional thinking reflects insufficient attention to what Joseph Schumpeter emphasized and what today's business leaders know. Change is central to economic progress. The progression of species, their life, death, and renewal, gives meaning to their existence. The old must be cleared away to create opportunities for the next generation. The evolutionary ecology of business, the competitive, dynamic interdependence of your organization and your customers, can be difficult to account for in traditional thinking.

Sometimes we criticize ourselves too much. As a manager put it, "It's not that our assumptions were wrong to begin with, which is what our people used to think of when they rejected past strategies. We thought, 'Well, we were wrong but now we've got it right.' As it turns out, we were right, but things changed. Our old ideas outlived their usefulness."

But we need to preserve traditional thinking. Traditional ideas provide insights into success in relatively stable mass markets like automobiles, fast food, distribution, and retailing. Comprehensive approaches to setting strategy in the new economy must preserve the best of traditional thinking.

A step in preserving the best of the past while moving toward the future is to think in terms of the laws of competitive evolution. In our studies of economic time we came to see three laws at work. We termed them *convergence, alignment,* and *renewal.* They are shown in Figure 1.1. Each plays a role in the dynamic process of creating and renewing advantage.

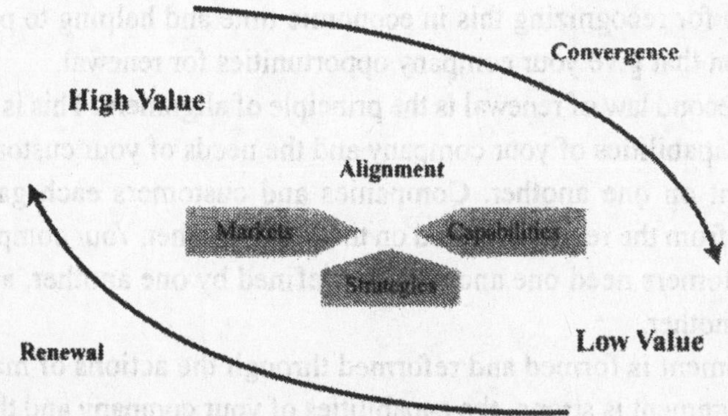

Figure 1.1. Laws of Competitive Renewal

The first law of competitive evolution is convergence. When you successfully innovate, profits follow. You operate high up the convergence curve. Then, just as surely, competitors offer newer products or improved products at lower costs. As your products move down the convergence curve, profits fall. Profits become low, zero, or even negative.

You can slow down convergence through isolating mechanisms but you cannot stop it. Convergence formalizes the idea of economic time that nothing lasts forever.

At the top of the convergence curve, the upper left-hand corner of Figure 1.1, are profitable, noncompetitive markets. When your products are located here, your profits are the highest possible. At the opposite end, the bottom of the convergence curve on the lower right-hand corner of the figure, are highly competitive markets. Here your products are indistinguishable from those of your competitors; you are forced to drop your prices down to the prices of the most efficient producer in the industry. If you and your competitors continue to attack each other at this point, you will move down the convergence curve to the point where all of you lose money on every product sold.

Profitability depends on how long you can hold off convergence, reverse it, and how well you can introduce products high up on the convergence curve. This, in turn, depends on how your core competencies operate in economic time, that is, how well they generate value and isolate your products from competitive imitation, substitutes, or obsolescence—what can be thought of as competitive displacement.

Each product has a position on the convergence line and a distinctive rate of movement. Products move inexorably, slowly or quickly, down the convergence curve toward competitive extinction. As a leader, you are responsible for recognizing this in economic time and helping to put plans into action that give your company opportunities for renewal.

The second law of renewal is the principle of alignment. This is the idea that the capabilities of your company and the needs of your customers are dependent on one another. Companies and customers each gain their meaning from the requests placed on them by the other. Your company and your customers need one another, are defined by one another, and exist for one another.

Alignment is formed and reformed through the actions of managers. When alignment is strong, the capabilities of your company and the needs of your customers are well matched. For any product's location on the convergence curve—anywhere from profitable to nonprofitable markets—the full amount of profits *possible* flow to your company.

Alignment is gained through business strategy, your pattern of day-to-day activities, the operating procedures by which your company maintains its relationships with its environment. Corporate pronouncements of strategy don't matter much in understanding alignment. What matters is how people in your company *actually behave,* toward suppliers, customers, and competitors, day after day.

The third law of competitive evolution is renewal. The purpose and responsibility of renewal is the recapitalization of aging assets. Renewal is required by the certain knowledge that what you are doing today, no matter how successful, will become obsolete. Renewal has as its goal the renaissance of your company, away from the slide toward competitive markets brought on by convergence. Renewal repositions aging products and introduces new products higher up on the convergence curve. Leadership is the process of giving your organization every opportunity for recapitalization to happen.

Renewal reflects how well a company's growth engine capitalizes the resources available to it and transforms its capabilities into value. As we will see, about 70 percent of the value of a typical company comes from renewal. Economic time orients managers to success drivers beyond the current period—how competitive progress will reshape advantage into the future.

MULTISPEED COMPETITION

Economic time can make sense of problems that in our day-to-day experiences we tend to see as unrelated. Sometimes these insights can be unexpected. Ask yourself if you know:

- When bigger is not better
- When faster is not better
- When it is better to say "no" to customers
- Why great ideas for good products fail
- When market share goals can destroy a company

Answers to questions like these help to uncover the leverage points in a business problem, where concentrated efforts lead to high payoffs. Economic time sets a balance in thinking about long term and short term. The main operating sequences, your company's central, value-added processes, are accented and compared to the short-term activities that consume your day-to-day energy. Thinking in terms of economic time puts the focus on the deeper patterns of behavior, the underlying forces central to organizational regeneration.

To understand what their companies can do, we encourage managers first to understand their company's growth history in terms of economic time. Look at how your company's growth engine has operated in the past. Confirm how you are similar or different from your competitors in terms of how you replicate your advantage. Distinguish a history of continuous change from framebreaking change.

Emulating the practices of another company, or adopting a new strategy without a grounding in economic time, can be like starting a game without being certain that you know what the rules are, whether the game is changing, or whether your company is likely to be good at it. In one Fortune 10 company that we worked with, this danger became apparent. On the surface of it, the problem was that company managers needed to understand the challenges brought on by the faster-moving markets into which their product was headed. But as discussions unfolded, a deeper problem surfaced. Company officers did not know how economic time had operated for them in the past.

As we discovered, hidden growth barriers were present deep within the company that would have remained undetected well into the process of commitment to the new strategy. A barrier to growth in economic time within the company's information systems could have driven the enterprise into bankruptcy. Eventually, it became clear that managers needed to reset their cultural clocks to a new management style. Before decisions could be made on what direction to take, managers needed to think through what kind of company they wanted to be.

Ask yourself: Do you think of your advantage as merely sustainable—or as dynamically *renewable?*

There are few free rides in economic time, few tricks or one-shot tactical maneuvers to create advantage. What you get is a dynamic road map among the outcomes that may be possible and indicators of which styles of management may be best for you. As the research illustrates, managing through economic time opens up new ways to get from here to there. Still, the question you will be left with is, "What kind of a company do I *want* to be?"

RECAP: ECONOMIC TIME

This book is about economic time, the emergence of multispeed competition. Managers sometimes think in static terms, as if management is the task of arranging elements of a still-life painting: the structural characteristics of an industry, relative company size, bargaining power, and entry barriers. Others interested in dynamic perspectives, such as learning, innovation, and technology diffusion, see all advantage as fleeting, as if all choices managers make operate on fast forward. The reality encompasses all of these views, is more complex, more interesting, and filled with opportunities.

The heart of economic time is the understanding that competitive forces drive the value of products down to zero at different rates of speed. The classification of markets by economic time refers to how quickly and by what means this happens. Rather than rely on one or a few drivers of competition, economic time compares a wide range of competitive options in terms of how aging advantage can be renewed.

Economic time is universal. All companies operate, somewhere, in economic time. Economic time provides a unifying business language for the multicycle manager, by which to compare the renewal opportunities of widely diverse different products, companies, and markets.

The key idea in economic time is to manage products and organizations by the speed and means by which economic value arises, decays, and is renewed. Economic time recasts the traditional idea of strategic groups into economic time zones, according to the strength of isolating mechanisms prevalent in each. Up to five economic time zones can be formed in any industry (slow, standard, fast cycle, shifting cycle, and mixed cycle) depending on the diversity and stability of isolating mechanisms at work.

The drivers of economic time are *isolating mechanisms,* features of a company's market or its capabilities that slow down convergence, or that delay product obsolescence. Another way to denote isolating mechanisms is to refer to a product's, an organization's, or a market's *cycle time drivers.*

The central measure of economic time is *product half-life,* the amount of time that passes (or, more precisely, would pass with no reinvestment) until the per-unit profit margin for a product drops to one half of its highest amount. Product half-life is related to a product's *profit cycle,* the amount of time that passes before a product ages to the point where attractive levels of profit are no longer possible. The aggregate profit cycle of a company or a market is the combination of all of its product profit cycles.

Economic time reflects three basic, universal laws of competition: (1) *Convergence* is the transforming assumption that nothing lasts forever, or that products become less profitable with the passage of time, absent reinvestment. The location of a company's products on the convergence curve accounts for current profits or 30 percent of its value. (2) *Alignment* reflects how a company maintains its relationships with its customers; it comprises short-run (reactive, fine-tuning) and long-run (proactive, framebreaking) strategies. and (3) *Renewal* refers to that part of a manager's job that is responsible for recapitalizing the company's aging assets, accounting for 70 percent of a typical company's value. The location of a company on the renewal curve is associated with the company's price/earnings ratio.

In our work with organizations we found that economic time can help to understand where hidden growth barriers may be present in otherwise well-conceived strategic plans: the relative importance of controlled growth, cost leadership, and speed-to-market objectives; the different long-term price pressures different products face; and when faster is better and when it is not. Economic time helps to forecast life-cycle manufacturing goals; to know the extent to which a manufacturing process will come under pressure to meet productivity and time-to-market objectives; to establish meaningful human resource policies; to determine product-specific success factors like quality and standardization; to compare different styles of management as to whether they work for or against each other; to match control systems with cultural norms; and to guide policies on innovation and, ultimately, personal renewal.

When the rules of the game are changing, economic time helps to define important aspects of new opportunities, new critical success factors, and whether an organization can stretch itself enough to succeed. The benefits of economic time come about through the transforming behavior that business is about managing the ebb and flow of events, where nothing lasts forever.

The ancient Greeks had a way of putting it: "I can only discover what I am when I know what is unlike me. When I look to what is fundamentally different from me, then I know who I am." We have found that a useful place to start your journey in economic time is to look at companies that were brought into being in traditional markets. These familiar markets and the companies that define them provide an important starting point. Through them we see how traditional markets are changing, what new opportunities their managers face, and how you can begin to ask yourself where you want to operate in economic time.

CHAPTER 2

THE SCALE ORCHESTRATORS

At the end of the Renaissance, industries were slow moving and isolated. Then came cultural and technological changes: the standardization of goods and services, an abundance of energy, and the development of mass communication. Thus, the distinctive feature of the industrial revolution was created: economies of scale. Traditional markets exist where production is standardized and demand is uniform and extended.

Traditional, oligopolistic rivalry is the most common, century-old form of organized, large-scale commerce. It is analogous to trench warfare where territory is staked out and defended for drawn-out periods. In the steel industry, when either Bethlehem Steel or U.S. Steel tried to gain market share by reducing prices, the other would follow with price cutting to defend its territory. As these markets evolve, they become concentrated around large companies. Smaller companies drop out, become merger candidates, or hide behind market niches.

Competitive momentum is gained gradually. Moves are painstakingly thought out in advance. Alignment is maintained through near-flawless, repetitive execution, day after day. Success is seen through "three yards and a cloud of dust." ATT Communications, MCI, and American Express are multibillion-dollar companies that "make it on thirty cents a transaction," as an industry observer put it to us.

Fast food provides an example. McDonald's founder Ray Kroc's strength was in the way he selected and motivated his managers, his franchisees, and his suppliers. He had a knack for bringing out the best in people and discovering what each could offer in concert with the efforts of others. The supply system for McDonald's was built by working with fledgling vendors of food and equipment who became as entrepreneurial and as loyal to McDonald's as did Kroc's franchisees. Eventually, 2,500 independent companies were molded into one family with a common purpose.

Traditional markets and the companies that comprise them continue to be central to the economy. We will look at Starbucks, UPS, Chrysler,

Southwest Airlines, and Andersen Consulting, close cousins to the traditional archetype. These retooled four-hundred-pound gorillas not only survived the economic strains of the late twentieth century; they emerged anew or became stronger. They evolved, from size for the sake of size, toward a management style that we see as like *scale orchestration*. Scale orchestration benefits from economies of scale, but requires organizational capabilities that go beyond size for the sake of size.

BEYOND SCALE TO SCALE ORCHESTRATION

Scale orchestration requires a dynamic balance of qualitative and quantitative elements. Consider a symphony orchestra in this regard. We know that each of the four sections of a symphony orchestra, the string, brass, percussion, and woodwind sections, are difficult to master individually. Yet world-class orchestras achieve world-class levels of excellence and balance across all sections simultaneously. Excellence is more than the sum of the parts. So it is with standard-cycle, scale-orchestrated companies.

Scale

When prohibition ended in America, the beer industry comprised some seven hundred plants owned by local, regional brewers. Primitive production technology, inefficient plants, and high transportation costs prevented breweries from producing beer in large amounts. Beer was expensive to ship relative to its value, which meant that competition and scale economies were limited to a geographic area.

Then pasteurization and heating methods and improved refrigeration facilities increased minimum efficient plant size. Plants grew from 1 million barrels per year in 1960, to 2 million barrels per year in 1970 and 4 million barrels per year in 1980. Larger plants allowed the cost per barrel for a 4.5 million barrel plant to decline to one-third that of a 1.5 million barrel plant. The Coors brewery in Golden, Colorado, the world's largest, is a mile long. Anheuser Busch's St. Louis facility fills two hundred rail cars of beer a day.

Size conveys bargaining power, which can be used to gain concessions from suppliers and customers. But related to scale economies, as in the case of Coors, is the idea that scale economies multiply when they are coordinated with the evolution of product design, process improvement, and organizational learning. This brings us to the rest of the scale orchestra.

Product Design

In 1903 United Parcel Service (originally the Seattle Company) began by providing private messenger and local delivery services, a thriving market at the turn of the century when the post office did not offer the parcel post system. As the popularity of the phone increased, the company switched to the use of motor vehicles to transport and deliver packages. Over time the package delivery industry became concentrated around three competitors, UPS, the U.S. Postal Service, and Federal Express. The Postal Service offered guaranteed nationwide service. UPS offered mid-range prices while operating efficient regional services. Federal Express offered premium pricing with fast, reliable service to high-density markets. As time went on, UPS became wedged between a high-priced air carrier and a low-priced ground carrier.

In response, UPS managers redesigned their product around a pricing strategy that incorporated distance in addition to weight, traditionally the sole pricing factor in the industry. The approach allowed UPS to offer 40 percent discounts on short-haul, ground-based truck deliveries between concentrated customer locations, primarily large cities and corporate facilities. The approach recognized that 70 percent of the company's city-to-city shipments traveled less than seven hundred miles.

This strategy could not be easily duplicated. The U.S. Postal Service was required to deliver to all locations. Federal Express's nationwide twenty-four-hour delivery system, based on its airplane fleet and hub in St. Louis, put Federal Express at a cost disadvantage in short-haul deliveries.

Many aspects of the UPS delivery process were orchestrated to reinforce the strategy. Local managers were allowed to reduce the frequency of deliveries to out-of-the-way addressees, effectively providing later delivery to these locations. Truck drivers were told to knock on doors where finding the doorbell could take a few extra seconds. This strategy was one of many successful product adaptations that would allow UPS to remain viable throughout the century.

Process Improvements

In the early days of McDonald's, Dick McDonald designed a portable stainless steel lazy Susan that could hold twenty-four hamburger buns. Ed

Toman, who later became the company's first design engineer, developed a hand-held stainless pump dispenser to automate the hamburger dressing process. The dispenser required one squeeze on a trigger to squirt the required amount of ketchup and mustard evenly on a bun. A variation of the device is still standard equipment in 18,000 McDonald'ses worldwide.

Gradually the fast-food process became refined. The kitchen crew became specialists. There were "grill men," who did nothing but grill hamburgers, "shake men," who made milk shakes, "fry men," who specialized in making French fries, "dressers," who dressed and wrapped the hamburgers, and "countermen," who did nothing but fill orders at the cash registers. Some McDonald's stores today use robots to make French fries and soft drinks. Designed by Coca-Cola engineers, the robots save ten seconds per customer, a useful improvement across a customer base of 20 million daily customers. McDonald's process skills are so highly respected that Ford sent thirty of its top managers to McDonald's to learn how to improve the manufacture of automobiles.

Organizational Learning

Early on, Andersen established its Center for Professional Education in St. Charles, Illinois. New hires sent to St. Charles undergo three-week training classes to learn the concepts of systems integration, computer programming, and software testing. Training is required regardless of rank. The annual training requirements for consultants are two hundred hours for staff and senior grade employees, one hundred hours for managers, and fifty hours for partners. Even the most experienced partners participate in training programs as instructors or students.

Andersen employees are taught the same, universal Andersen language. A common core curriculum ensures that a shared methodology and a uniform approach are brought to Andersen customers. The teaching of Andersen's common methodology, Method/1, allows new-hires from a variety of backgrounds to be brought up to speed quickly and efficiently. Andersen consultants gain access to intelligence obtained by other Andersen consultants through the company's Knowledge XChange information management system.

The Andersen motto is that it's not the people you hire that count—it's what you do with them that makes the difference. Training expenses at Andersen run about 7 percent of gross revenue ($300 million in 1997). This is unheard of in standard-cycle companies that are less successful than Andersen is. Andersen consultants are referred to in the industry as Andersen Androids, a respectful reference to the efficient, no-surprises organization that Andersen passes along to clients.

At Andersen Consulting, as well as Anheuser Busch, UPS, and McDonald's, actions taken in each section of the scale orchestra are coordinated with one another. In traditional thinking, scale economies are the primary source of success. In economic time, economies of scale are important, but the growth engine is powered by the orchestrated balance of product and process improvements, as well as organizational learning.[1]

A good example is automobiles. It used to be that if you achieved scale economies, then you became successful. Now the emphasis is: If you continually evolve your product designs along with changing customer needs, *and* continuously improve your processes, *and* drive continuous learning throughout your organization—*and* orchestrate these activities among one another—*then* you can achieve economies of scale.

Scale Orchestrator Starbucks

Making a cup of coffee is easy. But what about a distinctive cup of coffee, prepared at high volume with carefully crafted, luscious coffee variations, offering the same delicious taste anywhere in the country? On the surface, Starbucks' business model appears to reflect a simple, low-capital process. Yet consistent high-quality coffee is difficult to achieve, as any coffee drinker will attest. Starbucks, in a masterful display of scale orchestration, designed business processes that ensure an attractive, repeatable experience in the Starbucks taste, regardless of where in the Starbucks system the customer purchases coffee. No national brand coffeehouse has been able to duplicate Starbucks' high-volume, no-surprises, high-quality consistency.

When on a coffee-buying trip in Milan, Italy, Starbucks founder Howard Schultz saw that Italian coffee cafes offered more than coffee. They provided a rich atmosphere for social gathering. Schultz came to realize that the success of these cafes was not only about the taste of coffee but also the orchestration of a range of coffee experiences. Schultz opened his first Milanese-style cafe in Seattle in 1986. Using standardized but carefully orchestrated designs and processes, Starbucks grew to a thousand stores in a decade. Here is a look at Schultz's scale symphony.

Scale. Early on, Starbucks pursued a strategy to reach a growing number of customers: urban coffee bars, channel-kiosks within bookstores and other retail outlets, catalogues, and direct-response advertising. Between 1990 and 1994 the number of Starbucks coffee shops increased ten times. Sales grew to 2 million customers a week. Yet growth was planned by sequentially entering cities and conquering each market in depth. The power of Starbucks' volume-oriented strategy was confirmed by repeated success in markets that it entered.

Product Segmentation. Starbucks designed a coffee-drinking environment with relaxing lounge seating that was crafted for a social setting. Window seating was provided for customers who wanted a convenient place to have a pleasing coffee and pastry before hurrying on their way. The design of every Starbucks store provides relaxed sociability, no surprises, and efficiency on the run. Every aspect is crafted to draw the customer's appreciation toward the natural goodness of coffee and its aroma through an artistry that captures the customer's imagination.

The product line (thirty varieties of coffee beans, teas, pastries, syrups, preserves, packaged goods, and specialty merchandise) is chosen to reinforce the Starbucks mission statement: "back to nature without the laid-back attitude." The core of Starbucks' identity, the siren logo, steam pattern, logotype, graphic character, and organic, earthy colors, is expressed on all of the company's packaging, merchandise, and serving materials. Attention to detail extends from refining the look of a coffee cup down to the color of a pastry napkin.

Process Refinement. Starbucks' engineers designed the outside of Starbucks stores to complement the mood and architecture of each particular location. But inside, each site incorporated the company's key, identifiable elements: its color palette, choice of fine woodwork, sparkling glass displays, tile floors, and cheerful lighting. No matter how individual the store might appear, overall store image reinforced Starbucks' uniform semblance: the clean, unadulterated crispness of the Pacific Northwest combined with the urban suavity of an espresso bar in Milan.

Organizational Learning. Company employees are highly trained and motivated. Eleven thousand employees of Starbucks have been trained in the company's own version of Method/1, to envelop the customer in the company's knowledge of coffee history and preparation. Another benefit of training is that the turnover rate of counter help at Starbucks is lower than the food service industry average.

In July 1992, master orchestrator Schultz took his company public, offering 2.1 million shares at $17 apiece. His hope was to raise $35 million. Two quarters later Starbucks' market value passed $500 million.[2]

FINE TUNING YOUR ORCHESTRA

Orchestration of volume growth, product design, process improvements, and organizational learning is challenging, even for products seemingly as straightforward as a cup of coffee. The high-volume symphony of standard-cycle scale orchestrators can be strengthened by the considerations discussed next.

Build a No-Surprises Reputation

Learning takes place not only inside your organization but also on the part of your customers. As they use your products their familiarity with your company grows. They become more comfortable with the features of your products as they incorporate them in their day-to-day experiences. From an ecological or dependency perspective, standard-cycle companies move their customers down market learning processes that parallel the company's organizational learning processes.

The customer has come to distinguish Wal-Mart by its ability to provide a one-stop no-surprises shopping experience at the best overall value. Conventional supermarkets use special promotions as loss leaders to build traffic. Wal-Mart does not follow this strategy; instead it provides everyday low prices across a bundle of goods. This business model is not new. Its origins can be found in the history of retailers like Sears and Kmart. What is new is that the orchestration demands placed on large retailers and their suppliers have become more complex.

The Wal-Mart experience? Reliable, best selection, lowest overall price. The Wal-Mart renewal engine relies on demanding inventory controls, disciplined procurement procedures, strict attention to work force training and incentives, and carefully designed facilities, with these elements in continual, evolving balance with one another. Consistency is maintained across thousands of products, even as the mix changes through changes in suppliers, products, and customer shopping patterns. In this way, Wal-Mart does a better job of scale orchestrating through "three yards and a cloud of dust" than their competitors.

Companies like Wal-Mart learn to produce and deliver product experiences with zero defects as their customers learn that they want the same experiences, repeatedly, with no surprises. The result is a mutual interdependence between company and customer. One benefit of this interdependence, as we will see, is brand loyalty. Nurturing a no-surprises relationship between your company and your customers helps to isolate your products from the forces of convergence.

Product defects unbalance a scale orchestra. Recall the rumor about sudden acceleration in Audi's automobiles, which, though never proven, severely hurt Audi sales in the United States. Or recall the well-publicized outage in ATT Communication's Northeast system, which shut down all three New York airports. Two days later MCI ran an ad in *The Wall Street Journal* advising readers that they could now enter a five-digit access code to bypass "that now defect-prone, hallmark of reliability. . . ." Product surprises upset customers' expectations for repeatability of experience, disturb the customer learning process, and weaken company/customer alignment. Product surprises bump your organization and your customers off their interdependent learning processes.

Control Innovation

With a focus on flawless execution, how much opportunity is there in the scale orchestra for innovation? Let's return to our musical metaphor. In a real symphony orchestra, new music is carefully chosen and coordinated with the overall repertoire. New performers are introduced selectively. If any player gets out of step during a concert, because of poor training, not enough guidance, inexperience, or lack of control, it is obvious to the audience.

How do orchestras innovate? Step by step, carefully and deliberately. Decisions about new scores, new members, new instruments and techniques, and new conductors are made selectively, with an eye toward harmonizing what each member of the orchestra has to offer. Consider MCI's Friends & Family, the first branded product in telecommunications. On the surface of it, Friends & Family was a simple discount offer on long-distance phone calls. It featured a discount on frequently called numbers between any two callers who belonged to the MCI calling circle. But look closer and we see how innovation in the MCI scale symphony was accomplished.

To raise interest, MCI ran TV teaser commercials. These were followed a month later by TV, print, and billboard advertising, offering a toll-free number for customers with questions. As momentum for Friends & Family grew, responses came in from prospective customers, listing their calling circle friends. This provided large amounts of information that needed to be entered and organized within MCI's databases. MCI followed with a telemarketing campaign offering five free minutes of long-distance calling per nominee. A direct mail campaign followed two weeks later with a promotion giving customers the initial list of calling circle participants. Eight weeks later, a list was sent out to customers listing their new MCI calling circle family. Throughout the process, MCI employees were trained to insure a consistent, friendly exposure to the new product. A "simple" product like Friends & Family required coordinated planning and harmonized execution over a large, complex operational base.

This is why in the scale orchestra innovative ideas are often met with a volley of questions. Will innovation raise costs? Will it create inefficiencies or upset time-proven processes? What will innovation do to quality? To our training programs? To our supplier relationships? How will change affect customer expectations? These questions should not be seen as obstructive, but as an expression of the orchestration requirements that power standard-cycle organizations.

American International Group, a life insurance company, maintains special risk assessment criteria for new products. No matter how much in demand new insurance products or services are, managers will not introduce the product unless it passes the company's tests for consistency and quality. No-surprises life insurance? Yes. Customers are more interested in the long life of their insurance carrier's products and consistency of coverage than the ability of insurance carriers to innovate.

In a real orchestra, skilled musicians contribute their talents in ways that enhance and distinguish the whole organization. Each is a skilled individual. Learning is continuous, as the musicians seek to perfect their craft and extend their individual abilities. In this way, they bring out the best talents of each other. When it comes to performing, all operate in unison, at a carefully dictated pace, and by the same score. In scale orchestrated companies, empowerment means that people are allowed to make a mistake in order to learn, but they are not allowed to repeat it. They are encouraged to question a process with the goal of improvement in mind. But once the process is set, the window of experimentation narrows. In this way, controlled innovation represents a balance between the demands of customers for cost-effective, no-surprises experiences and the need to continually improve.

Balance between old and new defines the innovation symphony. Managers must be responsive to new opportunities, changes in customer tastes, and potential shifts in customer preferences, but they should balance these responses against the expectation for no surprises, both inside and outside the company. If renewal in standard-cycle markets proceeds through "three yards and a cloud of dust," then innovators in standard-cycle organizations are like football coaches who introduce new football plays carefully, while practicing for next week's game. And like innovative symphony conductors, innovative scale orchestrators rework their competitive score over time, to appeal to the gradually changing tastes of customers.

Say No to Customers

Can you have *bad* customers? While we don't normally think this way, customers can be wrong for you if they draw people in your organization away from their competitive score. Bad customers upset the task of crafting no-surprises dependencies between you and your customers.

Brand loyalty, for example, can be put at risk by setting customer expectations unrealistically high. The problem arises when high expectations created in one setting cannot be met in another setting. In the early 1980s, there was considerable variation among the properties that made up the Holiday Inn brand. A customer could go to one Holiday Inn franchise that was new and upscale; the experience was pleasant and reinforcing. But the customer could later stay at a Holiday facility that was old and poorly maintained. Variation in brand experience, rather than providing market coverage, confused customers, resulting in a fuzzy, weakened brand image.

In response, Holiday management imposed strict systems-wide standards on facilities design, training, and marketing. The company also spun off 300 downscale *and upscale* facilities. The result of a tightly controlled no-surprises approach to the brand? Within a few years occupancy levels in the remaining 1,400 Holiday Inns rose to the highest in the industry.

To be sure, customer expectations should be set as high as your organization can meet, repeatedly, across the whole enterprise. At Starbucks Coffee, customers who bring back purchased bags of coffee for any reason are cheerfully given another bag of coffee in exchange, no questions asked. Considering that a bag of Starbucks Coffee costs $10.00, this commitment to excellence requires confidence that expectations can be crafted carefully, controlled, and met, with no surprises throughout the organization.

Consider the idea of mass customization, the concept that through the use of information systems and computerized manufacturing, one-of-a-kind products can be made for mass markets. Customers get individualized products, tailored to their special requirements. Levi Strauss makes customized jeans for customers based on individual measurements. Health food retailers mix vitamins and health care supplements to the needs of individual customers. Bowling balls can be customized to fit customers' hands. These mass customization efforts are successful in part because they are relatively straightforward from an orchestration standpoint. But what about situations where orchestration needs are higher? We find that mass customization has limits.

It used to be possible to order any combination of options on automobiles. A manager at General Motors put it this way: "We made two million Chevrolets this year, and every one was different. It's easy to make one-of-a-kind cars when you have no competition." But automobile competition became more intense, and the 1990s saw a move away from variety. Toyota reduced the varieties of its Corolla model from eleven to six.[3] Mazda cut seventy-six variations of its 929-model car. Nissan announced a reduction in the number of types of engines by 40 percent. Kao, Japan's Procter & Gamble, announced that it was trimming its product line from 600 to 550. Lion, its main rival, announced plans to reduce its product lineup by 30 percent.

The limits to mass customization are not on the shop floor. Impressive advances have been made in the capability of organizations to customize products for customers and to make manufacturing dynamic.[4] But challenges remain in the processes outside of manufacturing, elsewhere in the scale symphony. As products become customized, inventory support requirements increase. Service and maintenance become more costly and time-consuming. Special training is required to handle the diversity of service calls. Distribution becomes more difficult to coordinate as combinations of replacement parts and subassemblies show more variety. Organizational learning slows, as knowledge gained from specialized experiences becomes difficult to codify and as learning from individual experiences becomes more difficult to relate to the larger processes.

A compromise between mass customization and one-size-fits-all is found in what we think of as *orchestrated variety.* In 1988, the average number of parts for a midsize GM car was 3,200. There were 1.9 million build combinations possible when all combinations of options were taken into account. Ten years later the average number of parts for a midsize car was reduced to 2,300 and the number of combinations was reduced to 1,000. An option package available on the Buick Skylark featured floor mats, air conditioning, and wheel covers. Another package offered leather seats and alloy wheels. But you could not get the wheel covers without buying the air conditioning and you could not get alloy wheels and air conditioning unless you bought both packages.

Good strategies determine what companies should *not* do. A good test of standard-cycle strategy is to find evidence that managers have established guidelines by which to say no to customers in a carefully orchestrated way. "We will not meet certain demands." Ask yourself: Are standards in place to turn down business that does not meet your company's renewal criteria?

Make Them Want It

Toyota, Wal-Mart, and McDonald's care deeply about what their customers want. Indeed, their market research and advertising budgets are among the highest of all companies. But none of these companies gives customers everything they ask for. Instead, they spend the bulk of their research dollars deciding what to give and what *not* to give customers. In this sense they are best at saying no to customers *while making them like it.*

Customer needs are not just "out there" waiting to be satisfied. While satisfying customer needs is important, this thinking assumes that customers already know what they want. Yet, in many of the world-class companies that we studied, we find that customer expectations are *created.*

Carnegie's steelmaking processes, Edison's light bulb, and Ford's Model T were products that customers did not know they needed until demand was created. Later examples from fast food (McDonald's), cellular phones (Motorola), and computer mainframes (IBM) show that brand loyalty, and indeed market demand, are the result of purposeful efforts on the part of managers to create demand that does not exist previously.

The classic story of the invention of the light bulb shows that, in addition to persevering in the face of ten thousand failures before his research team got it right (a carbon filament), Edison had to overcome strong customer beliefs that gas lanterns could not be improved upon. One approach Edison employed to shape customer expectations was to refer to his product as an "electric lantern," thereby evoking experiences that customers were familiar with. There are exceptions, of course, but few companies become great by giving customers everything they want. More often, master orchestrators renew their organizations by carefully estimating what the customer *may* want and then by *making them want it.*

Defend Your Brands

Brands have existed since the time of ancient Egypt. Brick makers placed symbols on their bricks so their products could be easily identified. Whiskey distillers of the sixteenth century burned their name on the top of each barrel so customers could distinguish their products from cheaper, lower quality alternatives. The beginnings of today's Ivory Soap, Vaseline, and Quaker Oats can be traced to the mid-1800s.

McDonald's with a media budget of $295 million in 1992 was the most advertised brand in the world and the fifth most widely recognized brand on the planet. Standard-cycle companies account for the largest advertising spenders. Famous brand names like McDonald's, Wal-Mart, IKEA, and Perdue Chicken are the result of purposeful efforts—indeed, long-term commitments—to create a specifically targeted need where none previously existed.

The implication is that brands are difficult to create, and once a brand has been created, it can be more effective to retain existing customers than to create new ones.

Renewal requires a willingness not to overreact to pressures to improve current profits at the expense of capitalized brand value. Also, it is important not to overreact to temporary downturns in a market by taking actions that accelerate the erosion of brands.

Brand loyalty is not easily quantified. This can make it difficult to measure the value of a brand or the payoff from reinvestment in a brand. For example, sales promotions and cost-cutting efforts have more impact on current profits than forward-oriented, brand-renewing activities. Similarly, coupon offerings and trade promotions, done in the interest of short-term revenues, can accelerate the transformation of brands into commodities.

Changes in retailing can put additional pressure on brands. Computers allow retailers to track the profitability of every square foot of retail space. The growth of chains and the use of scanner data help stores understand customers' preferences and purchasing patterns. This can tip the balance of power to retailers. Wal-Mart developed store brands Sam's Choice and

Great Value that increased sales by $1 billion. Some store brands have become as strong as national brands.

In spite of these pressures, brand expert David Aaker warns against the temptation to pursue new customers at the expense of existing customers.[5] Brands can be strengthened by approaches that include database marketing, as done by MCI in telecommunications, or involving customers directly in marketing, as Saturn did with its campaign to let customers nominate a marketing spokesman for the car line (often themselves). Frequent shopper programs reward consumers with credits for repeat purchases, such as done in the national airlines' frequent traveler programs. Similar programs have been initiated by AT&T and MCI in long distance.

Failure to support time-honored brands can accelerate market convergence. Unfortunately, because of the competitive momentum of standard-cycle markets, brand abandonment can be an expression of imbalance across the scale orchestra that can take years to detect and remedy.

Orchestrate Suppliers

McDonald's converted its distribution system into the model for the food processing business. It reduced its beef suppliers from 175 to five; these hamburger processing plants were the largest and most efficient in the meat processing business. The Simplot Company replaced independent companies that had provided fresh potatoes but often not the type or exact number that McDonald's ordered. Simplot's four potato processing plants dominated the North American French fry business, supplying 80 percent of McDonald's 9,000 U.S. stores. Traditional thinking might see the relationship between a large customer like McDonald's and a large supplier like Simplot as a competitive battle, based on which company had the greatest bargaining power to force concessions upon the other. In reality, many of the contracts between Simplot and McDonald's were based on a history of good will and a handshake.

Chrysler provides another example of how to bring suppliers into harmony with a scale orchestra. Chrysler gives suppliers responsibility for design and manufacture of prototypes, as well as for volume production of components. This contrasts with the industry practice of throwing a design at suppliers and selecting the lowest-cost bid. Chrysler's focus is on harmony and coordination throughout the design and manufacturing process. Suppliers that generate cost savings have a choice of keeping half of those savings, or of sharing them with the company, which boosts the supplier's performance qualification; this, in turn, helps a supplier gain future business.

One Chrysler component systems supplier, Magna, suggested 213 proposals for cost savings. Chrysler management selected 129 for cost savings of $75 million. Magna then gave the savings back to Chrysler. Magna's sales to Chrysler doubled to $1.45 billion. As of December 1995, Chrysler had implemented 5,300 supplier-based ideas that generated over $1.7 billion in savings for the company. Orchestration of buyers and suppliers is an enormous step beyond the win-lose attitudes that can dominate traditionally managed companies.[6]

Above All: Master the Balance

World-class symphony orchestras are known for specific strengths. The Philadelphia Orchestra under Eugene Ormandy excels at the Haydn, Mozart, and Mendelssohn repertoire. The Chicago Symphony, under Georg Solti, applies its exceptional brass and winds to Mahler, Wagner, and Richard Strauss. World-class scale orchestras excel in particular areas, but only if each of the supporting sections achieves a minimum level of competence.

Ford's renewal in the 1990s U.S. market was marked by solid product designs and the best assembly labor productivity of the Big Three. Yet Ford was not able to drive overall costs down as much as Chrysler did, as discussed above. Chrysler's product development costs, by then the lowest in the United States at $471 per vehicle, ran 56 percent of Ford's. Chrysler for its part, despite the best car designs in North America, was hindered by a perception of lower vehicle quality.

General Motors sought to improve its scale orchestra by investing tens of billions of dollars on industrial robots that had been observed in abundance in Japanese plants. The company did close outdated plants, but it did less to address its internal labor problems. The result of spending billions on automation but ignoring labor productivity? In ten years GM went from being the most cost-efficient American automaker to the least efficient producer. Lack of sufficient attention to product design and labor-management practices left GM in an unbalanced state.

In seeking to regain balance, GM entered into a joint venture with Toyota whereby each could benefit from the strengths of the other. Their Fremont, California plant allowed Toyota managers to see GM's state-of-the-art automation technology while GM managers learned about Toyota's labor management practices. GM also regained balance through the greater use of common systems and parts, fewer parts per subassembly, and by reducing process variation so that several models could be assembled more easily. These efforts required orchestration between previously autonomous plants. The improvements piggybacked on GM's scale advantages, but they required cooperation and coordination between GM groups that had operated autonomously. Several years later, three quarters as large as before, the revitalized GM had rebalanced their fifty-year bigger-is-better philosophy by putting scale orchestration before size alone.

DIFFERENTIATED COST LEADERSHIP

Traditionally there have been two primary ways to position products in markets dominated by economies of scale: through cost leadership or through differentiation. As Michael Porter has shown, cost leaders win through the ability to sell at lower prices, while differentiated producers gain from selling higher-priced products that customers perceive have additional value.[7] It can be difficult to excel at cost leadership and differentiation at the same time where the two efforts require opposing types of investments. Yet, in a dynamic sense, many of the benefits of scale orchestration come when cost leadership and differentiation are combined, a process that we see as differentiated cost leadership.

Consider L.L. Bean. The successful mail-order company offers neither the most unique product, nor the cheapest mail-order delivery. Yet it does well based on high quality, an upscale identity, and efficient orchestration of back room processes. Also recall Starbucks, which positioned itself as the most efficient provider of mid- to high-priced coffee. Other examples of differentiated cost leaders include American, United, and Delta, the largest air carriers in the United States. Later we look at Southwest Airlines, successfully positioned as a cost leader, with attractive levels of differentiation and an unbroken stream of profits unmatched in its industry.

The relationship of costs, differentiation, and profits that results from scale orchestration is shown in Figure 2.1. The differentiated cost leadership map shows what managers know: Many different levels of profits are possible from many combinations of cost leadership (lower costs) and differentiation (higher prices). The curved lines on the map can be thought

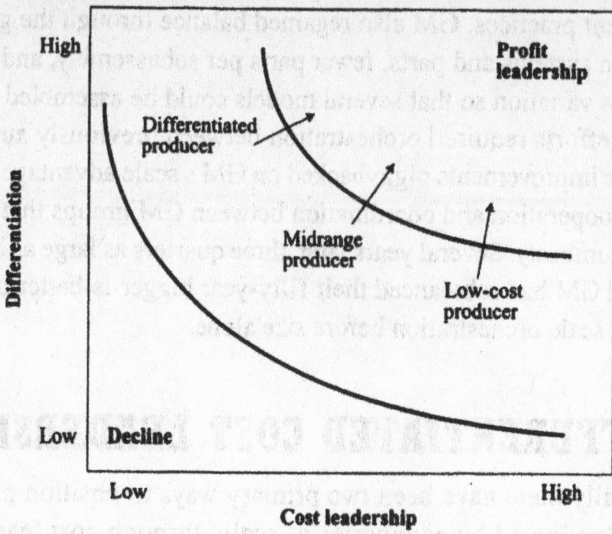

Figure 2.1. Differentiated Cost Leadership

of as isoprofit, or equal profit curves; regions of a market where similar levels of profit result from tradeoffs of cost leadership for differentiation, and vice versa. Along any isoprofit curve, there are many profitable product combinations possible, based on different positions of cost leadership and differentiation.[8]

It is straightforward to imagine that lowering the cost or raising the price of products is good. What is more useful is to know how some combinations of these two investments will generate greater profits than others. The differentiated cost leadership map gives an indication of this, depending on where you are positioned and where you are headed in your industry.

As the figure illustrates, differentiated, mid-range, and low-cost products all benefit from cost efficiencies and abilities to premium price. But notice that their routes to renewed profitability are different for each based on their initial positions.

Regardless of starting position, the goal is to move as far as possible toward the upper right-hand portion of the map, where profits are highest. In discussions with managers we refer to this region of a market—where costs are lowest and prices are highest—as business Heaven. For differentiated companies, movement toward Heaven is achieved by efforts to reduce costs, whereas for-low cost companies, movement toward Heaven requires successful efforts at making the product more differentiated. This is another expression of balance in the scale orchestra.

If cost leadership is overemphasized—that is, when products are configured with levels of differentiation that are too low—profits fall. The failure of People Express, the one-time cost leader in airlines, to achieve profitability resulted in part from a business model that set the airline's level of product differentiation too low. Cost leadership was achieved, but at a price point that was so low that even during its best years People Express showed low profits.

Pushing differentiation too far, with insufficient regard for cost, can lead to imbalance on the other end of the differentiated cost leadership map. The Mercedes-Benz 12-cylinder 600 SEL, priced at $125,000, was panned by the German auto press as a cathedral on wheels (the car was so large that it could not fit on standard German railway transports). Demand fell, but what also hurt Mercedes was that production costs in the company's plants became too high relative to BMW and Lexus. Layoffs by Daimler Benz in Germany, accompanied by a redesign of the Mercedes flagship, were necessary before balance was restored.

Convergence is continually at work on standard-cycle companies. Profits fall when any combination of poorly thought out, poorly executed investments or superior competitor moves forces products down, toward the origin or lower left-hand corner of the differentiated cost map. We think of this as competitive Hell, where your rate of return falls below your cost of capital. One manager remarked that this region is more like Purgatory, where you may have another chance to work out your sins before the Final Judgment.

Improvements from cost leadership and differentiation are also dependent on gains your competitors achieve, or how rapidly competitors are improving relative to you. Your organization can get pushed down closer to competitive Hell even as you are improving *if your competitors are improving faster.* Chrysler slid towards competitive Hell (or Purgatory as it turned out) in the early 1980s. To a lesser degree so did General Motors, which improved its processes at a slower pace over the period than did Toyota and Ford. The ability to reposition yourself is also dependent on the degree to which you can redirect your core competencies in the direction desired, a process that may require considerable change in historical practices.

As in all aspects of the scale symphony, balance is the key. The relative commitments that you make toward differentiation and cost leadership affect all four sections of the scale symphony. Changes in volume, product design, process improvement, and organizational learning associated with product repositioning occur gradually and take on momentum.

Thus, you should think years ahead as to where you want to place yourself and to the actions your competitors are likely to take. Leadership—moving your organization closer to Heaven—requires long-term commitment to your product strategy, the ability to move more effectively than competitors, and the ability to execute efficiently through three yards and a cloud of dust, not just for a while, but continually.

Focus and Renewable Scale

Related to differentiated cost leadership is what can be thought of as renewable scale, the amount of volume that a market segment will absorb at any combination of price and cost. To estimate renewable scale, compare the actual volume likely to be sold in a market with the minimum volume necessary to break even. Where market demand is sufficient to satisfy the investment needs of only one company, that segment of the differentiated cost leadership map will be focused.

When markets are focused, renewable scale is too low to make it profitable for large companies to enter and compete for the business in that segment. Thus, convergence does not occur. Still, scale is high enough for a smaller, focused company to survive. A focused segment can arise at any point on the differentiated cost map.

Renewable scale has an important implication. In order for a focus strategy to remain viable, your market *must not grow significantly.* The reason? Growth makes a focused market attractive to larger companies, encourages their investment and entry, and brings on convergence. Consider the history of American Motors. In the 1960s AMC was the small car leader in the United States. As the demand for small cars grew after the 1973 oil embargo, AMC's leadership and profits declined. How can we understand that a market leader loses market leadership as its market grows?

It is easier for scale-orchestrated companies to copy the products of smaller, focused companies than it is for a focused company to copy the processes of larger, scale-orchestrated companies. Thus, ironically, sometimes it can portend trouble for a focused competitor to see demand in its market grow significantly. As renewable scale rises to the point where larger competitors see the opportunity to enter, demand and supply will realign around larger competitors, effectively blocking the renewal path for the focused company.

Taking into account renewable scale at any projected price/cost point on the differentiated cost leadership map helps to choose between mainline and focus strategies and, thus, to balance your orchestration of cost leadership and differentiation. Other considerations helpful in pursuing differentiated cost leadership are discussed next.

Leverage Economies of Scope

Economies of scope result from sharing similar internal processes across different product lines. By using similar processes to produce products that sell at different levels of differentiation, economies of scope can reduce costs overall. At Ford, marketing themes are different for the lower priced Taurus and the higher priced Mercury Sable, but the common use of technology in the two car lines is widespread. Virtually all of the global automakers employ economies of scope to various degrees to achieve the most advantageous mix of cost leadership and differentiation. Global automakers strive to most effectively share auto platforms, systems, and components across the widest spectrum of global automobile price points.

Stress Inexpensive Visual Differences

Alfred Sloan's original concept of product segmentation stressed distinctive body styling for the Chevrolet, Pontiac, Oldsmobile, Buick, and Cadillac. In the 1980s GM's management, concerned about cost reduction, allowed GM's body designs to become too similar, causing market segmentation to break down and brands to overlap. The renewal pathway for the time-honored Oldsmobile brand nearly closed.

In a return to the original strategy of stressing visual differences, GM established a corporate marketing center to help negotiate separate market images for various GM models. Vehicles were required to fit within twenty-six carefully defined market segments. The differences might be small in some segments, interior and exterior trim, for example. But if a proposed Buick Regal design resembled a Pontiac Grand Prix too closely, they went back for redesign. This example illustrates the role that marketing plays in orchestrating differentiated cost leadership. The task is to accentuate the perception of differences between brands where, in reality, the most expensive differences are minor.

Promote Distinctive Channels

The Lexus ES300 and the Toyota Camry are made side-by-side on the same assembly line in Japan. (In Japan the Lexus LS400 is sold as a Toyota-brand Celsior and the Lexus ES300 is sold as the Toyota Aristo.) When Toyota entered the U.S. high-priced luxury car market with the Lexus, it opted to create a distinctive distribution channel for the car. Strong control was exercised, stressing separate showrooms, advertising, and training of dealership staff. Partly as a result of a distinctive distribution channel, with roughly similar production costs, Toyota achieved a $7,200 premium in the 1994 sticker price of an ES300 over a Camry.

It's a delicate balancing act. Ford managers used the same distribution channel to sell German-built Fords as Merkurs in Lincoln showrooms, but without success. Mazda faced a similar problem with its Millennia model, which shared showroom space with lower-priced Mazda Proteges and Miatas. These examples illustrate that the balance between differentiation and cost leadership is delicate, and that it requires careful orchestration of all aspects of the company/customer relationship.

Expand Strong Brands Downward

Mercedes cars range from $30,000 to over $100,000, have the same overall appearance and similar names (190, 300, 420), *and are sold on the same showroom floor,* yet each maintains its own brand identity. How? At no point in Mercedes's differentiation/cost portfolio do market segments collapse into each other. High-end brands benefit from the scale economies generated by common components, while low-end brands benefit from the exclusive image of the high-end brands. It appears that the image of high-end flagship brands spills over downward, to lower-priced offerings, without affecting upscale volume, allowing each to sustain renewable scale.

Leverage Differences in Location on the Convergence Line

Singapore Airlines (SIA) pursues a range of cost and differentiation strategies by segmenting its markets by degrees of competition. In the price-sensitive Asian market, SIA pursues a medium-cost, high-quality strategy relative to competitors like Thai Airlines, Malaysian Airlines, and Korean Airlines that follow a low-price strategy. In the transatlantic market, SIA positions itself as a low-cost, mid-range quality carrier where competitors like Swissair, British Airways, and Lufthansa benefit from ties to their host countries. In the transpacific market, SIA benefits from a lowest-cost, highest-quality strategy relative to competitors United and Northwest. The ability to orchestrate relatively similar products at different price points in international markets can be a means of inching international companies toward profit leadership Heaven.

These considerations, taken alone or together, point out how, in the new economy, even dominant companies must maneuver carefully. Small margins of error separate success and failure. The complex task of orchestration is accompanied by considerable competitive momentum as managers seek to move their companies toward Heaven and their competitors toward Hell.

Managing standard-cycle companies is a task analogous to commanding large battleships. It takes a long time to gain momentum and direction. Once established, momentum continues in the same direction unless altered through strong leadership or the actions of competitors. Changes in direction that are desired two or three years from now should be carefully thought through and initiated early on.

Master Orchestrator Southwest Airlines

Southwest Airlines president Herb Kelleher is a master scale orchestrator. Early on, Southwest's musical score did not position the air carrier against the major airlines but rather the automobile. Southwest's orchestration of volume growth, product design, process improvement, and organizational learning provides an illustration of how the elements of a scale orchestra come together in a service business.

Scale. Southwest Airlines, the eighth-largest U.S. air carrier in 1997, offers flights to 48 cities. It carries 44 million passengers annually on 2,100 flights daily. Southwest ignores traditional long-haul routes and positions itself as a short-haul, city-to-city carrier with a low-cost, no-frills, highly reliable reputation.

Product Segmentation. Southwest flies to low-congestion airports like Phoenix, Dallas Love, Houston Hobby, Chicago Midway, St. Louis, San Diego, and San Jose (the short-haul, city-to-city strategy). Although these airports are smaller and less convenient to get to, Southwest's lower price compensates customers for having to go out of the way. Lower congestion at airports enables the airline to schedule more frequent flights since there is less risk of delays. Seventy percent of flights have a turnaround time of fifteen minutes, the fastest in the industry. Confirmation numbers and IDs are all that customers need to receive a boarding pass and enter the airplane. The savings to Southwest from ticketless travel (which they pioneered) are $100 million annually.

The Southwest passenger experience consists of a drive to the airport, which, because it's not a major airport, is less subject to overcapacity and traffic tie-ups; a plane that arrives at the gate on time and departs on schedule, due to the lack of congestion and efficient handling of passengers and baggage; cheerful service by flight attendants; luggage that shows up at the carousel in a timely manner; and a quick trip out of the airport because it's not overcrowded. A lot of little details that cannot be duplicated by competitors come together to power the growth engine for Southwest.

This set of carefully crafted customer experiences requires that Southwest say no to customers. There is no first-class section; there is no meal service; there are no movies. Southwest customers expect this. Southwest *created* these expectations. Customers consistently rate quality of service high, at 0.21 complaints per 100,000 passengers. Southwest ranks at the top of the Department of Transportation's ratings for best on-time performance, best baggage handling, and lowest rate of customer complaints.

Process Refinements. Southwest uses only one aircraft type, Boeing 737s. This strategy enables Southwest to maintain lower costs in maintenance and inventory and to eliminate the cost of training personnel on other types of planes. The 737 is Boeing's smallest narrowbody, tailored to short-haul flights of less than 1,500 miles. Because Southwest's fleet consists exclusively of 737s, it is possible to order only those parts that are vital for the maintenance of such a fleet and to provide high levels of equipment maintenance. Southwest's flight record is perfect, with no flight accidents since its inception in 1971.

Organizational Learning. The Southwest work force dresses informally to promote a relaxed atmosphere. Customers think of Southwest as casual and fun. Flight attendants' uniforms are multicolored Hawaiian print shirts, and shorts or slacks. Traditional uniforms cost hundreds of dollars more than the more relaxed outfits, yet Southwest's customers prefer casual uniforms.

Ticket clerks and baggage handlers are cheerful, patient, and treat baggage with care. Stewardesses sing songs and tell jokes (it's in the training manual). Employees are preselected by their inclination to keep people happy. All of the airlines want people like this, but Southwest employees are all steeped in this culture. Careful selection, intensive training in procedures, and immersion in Southwest's culture are part of Southwest's competitive score.

Still, nothing lasts forever. There are challenges to Southwest's business model, from small start-up carriers and from larger carriers streamlining their operations and imitating Southwest's personnel practices. And new cities that meet the company's low-congestion criteria are in short supply. Yet, since 1971, against a backdrop of corporate carnage wrought by air carriers on each other, Southwest steadily captured—indeed they created—a segment of the airline industry where passengers expect to get from Point A to Point B quickly, efficiently, and with no surprises. Through three yards and a cloud of dust master orchestrator Southwest tells customers what to expect and makes them love it.[9]

RECAP: SCALE ORCHESTRATORS

The ideas in this chapter can be found in competitive thinking that sees scale-driven companies as evolving through continual realignment with gradually changing markets. Simple economies of scale-based organizations have evolved into dynamic symphonies that renew themselves by balancing growth with product segmentation, process refinements, and organizational learning. A dynamic perspective on extended rivalry shares these points:

BUILD A NO-SURPRISES REPUTATION

Produce and deliver products with no surprises at the same time that customers learn to demand the same experience, repeatedly, with no defects. Stress a high repeatability orientation toward customers to build brand loyalty.

CONTROL INNOVATION

Balance product and process improvements. Harmonize innovation with long-established expectations, familiar usage patterns, and operational efficiencies.

SAY NO TO CUSTOMERS

Look for bad customers, those that draw your organization away from its game plan. Insure that your products have carefully-defined boundaries that keep your organization and your customers matched in their experiences. Direct market research toward expanding customer expectations gradually.

HARMONIZE SUPPLIERS

Work toward seamlessly integrating suppliers within the organization. Innovative contracts can make separately owned suppliers part of a company's scale symphony.

MAKE THEM WANT IT; DEFEND BRANDS

Decide what customers should want and make them like it. Remember that often demand does not exist until it is created. For established brands, resist the temptation to improve short-term profits at the expense of brand capitalization.

STRIVE FOR DIFFERENTIATED COST LEADERSHIP

Whether you excel at cost leadership or differentiation consider the relative benefits of improvements in both. When setting benchmarks for cost leadership and differentiation, goals should be set relative to the progress expected by competitors. Harmony between cost leadership and differentiation can be aided in several ways, by tactics designed to share similar processes across products that look different to the customer and by careful choice of market segments. Long-term commitment is important, as is attention to detail and effectiveness of execution.

ORCHESTRATE FIRST; MASTER THE BALANCE; THEN GROW

Guard against acting as though size for the sake of size is enough. Instead, master the intricacies of enterprise-wide learning, and the benefits of product and process synergies. *If* you learn how to orchestrate, *then* you can achieve economies of scale and long-term growth.

ABOVE ALL—FIGHT ENTROPY

A common hazard in standard-cycle organizations is benign neglect, the tendency to take past success for granted and to drift out of a renewal mind-set. Competitive momentum can lull managers into a frame of mind where small mistakes are tolerated at first. No obvious harm is done. Scale complexity makes responsibility difficult to assign. A thousand small mistakes add together to become common practice. Like an old soldier, once-great companies begin to fade. The final paralysis, reorganization, spin-off, or liquidation is accompanied by a low-energy numbness, the final diagnosis of progressive entropy that works to age once-great companies.

The leadership challenge in standard-cycle markets is to fight creeping mediocrity, avoid the loss of stamina, and resist that part of human nature that follows the pathway of "good is good enough." The successful scale orchestrators that we studied, those that evolved beyond their once-safe competitive foundations and created new markets, are distinguished by a continual, enterprise-wide desire to improve.

How to win? Inspire your people to stretch toward performance targets that are continually improving, through any number of modest and carefully coordinated steps.

In these and other dynamic ways, standard-cycle companies are reshaping the traditional, oligopolistic landscape. Economies of scale are still vitally important for these companies, but now scale efficiencies require more sophisticated approaches that treat the enterprise and its customers as part of a highly interdependent symphony. As difficult as this is, the rewards of success can be great, and advantage long-lived, as the examples of UPS, Andersen Consulting, and Starbucks demonstrate.

Ironically, however, as challenging as the new scale orchestras can be, excelling within them may not be enough. Economic time challenges us to look ahead, and around, for changes in business that are potentially framebreaking. The task is to know when your markets shift from those that require scale orchestration to something so different that still another, new leadership style may be required.

Efforts to radically streamline your company, to simplify the way a product is made or used, or to innovate wholly new products—if successful and if duplicated by competitors—can *speed up* economic time. The result can be to bring on a different set of competitive opportunities associated with faster-cycle markets.

In the next chapter we discuss markets where it can be limiting to rely on scale orchestration. When economic time speeds up, your managers will need to learn different rules and new management styles, including how to "eat your own children."

CHAPTER 3

THE CHILDREN EATERS

As the industrial revolution gained momentum in the eighteenth century, the mass markets that we know were created. Then another class of markets emerged. These markets operate according to ideas put forth by the economist Joseph Schumpeter, who saw competition as the chase after the innovator. These markets continually reshape product advantage through a gale of creative destruction.

Accelerated market convergence is common for technology-driven products like Intel Pentium microchips, Compaq personal computers, Ericsson cellular phones, and Sony MiniDisk music players. Products that operate in fast-cycle economic time also include toys like the Mattel Cabbage Patch doll and adult accessories from Sharper Image (one big seller was a solar powered hat that ran a small fan to keep your head cool on hot days).

Consider also the pace of innovation in derivative securities offered by companies like Salomon Brothers. Examples include currency and interest rate futures, index options and futures, mortgage-backed securities (MBS), asset-backed securities (ABS), collateralized mortgage obligations (CMO), and securities with exotic names like butterflies, bullets, and barbells. These are called derivative securities because their value depends on the value of other underlying assets. Profitable at first, these products are easily copied. Popular belief is that Wall Street comes up with a new product each working day. Since each derivative security is a combination of a few underlying securities, the number of possible combinations is huge. With ten commodities, five currencies, five stock classes, five bond classes, five foreign equity market indices, and five foreign bond market indices, the number of derivative security combinations is vast.

Ask yourself: How is a 333-megahertz Pentium microchip like a Cabbage Patch doll? Or an original offering of mortgage-backed securities? Like microchips, toys, and financial securities, Pentium chips are information intensive. Value is idea-driven. Profit cycles are short. There is little that slows down the copying process or retards the fast commercialization of attractive alternatives. Complementary assets are weak. Isolating mechanisms like scale orchestration, as well as geography, patents, and close customer relationships are rare. Fast-cycle markets and the products sold in them are based on freestanding, portable ideas. Value is high upon introduction but erodes quickly as ideas become commonplace.

To borrow a phrase from a Hollywood movie: in fast-cycle markets there are two kinds of companies: The Quick and The Dead. As an example, consider the history of Pulse Engineering.

Pulse Engineering

Apple Computer dominated the personal computer market in 1982 with its Apple 1 machine, with competition from Commodore and Osborne. IBM was developing a competing machine that would utilize off-the-shelf components and technology, including two or three delay lines, for which Pulse Engineering was a qualified supplier. Delay lines regulated the flow of digital signals in the computer circuitry.

Pulse Engineering manufactured delay lines for mainframe and minicomputers and central office phone switching equipment, products where customized designs, specialized applications, and high prices were the norm. With $6 million in annual revenue, Pulse was the second-largest delay line supplier to the industry and the largest supplier to IBM for these kinds of products. Pulse could build delay lines at a rate of 15,000 units a week.

When Pulse Engineering became a supplier for IBM's personal computer, little was known about the machine's market potential. IBM gave little indication of its long-run volume needs or whether Pulse had competition for the delay line business. Pulse had difficulty forecasting capacity needs.

In early 1982, Pulse was notified that it had won the contract at $5.25 per part and should begin shipments immediately. Pulse boosted production in Mexico as IBM announced its intention to market the PC. Delay line production volume quickly jumped to 35,000 units per week but demand rose even more quickly, leaving IBM short of delay line parts. Pulse struggled to reduce manufacturing costs. Management was able to cut labor minutes per part from 18 to 8 and increase yields from 88 to 92 percent. Still, IBM added more delay line producers and the increased competition contributed to a price drop to $2.20 within nine months.

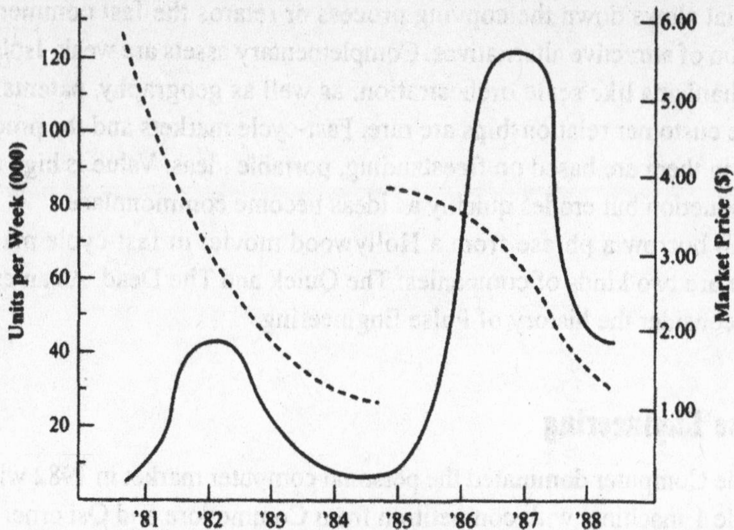

Figure 3.1. Pulse Engineering Delay Line Sales

Then, in late 1984 demand evaporated. Delay line sales shrank to 6,000 units per week. Prices declined to $1.90. Despite operational enhancements, Pulse could no longer create value from the business. Attempts to win back customers with delay line applications outside the PC business were unsuccessful. During this time, which Pulse management termed "the great drought of 1985," Pulse laid off much of its production force and took large inventory write-offs. See Figure 3.1.

Then in 1986, the market improved. IBM's new PS/2 called for up to seven delay lines, but Pulse could build only 100 of the new units a week. IBM's sales estimates called for 25,000 to 35,000 units per week. Still, Pulse bid on, and won, a contract as a sole source at $3.87 per part.

Almost immediately IBM began adjusting its forecasts upward, from 20,000 units per week to 123,000 units a week nine months later. Pulse moved labor-intensive production to the People's Republic of China, and added just-in-time production methods that utilized statistical process controls. Labor minutes per part dropped to 4 and yield increased to 96.4 percent. Despite daily deliveries and round-the-clock production by 1,000 employees in Mexico, Ireland, and China, Pulse could not meet IBM's demands. As before, IBM turned to other delay line manufacturers, which drove the price down to $1.15.

Late 1988 brought another drop-off in demand. The PS/2 failed to gain the market dominance that had been forecast. Additionally, some of the timing functions of delay lines had been incorporated into newer versions of computer microprocessors. Delay lines were becoming unimportant. After several attempts at restructuring Pulse abandoned the entire product line.

From traditional perspectives, Pulse's delay line experience could be called a failure. Although Pulse had become, at one point, the world's largest delay line supplier at $14 million, the company lost customers in other markets in its focus to meet IBM's orders. The division suffered financial losses when it ceased production of the PC delay line.

Yet the company had also enjoyed several years of solid profits. Competencies had been developed that could be transferred to new product lines. These prepared managers at Pulse for competition in other product areas. To understand what happened at Pulse, let's look at some features of fast-cycle competition.

Beyond Time-based Competition

Why now? Why do we see so much acceleration in the pace of competition, of the potential for success and the risks of failure? Radio existed for 38 years before it had 50 million listeners. Television took 13 years to get 50 million viewers. The Internet? It reached 50 million U.S. users in four years. What has caused this acceleration and is it really a different kind of business economics?

Time-based management, an important, dynamic idea originated in the 1990s, focuses on reducing the time it takes to deliver products after a need is understood and an order is placed.[2] The goal in time-based management is to shorten the elapsed interval between the customer's identified need and the fulfillment of that order. Time-based management calls for analysis of each individual step in the development, production, and delivery process so that managers can determine whether the step is needed at all or if it can be carried out differently to speed up delivery of the product to market.

Time-based measures include: the time from idea to market, the rate of new-product introduction, value added as a percent of total elapsed time, time lost waiting for decisions, response time, quoted lead time, the percentage of on-time deliveries, and the time from the recognition of a need to delivery. These important measures encourage shortening the time between orders and fulfillment, important to strengthening advantage.

Table 3.1. Time-Based vs. Fast-Cycle Principles

	TIME-BASED MANAGEMENT	FAST-CYCLE MANAGEMENT
Source of value	Wait-time reduction	Innovation
Isolating mechanisms	Moderate to strong	Weak
Additional value	Incremental	High
Advantage	Sustainable	Temporary

How does fast-cycle thinking fit with this? Fast-cycle management shares with time-based management a concern for speed, but fast-cycle management draws a principal distinction. In contrast to time-based management, value that can be created in fast-cycle markets is extremely high, typically several orders of magnitude above existing products. Also, in contrast, fast-cycle management sees the advantages to be had by speed as fleeting at best. See Table 3.1.

Consider the Internet brokerage business. Industry leaders eSchwab, Fidelity, and E*TRADE sustain only brief advantages over their competitors as they upgrade their web sites to lower costs or improve customer service. Compared to the labor-intensive discount brokerage business, automated Internet brokerage sites can reduce labor costs, processing costs, and marketing costs by 80 percent or more. Internet traders, because they are relatively active, give early site innovators two and a half times the income per account of a discount broker (the $40 customer acquisition cost of a typical site is recovered in a month).

E*TRADE Securities, Inc. is not a complex organization. Three hundred employees staff their touch-tone phone, on-line, and Internet-trading systems. To keep costs low, E*TRADE outsources their raw materials by purchasing the data, news, and other information services that they supply to customers. E*TRADE has only a small staff to handle customer inquiries or requests for information.

eSchwab gained 35 percent of the early Internet brokerage business through rapid innovation. Products included college and retirement planning, term life insurance, mutual fund wrap accounts, institutional on-line trading, and introduction of financially oriented speech recognition software. Still, eSchwab's competitors react to its product introductions quickly. Use of Java applets allows brokerage sites to add free and fee-based informational resources (quotes, news, graphs, research, and commentary) with little delay. In two years Waterhouse lowered its commissions from $35 to $12, forcing Schwab to lower its commissions from $68 to $30. Oxford offered to execute a trade for $2 for an account greater than $250,000. First-mover advantage in the Internet-based financial service industry is temporary.

Yet value creation is high. Recall that a company's P/E ratio is its primary measure of renewal. In the early days of Internet trading, eSchwab, Ameritrade, and E*TRADE had P/Es of 39, 35, and 135, respectively. These expectations of profitable growth compared to a P/E range of 10 to 18 for comparable full-service brokers. Forecasts were that Internet trading would surpass the combined volume of all other trading processes by the year 2000.

Why does first-mover advantage for some products, such as cellular telephones, DRAM computer chips, children's toys, and Internet-based services, yield such tenuous advantage? Companies producing these products, like Ericsson, Sony, and Salomon Brothers, are well managed, and their industry structure is not notably different from industries in slower economic time.

Let's go back in time. We know, for example, that Leonardo Da Vinci invented the helicopter. At the time there was no consumer demand. Da Vinci also lacked the manufacturing technology for building helicopters. Even if he had solved these problems there were few ways for Da Vinci to bring together manufacturers and consumers at the volumes needed to justify the investment. The information infrastructure was primitive.

Now move the clock forward to today. Worldwide, wealthy, educated customers are predisposed to try out new products with little delay. Global capitalism generates ever-rising amounts of capital for investment. Technology can be employed to build or to copy any number of configurations of products, quickly and efficiently. Global communications have transformed international markets into an electronic village where distance no longer matters. Imagine a marketplace where thousands of idea-driven, well-financed companies have quick access to millions of customers who, as they say, "have so much money that they don't know what to do with it." These are the building blocks of fast-cycle markets.

Predicting the Onset of Fast Economic Time

Consider the bicycle industry, which has been reshaped through the introduction of high-performance aluminum, titanium, and carbon fiber. The first suspension fork was introduced in 1989 and nearly laughed out of a trade show; yet, a year later, bike companies began putting suspension forks on bikes in response to widespread customer demand. In 1991, nearly every company building mountain bikes had some with front suspensions, and some were introducing rear suspensions. In 1992, many companies had bikes with full suspensions (front and rear). That year the European ten-speed race over cobblestone roads, the Paris-Roubioux, featured a bike with a front suspension. In 1993, virtually all companies had fully suspended bikes. Fast-cycle products generally share the following characteristics:

- They are freestanding and idea-based. They are information intensive and available to many competitors, either through imitation or licensing.
- They can be copied or improved upon quickly. They are made of non-proprietary components that are widely available. Profit cycles are short.
- They experience supernormal productivity gains. Rapid learning and fast technology improvements diffuse throughout their industries. This enables followers to enter the market with lower costs of production than first movers, thereby turning first-mover advantage into a disadvantage.
- They see economies of scale for a brief period only. Although volume is high, advantage based on size is temporary. Rapid product obsolescence works against sustainable scale economies for even the largest of companies.
- They originate from uncontrolled innovation. Technology spillovers between competitors keep any single company from dominating a market for long.
- They are culturally neutral and innately global, with few physical, regulatory, or geographic barriers.

Bicycles are simple to build and require little organizational coordination. We can see how *Bicycling Magazine*'s 1993 Buyer's Guide could list 89 bicycle companies with 1,043 models, not including an additional 73 custom builders and specialty shops. Bicycle companies rely on outsourcing—designing, engineering, and marketing bicycles in-house and having them built by overseas companies. This allows rapid changes without investments in machinery. As new designs and technologies are copied and appear on competitors' bikes, prices fall rapidly, with premium models selling for as low as $280 that were $750 a few years earlier. In 1993 the median price of fully suspended bikes, at $2,400, had dropped $500 from a year earlier.

THE GALE OF CREATIVE DESTRUCTION

Recall that Compaq's ProLinea originated in a hotel room during a Comdex trade show. In three days Compaq managers bought components and built the prototype that became the ProLinea computer line. Fast-cycle markets converge quickly because the products in them are organizationally simple: they can be produced quickly in large numbers, at rapidly falling costs.

At the same time, the capabilities that allow for fast and cheap reproduction are possessed by competitors. Hence managers in these markets, despite their best efforts, lack effective ways to slow down economic time. Compaq, for example, has strong capabilities and is well managed, but isolating effects are weak. Its capabilities do not prevent rivals from quickly imitating its products.

DRAM chips can be manufactured with simpler administrative structures than found in the standard-cycle automotive, hotel, or telecommunications industries. Fast-cycle companies can be so organizationally simple that managers can locate the production process in an automated facility and effectively turn out the lights, leaving the operation to run itself.

Products like ProLinea have few isolating mechanisms like localized needs, the inertia of traditional assembly line processes, customer loyalty, and transportation costs, all of which slow down the ability of competitors to enter a company's markets. The first ProLinea computer had 100 parts, most of which could be purchased on the open market. ProLinea is subject to significant improvements in performance by changing a few components. ProLinea is a collection of ideas that can be produced almost as quickly by Compaq's rivals as by Compaq.

Fast-cycle markets are unencumbered. Products are idea-driven, technology- or information-based, valued in their purest forms, unconnected to isolating mechanisms. Knowledge-based advantage is slippery, easily dispersed and copied. Momentum is low, but velocity—the speed at which revenues rise and fall—is high. Thus, fast-cycle innovators can be pushed off their renewal pathways by fast followers in little time. Let's look at other features of fast-cycle markets.

Hypergrowth

Growth rates of 30 percent per year or more are common in fast-cycle markets. The value of personal computers, telephones, and other electronic gear made each year is projected to surpass $1.2 trillion by the year 2000. Sales of personal computers, computer chips, and communications and multimedia devices are estimated to grow to $2.2 trillion by 2010.

Hypergrowth, often seen in fast-cycle markets, often causes demand to outstrip the ability of companies to build capacity. The result is to encourage quick entry for fast-follower companies of all sizes. This is so regardless of how dominant the innovating company may appear to be. Texas Instruments had gained an estimated 90 percent market share in low-priced digital wristwatches as of 1976. Yet six years later, the world price of the digital wristwatch had fallen to $3.00, a price that could not sustain TI's infrastructure. When company managers announced that they were abandoning the electronic watch market, their actions signaled a transformation—from market dominance to market exit in six years.

Growth, rather than creating alignment with loyal customers, creates windows of opportunity. During this time growth goals must be achieved quickly. Uncertainty about alternatives under development by competitors is high.

Escalating Commitment

Intel's development expenses rose from $100 million for the i386 chip to $300 million for the i486, to $500 million for the P5, and to $600 million for the P6. The costs of building semiconductor fabrication foundries rose from $422 million in 1989 to $680 million in 1990, to $1.0 billion in 1991, and $1.2 billion in 1992. At the end of this period Intel managers were investing billions of dollars a year in fabrication plants before reliable estimates of demand were available. Intel's Craig Barrett explains, "We build factories two years in advance of needing them, before we have the products to run in them, and before we know that the industry will grow."

During a hypergrowth phase disagreements will arise as to how much demand will materialize. Opinions will differ as to how fast the market will grow, how much competitive capacity will enter the market, whether rivals will introduce effective substitutes, and what the most profitable rates of investment are. The combination of uncertainty and escalating commitment can create tension among management teams. These strains should not be avoided, covered over, or seen as a failure to work together. Andrew Grove says, "Our fabs [wafer fabrication plants] are our fields of dreams. We build them and hope people will come."[3]

Why not wait for the dominant product design to emerge and for reliable sales estimates to materialize? Because by then market opportunities will have changed. To hesitate is to concede a product's profit potential to others. Thus, the challenge is to encourage investment alternatives that allow for reversibility of investments while allowing full profits to flow to the company where it succeeds.

Multiproduct companies, for example, may have an advantage over their single-product counterparts if they are structured to facilitate quick resource movements between divisions. One example is Canon, which shares development costs across many products. Should any one product fail, Canon management can shift resources to related products efficiently and quickly. More generally, competitive flexibility and a focus on reversible investments may reduce the risk of escalating commitment.

So Little Time to Grow Up

In pioneering the Internet browser market, Netscape's management found it difficult to grow the organization fast enough. Within two years of Netscape's founding, Netscape's management was forced by competitive pressures to operate as a fully developed, mainstream company in competition with well-established Microsoft.

Adam Osborne, president of Osborne Computer, reported similar growth problems in the early days of the personal computer industry when Osborne's growth rates were doubling every three months.

Irrepressible Innovation

The product half-life of a modem, the device used to carry computer information over telephone lines, is about eighteen months. Each of the early-generation modems was introduced at approximately $300, and was essentially given away three to four years later. These innovations took place even though each modem generation at the time was declared by experts to be the "fastest possible" because of fundamental physical limitations. In this way the modem industry is similar to other fast-cycle industries, which see generation after generation of ideas proclaimed to

Table 3.2. Irrepressible Innovation

YEAR	MODEM SPEED
1978	300 bits per second
1980	1,200 bits per second
1984	2,400 bits per second
1987	9,600 bits per second
1990	14,400 bits per second
1993	28,800 bits per second
1995	33,600 bits per second
1997	56,000 bits per second

be the fastest or smallest possible, only to have them superseded by something better. See Table 3.2.

Industry leadership affords little protection from competitors. When digital audiotape (DAT) technology was commercialized, it promised a great improvement over compact disk technology because it allowed customers to record their own digital music. Yet, Sony managers considered slowing down DAT's introduction, concerned that the new technology would cannibalize still-growing sales of compact disk players. However, within months, a dozen Japanese companies acquired the technology to commercialize DAT. Unable to stem the introduction of DAT into the industry, Sony management accelerated their own plans to commercialize DAT machines. (As it turned out, DAT did not create competition for CDs.)

The commercialization dilemma in fast-cycle markets can be likened to sitting in the front of a roller coaster at the top of the ride. You look forward to the ride but you are concerned about the dangers ahead. Are you really prepared? The roller coaster is about to move. What do you do? Your choices are to stay on—or to unbuckle your seat belt and jump off. Either way you cannot slow down the ride as can your traditional, slower-moving counterparts. You have invested considerable resources and are in a position to commit to production. Still, you are not sure of the market growth potential or the attractiveness of your product. Nothing quite like it has been offered before. You have two choices: you can quickly commit funds for production (stay on the roller coaster) or you can get out (jump off). But, and this is the difference from the investment choice in slower-cycle markets, you cannot slow down the ride or prevent it from taking off.

You must do something. And you must do something quickly. Why not take a go-slow approach? You can, of course, but this will limit your market potential and certainly abdicate your leadership of the industry. Even as market leader you should operate at at least the same competitive speed as your competitors. To gain leadership, your managers must chase after themselves as fast as—actually, faster than—your competitors chase after you.

Price Compression

Prices fall quickly in fast-cycle markets:

- When one model of Nike's Air Jordan shoes was introduced they were priced at $112.63 (our experience at one local store). Two years later a price of $39.95 could be found at Wal-Mart because Nike had introduced newer models of Air Jordan shoes. Price decline: 65 percent in two years.
- The price per megabyte of a DRAM chip was $378 in 1988. Three years later the price had dropped to $35. Price decline: 91 percent.
- Remember that the Cabbage Patch doll originally sold for $850? A decade later you could purchase one for $39.95. Price decline: 95 percent.
- Prices for cellular telephones, introduced at $3,500, dropped over the subsequent decade to $100 exclusive of service plans. Price decline: 97 percent.
- From 1973 to 1983 the market price of the liquid crystal display (LCD) electronic wristwatch fell from $2,100 to $3. Price decline: 99.9 percent. At this point the original product is effectively being given away.

As prices fall, they open up unfamiliar markets with new competitors. Alignment between the company and its customers changes. The focus of competition passes from early adopters, who are predisposed to pay high prices, to fast followers who are price sensitive, and finally to late adopters who see the product as a low-priced commodity (more on this later).

Zero-coupon bonds and mortgage-backed securities were immensely profitable for their originators because they offered a novel way to package claims on assets and cash flows associated with debt. But the value resided in their novelty, which, once understood, could by copied quickly. Wall Street competitors drove down value creation opportunities quickly. Profit cycles were eighteen months.

Fleeting Brand Loyalty

Uncontrollable innovation and falling prices make it difficult to sustain brand loyalty. The Sony Walkman is recognized throughout the world, but Sony managers were required to introduce 160 Walkman models in ten years to sustain brand identity against an onslaught of Walkman clones.

Ask yourself: How long would your brands retain their value if you stopped investing in them? Brand loyalty for slower-cycle companies, as for McDonald's, Toyota, or Ikea, would last for years, although it would surely decay.

In fast-cycle markets, within a year or two, your brand would be buried by competitors.

Yet, branding, such as that gained from the "Intel Inside" campaign, can be valuable. Branding can help the innovating company reach a larger number of customers more quickly. Exposure allows more products to be sold while prices are high.

The goal of brand awareness in fast-cycle markets is not to encourage repeat business; the goal is to expand the amount of product that can be sold before price erosion sets in. Brand awareness, rather than creating a defensible barrier to entry, sets the stage for competitive entry.

In this sense, branding can accelerate product obsolescence by speeding up the rate at which newly commercialized products come to the attention of competitors. When considering branding campaigns for fast-cycle products, be prepared to act quickly to ensure that short product life cycles can be compensated for by the sale of more products over the shorter anticipated amount of time.

Fast-shifting Strategies

Alignment between a company and its customers undergoes redefinition in fast-cycle markets faster than in traditional markets. Until the entry of Advanced Micro Devices into microprocessors, Intel enjoyed a relatively competition-free market. Intel introduced each of its microprocessors, from the 4004 controller to the i286, at a price level of $360. OEMs had to purchase the peripheral chips (the math coprocessors and the controller chips) separately from other vendors. Intel kept the prices of its chips at profitably high levels, lowering prices on average by only 12 percent annually.

When AMD introduced its own version of the i386 at a price of $299 in

1989, Intel was required to alter its strategy. Intel reduced the price of its 386 chip to $190 and brought out the 486 chip. It stopped requiring OEMs to procure and mount the necessary peripheral chips. It added the functionality of peripheral chips to the 486 and raised the price to $950. OEMs were encouraged to stop manufacturing 386-based machines in favor of the newer 486 machines. Thus, Intel's competitors, AMD and Cyrix, were forced to price their products comparable to Intel's $190 price for the 386, drastically shortening their profit cycles. Additionally, as 486 circuit boards would no longer accept the 386 processor chip, AMD and Cyrix were forced back to the drawing board to come up with an equivalent to the 486 chip. These kinds of fast-shifting strategies, blocking maneuvers, and product end-runs are characteristic of competition in markets with weak isolating mechanisms and compressed action-reaction cycles.

SPAWNING AND CANNIBALIZING

Fast-cycle markets realign companies with customers at a faster pace than their slower-cycle counterparts. To be sure, traditional strategies like preemptive capacity expansion, brand advertising, use of bargaining power, or limit pricing can be effective in these settings. But these strategies are likely to have less effect when convergence pressures are severe and strategies achieve temporary alignment at best. Thus, traditional approaches should be supplemented by strategies designed to extract value from fast-moving profit streams that rise and fall quickly. These nontraditional strategies are discussed next.

Create Demand

Like fast-cycle products, fast-cycle demand is unstable. Ongoing renewal requires that the fast-cycle company pay particular attention to creating demand on a continuous basis. As one manager put it, "This treadmill could stop. If people don't buy a chip with more functions, there's no money to develop the next round."

One way to encourage demand to materialize on a regular basis is to focus on standards and related applications that favor the growth of your products. Think ahead to what David Teece calls product complementors, where two companies are not customers, suppliers, or competitors but share market dependencies. An example is Microsoft (software) and Intel (microchips), the "Wintel" alliance, whereby increasingly large software programs require increasingly fast microprocessors.

In 1997 the International Telecommunications Union, a standards-setting body of the United Nations, was to pick one 56-kilobit technology as the standard for all 56-kilobit modems. Three companies, U.S. Robotics, Rockwell, and Lucent, were competing to have their technology adopted as the industry standard. To encourage adoption of the U.S. Robotics standard, U.S. Robotics marketed its slower modems as 56-kilobit upgradeable. The company told customers that, even if U.S. Robotics lost the standards battle, its customers could easily upgrade their modems to the new standard. This encouraged customers who might otherwise have held off because of concerns about technological obsolescence to buy U.S. Robotics modems. By the time the standards body met, 200 Internet service providers serving 18 million subscribers had announced their support of the U.S. Robotics standard.

When the Pentium chip was under development, Intel engineers knew that the microprocessor would outperform the associated architecture of the rest of the PC. They isolated the problem to a slow PC bus design that came from IBM. In response, Intel proposed and promoted a new PCI bus design that overcame the problems of the older design. By 1993, through aggressive promotion efforts, this new bus had become the industry standard. The PCI bus also worked better with Intel chips than with chips from its competitors, further strengthening Intel's position.

Intel's efforts to speed growth of data-rich microprocessor-based applications include a microprocessor-intensive video phone with ProShare, interactive games on the Web, and a joint project with MCI to increase information network bandwidth. According to Grove, "If we don't make computers more useful, there won't be demand for the chips we'll be making in a few years. So we have to create users and uses for our processors. We get the market growth we earn by our development efforts, our investments, and our proselytizing." With spending on market development at $500 million in 1996, Intel has gone from basing its business on the premise that demand exists "out there" to creating demand itself.

Accelerate Market Reception

Product preannouncements can speed up the rate at which innovations are adopted by a market, particularly if the company has built a reputation for delivering on its new product announcements in the past. Software companies preannounce products before they are available. By preannouncing, companies encourage customers to defer their purchases until new products are available. Preannouncements also encourage third-party vendors to begin work on products and applications that complement the innovator's products.

Product development alliances can encourage the growth of new product applications that would otherwise develop later on. Intel and Compaq maintain close contact in the development of microprocessors and personal computers. By sharing information about predicted market needs and anticipated usage patterns, both companies can develop follow-on applications early on, thereby reaching more customers at higher prices than if each operated alone.

Also helpful in accelerating market exposure are assurances to customers that the risk of adoption is low or that the customer can return the product if it is not wanted. The goal is to move potential customers to a favorable attitude about new products, and then through the purchase decision process without delay. In this regard, it can be helpful to be ready to reposition products quickly if technical problems develop or if the product design proves less attractive than anticipated.

Distribution prearrangements can encourage market exposure. Details can include the timing of introduction, responsibilities for absorbing rapidly rising production, and can spell out what to do with discounted and obsolete products. Radio Shack uses its ten thousand retail outlets this way, which gives the company an advantage in commercializing short-lived products.

Because fast-cycle products are global, when early distribution is confined to a local market, the effect can be to give global competitors early notice of a company's best ideas. This can create an imitation target for competitors, while providing limited sales for the innovator. Imitations of test-marketed products can arrive in regions of the world before the innovators' own products appear.

Japanese electronics companies tes' market products widely in Tokyo. The strategy is to produce a wide variety of designs and applications in limited numbers, to see which are most attractive. This tactic has the advantage of lowering risk, but may have limited value if the product is accepted differently elsewhere. The Sony Minidisk, for example, sold well in Japan but not in the United States. An alternative strategy for Sony would be to enter the U.S. market more aggressively by supporting the Minidisk with dynamic pricing and awareness advertising, accompanied by prearranging distribution on a large scale.

Dynamic Pricing

Dynamic pricing is important to the successful commercialization of short-lived products. The process should not be driven by cost considerations, but rather by the willingness of customers to pay high prices for innovations that have high marginal utility. The tactic is to charge a high premium initially, followed by a rapid decline in prices later in response to competition. Dynamic pricing is different from the traditional idea of penetration pricing, where the objective is to build market share. The goal of dynamic pricing is not to build market share but to extract value, to skim off as much value as possible as product value declines. Dynamic pricing can be difficult for several reasons:

- Determining an introductory price can be difficult. Typically there are few price benchmarks for new, first-time-ever products.
- Demand is particularly sensitive to different price points. If price is set high, demand will not materialize; if price is set too low, demand will grow faster than the innovator's ability to build capacity.
- As price declines, the capacity of the market to absorb large amounts of product will increase significantly. Falling price and growing demand attract followers whose own pricing and production plans make market projections on pricing even more uncertain.

Consider the experience of personal computer makers. When Apple Computer announced a 20 percent price cut on its mid-priced Macintosh line of computers, demand grew so rapidly that Apple was unable to satisfy demand for months. Similarly, Compaq Computer introduced its ProLinea line of computers at a 30 percent lower price than preceding Compaq models that had similar features. To the surprise of managers, market demand shifted rapidly away from preexisting Compaq models, faster than marketing estimates had forecast. During this time Compaq struggled to satisfy distributors' demands for ProLinea while older models languished on dealer shelves. The shortage lasted six months, creating ill will between Compaq and its distributors. In a similar result, IBM carried a three-month inventory of 286 computers when it introduced its 386 machines, which then sold as quickly as they could be made. Prices for the 286 machines had to be cut below the cost of the 286 chips alone.

Thus in settings like these it may be better to err on the side of setting prices too high rather than too low, as high prices can be dropped more readily early on than low prices can be raised later.

The goal in dynamic pricing is to lower price "just fast enough," that is, whereby production runs at capacity with no inventory and no stockouts (this is considerably easier said than done, of course). Importantly, the goal of dynamic pricing is *not* to build market share, as in traditional approaches to pricing. Rather, the objective is to skim the largest amount of profit possible, dynamically, as price declines and volume grows. Dynamic pricing requires real-time sales and inventory tracking. Policies should be in place to ensure that the company can respond to changing market conditions on a real-time basis.

Figure 3.2 shows the dynamic pricing strategy adopted by Intel. The data is for three chip sets, the 66 MHz Pentium, the 100 MHz Pentium and the 200 MHz Pentium Pro. As can be seen from the graph, new microprocessors start at similar price points. As the price of each processor comes down, newer chips are introduced at the higher price levels. At introduction, a 200 MHz Pentium Pro is priced comparable to the older 100 MHz Pentium at its introduction. As competitors catch up and undersell Intel, the company lowers prices to the $200 price range, exits the market

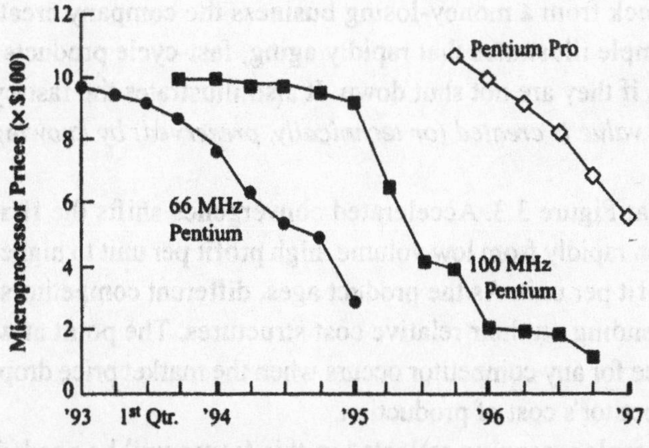

SOURCE: Intel Corporate Communications

Figure 3.2. Dynamic Pricing

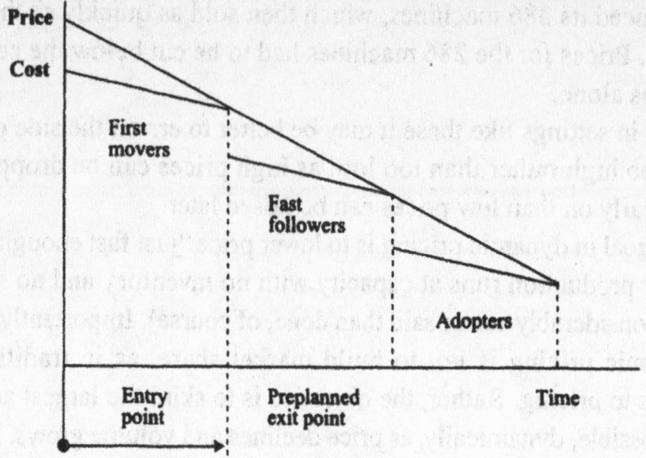

Figure 3.3. Preplanning Market Exit

with that generation product, and introduces its next generation microprocessor to start the cycle again.

Preplan Market Exit

Rapidly aging products create the need to preplan for market exit on an ongoing basis. When managers at Texas Instruments announced that they were giving up on the electronic watch market, the company's stock price *rose* 15 points. Investors believed that the electronic watch market would create a cash flow drain for the company if they remained in the market; by pulling back from a money-losing business the company created value. This example illustrates that rapidly aging, fast-cycle products consume resources if they are not shut down. It also illustrates the fast-cycle principle that *value is created (or technically, preserved) by knowing when to get out.*

Look at Figure 3.3. Accelerated convergence shifts the first mover's orientation rapidly from low volume, high profit per unit to higher volume, lower profit per unit. As the product ages, different competitors come on line, depending on their relative cost structures. The point at which exit takes place for any competitor occurs when the market price drops through that competitor's cost of production.

The simple reasoning reflected in this figure will be needed early on and frequently in fast-cycle markets. Managers should be encouraged to make projections as to when falling market price will pass through the company's cost of production. These estimates should be made, if possible, even before products are commercialized. Establishing benchmarks for exit encourages managers to see product withdrawal not as a sign of failure but as a natural part of competitive evolution. Preplanning market exit increases the effort that managers will devote to successive rounds of innovation.

Hewlett-Packard requires some divisional managers to replenish 20 percent of their product line every year. This goal does not explicitly encourage managers to retire products. It does so indirectly, though, in the sense that the 20 percent goal is more easily attained when, through regular product retirements, the overall portfolio is kept in manageable proportions.

During the planning stage for a new processor, Intel managers work with distributors to plan for the processor's obsolescence. A rollout table details the timing of new product releases and planned obsolete dates for existing products. One year before the Pentium was introduced, distributors and OEMs were given a schedule detailing the obsolescence schedule for the i486 and the Pentium, respectively. Distributors and OEMs were free to purchase the i486 up until the planned withdrawal date. After that, the i486was transferred to the company's Embedded Controller Division. The division uses aging processors to generate additional value, acting, in effect, as a latter stage adopter.

Several factors should be managed to prepare a market for product exit. Morale could suffer if managers feel they are giving up on a market, while loyal customers, if surprised by the decision, may feel abandoned, particularly if they have stayed with the company during difficult times. If replacement products are not readily available, wholesalers or retailers may switch allegiance and purchase competitor products. If a direct sales force is in place, they should be used to smooth the transition away from rapidly aging products.

Be particularly sensitive to the timing of product announcements. Errors in timing, announcing new products too early or too late, can occur on either side of windows of opportunity that are narrow and quickly changing. An example is Osborne Computer, which found that its announcement of the Osborne 2, the Executive, caused demand for the Osborne 1 to fall by half. Within months Osborne was left with large inventories of obsolete Osborne 1s at a time when the Executive was not yet ready for production. In extreme cases, as little as a month can separate product announcements that needlessly cannibalize mainstay products, or that concede the most profitable round of innovation to competitors. Sensitivity to product announcements is consistent with the freestanding, weakly shielded nature of idea-driven products.

Seek Time-based Alignment

As they mature, fast-cycle products pass the three stages shown in Figure 3.3: first mover, fast follower, and adopter. In fast-cycle competition, companies position their products along a timeline, dominated initially by first movers or product innovators. We see companies like Sony and Intel focusing on research and development that allows them to pursue innovation. Next, fast followers like Matsushita and Texas Instruments enter, by reducing cost rapidly and by increasing capacity quickly.

Some companies excel at first-mover and fast-follower strategies simultaneously. Intel has built capabilities across product and process development, allowing it to capture profits throughout the bulk of a microprocessor's life cycle. As we point out, this kind of approach, operating across competitive stages, requires high-stakes, you-bet-your-company commitments.

Ultimately, fast-cycle markets evolve to the final, adoption stage. At this point, the original idea becomes freely available and competition brings on a third type of competitor. Adopters use the original concept or technology in unorthodox ways that go beyond the commercialization opportunities imagined by first movers and fast followers. An example is placing a computer chip in the sole of a runner's shoe. Another example is Swatch, which adds value to commodity electonic watch technology through styling and marketing.

Adopters treat the innovator's ideas irreverently. Their core capabilities reside far from those of first movers and fast followers. By displaying unbridled freedom in adopting the original ideas to nonoriginal uses, adopters create additional value from innovation, in ways that are beyond the scope of first movers and fast followers.

Encourage Options-rich Opportunities

Fast-cycle competition, by its freestanding nature, generates a large number of competitive options. By this we mean that investment in the first round of projects opens up an extensive range of possibilities for future projects, more so than in traditional markets. However, this attractive feature of fast-cycle markets is not easily recognized in traditional capital budgeting processes, which generally find options difficult to value. Yet, without options considerations, projects that have considerable value may be seen as too risky for their more limited observable, traditional, benefits. Where options are present, but difficult to value, the result can be to unfairly penalize fast-cycle projects in the capital budgeting process. Consequently, special efforts should be taken to ensure that the options value of fast-cycle projects is recognized in the planning process (options thinking is revisited in Chapter 6).

There can be additional advantages to moving funds among a portfolio of fast-cycle projects. The time-consuming and intelligence-dispensing process associated with looking externally for funds can be avoided. Cash flows from maturing products can be used to commit to projects that are believed to be options rich without the necessity for disclosure and justification to the capital markets. Gaining access to capital more quickly and with a lower risk of information leakage to competitors gives an advantage to internal funding when investment decisions are made rapidly and often.

A company with a portfolio of fast-cycle investments, at different stages of development and commercialization, can enter and exit markets more quickly and with lower costs than its single-product competitors. The advantage comes from lower costs of reorganization and more efficient asset redeployment (the implicit costs of bankruptcy are lower than for a single-product company). Canon, as a multiproduct company, can enter and exit businesses more quickly and more efficiently than it could if its businesses were separately owned. Stockholders holding diversified portfolios of fast-cycle companies cannot create these benefits.

Identify Complementary Assets

Fast-cycle products age quickly because they lack isolating mechanisms, that is, they have few complementary assets to slow down imitation or competitive innovation. Thus, any actions that managers can take to link fast-cycle products to other, slower cycle isolating mechanisms can slow down economic time and extend the life of products. For example, in the Internet-based financial markets, slow-down tactics could include an emphasis on Internet consultants, analytical tools available only to brokers, and personalized sites for the user that are continually upgraded by analyzing individual customer activities. These services slow down economic time by directing customers to complementary products that are more difficult for competitors to imitate.

At the same time, strategies that slow down economic time may make it more difficult to innovate or to respond to competitor moves. It could become more difficult to introduce new products on the Internet, for example, if complementary analytical tools have computational protocols that are incompatible with fast innovation. Thus, to the extent that complementary capabilities slow down economic time, they also may reduce the number of options available.

HOW FAST-CYCLE ORGANIZATIONS SURVIVE

Joseph Schumpeter concluded that companies could not survive his gale of creative destruction. (His advice was to relax restrictions on monopolies to provide a stable source of funding.) Still, in modern markets, world-class companies like Sony, Intel, Hewlett-Packard, and Compaq bring out short-lived products from generation to generation. How?

Long-lived, fast-cycle organizations create ideas and transfer them to newer products, over and over again, more quickly than these ideas are generated and copied by their competitors. In our research, we sought to understand the types of resources and strategies that underlie this exceptional capability.

Selection Efficiency

Innovation is, of course, the capability to come up with something new. But for those organizations that wish to sustain growth through innovation for extended periods, there is another side to innovation. Think of it as *selection efficiency*—the ability to rapidly commit to promising new projects combined with the willingness to rapidly withdraw support from failing projects. Selection efficiency is the superior ability to choose between projects that become winners and losers—quickly and effectively.

Selection efficiency is important when a company faces a flurry of shifting investment choices. Fast-cycle markets generate fast-changing investment opportunities and the repeated need to shut down projects. With

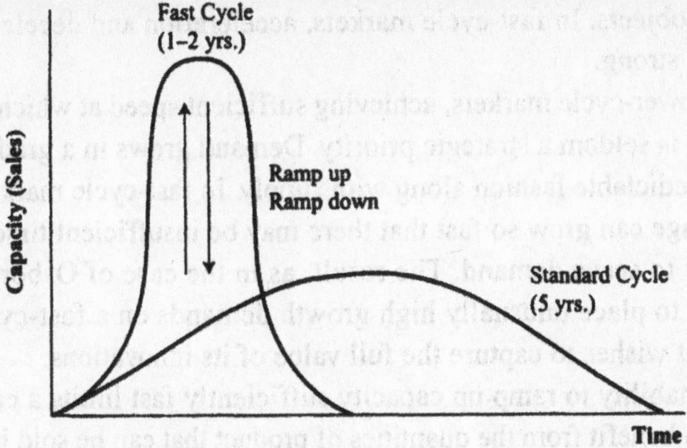

Figure 3.4. Capacity Ramping

selection efficiency comes the advantage of being able to shift resources away from destined-to-fail projects faster, with a greater sense of confidence. A pioneer in understanding and refining these kinds of important decisions, Robert Burgelman, has found that these skills are critical to renewal in companies like Intel.[4] With efficient selection, time and resources no longer needed on projects that ultimately fail are freed up for better uses.

The skill is like that of a high-stakes poker player in a fast-paced game. Selection efficiency gives managers, as Kenny Rogers put it, the ability "to know when to hold 'em and know when to fold 'em."

Selection efficiency increases the speed and accuracy by which an organization can choose between the alternatives facing it. It increases the ability to select projects that are likely to be successful, while discarding projects that are likely to fail. The capability is one of sharp investment discrimination, the ability to decide what to do and what not to do, repeatedly and effectively, in an environment of rapidly changing alternatives.

Capacity Ramping

Figure 3.4 compares product life cycles in standard- and fast-cycle economic time. Notice that the amount of product sold in the two cycles is not noticeably different. What is different is the rate of change of growth. In fast-cycle markets, demand increases rapidly but also decreases rapidly. Physicists call this effect acceleration, a change in the rate of change of moving objects. In fast-cycle markets, acceleration and deceleration effects are strong.

In slower-cycle markets, achieving sufficient speed at which capacity is added is seldom a strategic priority. Demand grows in a gradual, relatively predictable fashion along with supply. In fast-cycle markets, however, usage can grow so fast that there may be insufficient time to build capacity to serve demand. The result, as in the case of Osborne Computer, is to place unusually high growth demands on a fast-cycle company that wishes to capture the full value of its innovations.

An inability to ramp up capacity sufficiently fast limits a company's ability to benefit from the quantities of product that can be sold initially at high prices. The result of being unable to supply a fast-cycle market quickly is lost sales and greater competition. Fast capacity ramp-up is also necessary to gain the full benefits of dynamic pricing. In this way, capacity ramp-up and dynamic pricing complement each other in helping the fast-cycle company maintain profitable alignment with changing customer needs.

Equally important to capacity management is the ability to take capacity off line quickly. Shortly after peak sales are reached, demand will shift toward newer products. New products, product substitutes, and the entry of competitors at lower prices will shift demand away from the innovating company's products in short time. This has the effect of rendering manufacturing capacity obsolete faster than in more traditional markets. Capacity must be taken off line quickly at a minimum cost, and with low organizational disruption. The challenge is like being asked to run the fastest 100-yard dash of your life—but to be ready to stop instantly, on a signal, anytime into the race.

Intel's Grove recalls, "In 1983 and the early part of 1984 we had a heated-up market. Everything we made was in short supply. People were pleading with us for more parts and we were booking orders further and further out in time to guarantee a supply. We were scrambling to build more capacity, starting factory construction at different locations and hiring people to ramp up our production volumes. Then in the fall of 1984 all of that changed. Business slowed down. It seemed that nobody wanted to buy chips anymore. Our order backlog evaporated like spring snow. After a period of disbelief, we started cutting back production. But after the long period of buildup, we couldn't wind down fast enough to match the market slide. *We were still building inventory even as our business headed south* (italics added)."[5]

To minimize the onset of overcapacity it is important to revisit sales forecasts often. Systems should be in place to update changing sales often and to monitor price declines. Product loyalty should not be allowed to influence decisions to retire aging products. As Hasbro President Alan Hassenfeld puts it, "We have got to be able to stop on a dime if there's trouble. Once you have brought the product to market, all emotion should go away. You have to face reality as quickly as possible."

Fast Forgetting

Learning in new situations is essential for success. One expression of this is the highly regarded learning curve referred to in Chapter 2. However, in our work with fast-cycle companies we came to believe that also essential to fast-cycle success is the ability to *forget*. "Unlearning" or moving your company down a forgetting curve clears away old ideas, yesterday's notions, and knowledge gained in the past that is no longer needed.

Forgetting can be more difficult than learning. Letting go of long-held beliefs is difficult. It can be particularly difficult to "unremember" practices that were time consuming and expensive to learn, or that have become grounded in familiar notions, or that favor historical capabilities. When past practices get in the way of what needs to be done tomorrow, fast forgetting is needed to cast aside timeworn behavior and emotionally charged product loyalties to make way for more competitive attitudes and practices.

Fast-Cycle Decision Styles

Successful managers in fast-cycle industries are often analytical risk-takers. They have a deep understanding of their company's core competencies. They are aware of the dangers of confusing temporary product advantage with long-term renewable advantage. They are able to process information from a wide range of sources on a real-time basis so as to be able to change their mental maps of what is important.

Effective fast-cycle managers rely on real-time information. They blend formal and informal approaches, with a strong finance orientation. They build multiple, simultaneous alternatives, and do comparisons of possible outcomes. They maintain a fallback position if something should go wrong. They seek the counsel of experienced advisors as a sounding board and in order to build confidence. Consensus is with qualification in that if agreement is lacking, one person makes the decision, recognizing that to wait is to decide. Effective fast-cycle managers do not avoid conflict, they integrate decisions, and they maintain a web of information, sources, and contacts.[6]

Fast-cycle decisions are best managed as part of a system of decisions. It is understood that a decision in one area quickly affects a decision in another area, as in the case of price changes that cause demand to rise, inventories to change fast, and the need for production capacity to grow or shrink quickly. Special efforts are taken so that key decisions are not compartmentalized or made in isolation.

Smart Mistakes

Fast-cycle managers are required to make life and death decisions more frequently than are their slower-cycle counterparts. As a result, decision-making skills are highly valued and nurtured as an end in themselves. Toward this end managers in fast-cycle companies tend to encourage "smart mistakes." A smart mistake is one that leads to a poor outcome (does not favor the company) but is made within the confines of a high-quality decision process or for the purpose of expanding the organization's decision set. Smart mistakes are made for good reasons, in a sensible manner, following the best practices of the company or with the goal of augmenting best practices. Smart mistakes help an organization learn to make better decisions. Smart mistakes help a company move down its learning and forgetting curves faster.

The goal in rewarding smart mistakes is not to encourage mistakes. It is to encourage people to push their decision-making envelope, to learn more about market opportunities. Smart mistakes are valued for their ability to allow people to learn how to make better decisions. The knowledge gained is not so much what the decision should have been but how to enhance the company's decision processes overall. Smart mistakes help to build new capabilities.

Or as you may have heard . . . if you never fail, you're not trying hard enough.

The highly dynamic market success factors, unorthodox strategies, and unconventional capabilities that we observed in successful fast-cycle companies make fast-cycle organizations qualitatively different than their traditional counterparts. As effective as these new approaches are, we are left with Schumpeter's challenge: How long can an organization survive in markets that appear to be dominated by uncontrolled innovation?

Successful fast-cycle companies sustain renewal by adopting, even embracing, creative destruction as their central, ongoing way of doing business. Fast-cycle companies commercialize ideas, transfer resources to ever-newer products, and eat their children faster than their competitors do. It's that simple and that difficult. Successful fast-cycle companies *are* high-powered engines of creative destruction.

RECAP: CHILDREN EATERS

In fast-cycle markets the only source of advantage is innovation—and the only barrier to entry is time. While the risks of these markets are high the rewards can be high as well. If you are considering whether you wish to compete in fast-cycle markets you can keep the following points in mind:

WHAT YOU CAN EXPECT

1. During the hypergrowth phase there will be considerable debate as to how much demand will actually materialize and the degree of commitment that should be undertaken. There is no avoiding this; it is the nature of fast-cycle decision settings.
2. Unless you are well established you can expect that one of your challenges will be to learn how to grow up fast enough to take on the responsibility of operating in markets where customer expectations change rapidly. As you race to grow, you will experience enormous challenges to maintaining your core values and sense of purpose.
3. Collapsing prices open up unfamiliar markets and bring on new competitors. As alignment between your company and your customers shifts, your market's critical success factors will likely change. Be sensitive to the rapidly changing nature of critical success factors. Fast-changing strategies that may be required in response should not be seen as a sign of weakness but as a natural part of fast-cycle economic time.

ACTIONS YOU CAN TAKE FIRST

1. Don't identify strongly with individual products. Fast-cycle products come and go. Identify instead with the underlying processes or core competencies at work; these are more stable and will give you better predictions of which competitors are likely to enter a market, and their limitations—as well as yours.
2. Plan for product withdrawal at the time of product introduction. Hewlett-Packard, Intel, 3M, and Sony nurture a culture in which market exit is seen not as a sign of failure, but as a natural component to the competitive process.
3. Seek to create demand. Go from basing your business on the premise that others will create demand to taking responsibility for creating demand yourself.
4. Distribute across a range of markets, in high volumes, as quickly as possible. Brand awareness advertising, product preannouncements, product-development alliances and predistribution arrangements can help in this regard.
5. Lower price fast enough so that your organization runs at full capacity on one hand, with no inventory buildup on the other hand. Dynamic pricing requires real-time sales and inventory tracking and is made more difficult when the market's production capacity and elasticity of demand are increasing rapidly.
6. Condition customers and distributors in advance for product withdrawals. Helpful in this regard can be special contracts, training programs, careful inventory management, and a reputation for standing by distributors in a time of change.
7. Be sensitive to the timing of product announcements. Preannouncements of new products, particularly when made by companies that have credibility for delivering on product announcements, will have an immediate effect on the demand for existing products. Precise timing, announcing products neither too early nor too late, must take place within windows of opportunity that are narrow.

SUSTAINING LONG-TERM GROWTH

1. Base your strategies for product entry and exit on your underlying core competencies. Focus your efforts on the stage of market evolution that

creates best alignment with what you do well. Generally, the choice will be first-mover, fast-follower, or adopter. You can compete across these stages but your risks will increase due to the high levels of commitment required.

2. Encourage options-rich thinking. Make special efforts to identify projects that create opportunities beyond the foreseeable term. Internal capital markets that speed project financing, reduce liquidation costs, and minimize information spillovers can augment options-rich thinking.
3. Treat externally obtained information as a valuable resource. Seminars, corporate policies on information, and information technology can be used to encourage people at all levels to seek out and share information from a wide range of external sources.
4. Increase project selection efficiency. Develop within your managers the ability to sort out project winners from project losers. Increase the speed and accuracy by which you choose among many quickly changing alternatives.
5. Manage capacity aggressively. Explore ways to accelerate capacity additions and capacity withdrawals. Consider adopting a less efficient but more flexible manufacturing process.
6. Retain people who are eager to discard current ideas, who reason analytically under uncertainty, and change their competitive models as needed. Reward people for the quality of their decision making and their willingness to improve their decision-making capabilities.
7. Select managers who are willing to make decisions without delay, even if consensus is not possible, and to *do something*. Otherwise well-intentioned, skilled managers who move too slowly for fast-cycle markets can create bad alignment between their company and their customers without knowing it. Successful managers should be entrepreneurs, but with a strong command over the business aspects of their markets. It is particularly important to make sure that the styles and risk preferences of managers match those of fast-cycle markets.

Fast-cycle business practices will be brought into the mainstream of management, refined, and expanded. But the challenge and the opportunities do not end here. Our work revealed the importance of another class of mar-

kets that operates outside of traditional thinking. These markets operate at the opposite end of economic time, where product advantage is unusually long and enduring. Here product success can convey near-complete market ownership. At the same time, slow-cycle managers face special challenges in sustaining growth, in their own ways equal to that of their faster-cycle counterparts.

CHAPTER 4

THE NEW ARTISANS

Artisans' guilds flourished during the Middle Ages and the Renaissance. These individual businesses had little chance of achieving economies of scale and they faced little change. Each guild monopolized its immediate geographic area and produced by hand whatever goods the local population needed. Each maintained personal contact with its customers. These businesses operated within a shielded market. Human skills, geography, personal rapport, or religious and secular law built stable barriers to entry that effectively blocked competition.

Guilds operated within slow economic time. Transportation was measured by human bodily rhythms and was slow and cumbersome compared with the pace of the industrial revolution that would follow. The mechanisms available for telling time were primitive, reliable only to the hour, and in use only in cities. Because there was no one to beat to the market, time was not pressing. People were known by their life's work: Cooper, Carver, and Mason.

These artisan-like businesses and their protected markets are still part of the world marketplace. But today they are larger and more sophisticated and much more profitable. Consider:

Products and services based on naturally shielded property rights account for 7 percent of total U.S. GNP and the percentage is growing.

American-made films make up 89 percent of box-office receipts outside the United States. The entertainment industry in California has surpassed defense as the largest industry sector. The movie *Titanic,* released in 1998, earned $1.5 billion in revenues in two months, most of it outside the United States.

Company officials were astonished when Disney re-released *Snow White* in 1993; the $500 million in profits received was a greater return than the company made a half-century ago when it created this timeless classic.

The in-home video-game business reached $5 billion in 1992, on par with domestic movie box-office receipts. Sega Enterprises' *Sonic the Hedgehog 2,* released in November, sold 5 million units in sixty days. Its $300 million gross worldwide revenue was more than what all but a handful of movie blockbusters generate.

Two television shows, *Wheel of Fortune* and *Jeopardy!,* were responsible for keeping Columbia's studio profitable in the early 1990s—yet at the time, both game shows were over ten years old.

Eighty percent of profits on Wall Street still come from the old boy network: relationship-based underwriting and initial public stock offerings, markets that are a century old.

Bidders for wireless services on a fragment of the U.S. broadcast spectrum paid a record $8 billion to the U.S. Treasury in 1995. The market value of the digitized broadcast spectrum in the United States is estimated at $500 billion.

At the turn of the century Microsoft's influence in the global economy is unparalleled, and unprecedented compared to its relatively small revenue ($8 billion) and modest size (8,000 employees).

These examples have a common growth dynamic—the race for naturally shielded property rights. By this we mean *the near-total ownership of something essential to the functioning of a market.*

Property rights are one of the earliest recognized advantages. They originated with ownership of land, a nonduplicable factor of production in early agricultural economies. Opportunity for land ownership drove the development of the American frontier. Modern-day property rights are like land rights in that they are difficult to imitate. But *unlike* Will Rogers' famous quote, "buy land, they're not making any more of it"—they *are* making more of it.

Slow-cycle advantages are highly attractive from a strategic standpoint. Products and services operating in slow-cycle markets are shielded from traditional competitive pressures:

- They enjoy stable pricing.
- They face few cost-reduction demands.
- They experience long-lived profit cycles.
- They survive late delivery, poor quality, and even catastrophic failures.

Attractive, yes? Yet this class of organizations and their competitive opportunities are often disregarded, or at least underestimated. In an important study of specialist organizations, Glenn Carroll finds that in the music industry, specialist strategies often prove to be more resilient to recessions. Additionally, in book publishing, consistency of sales is higher and average book shelf life is longer for small press book companies than it is for larger publishers of mass-market books.[1]

These characteristics stand in contrast to thinking that advantage is becoming less sustainable. Still, as we will see, these naturally shielded markets come with their own special renewal challenges, in particular, a whole set of issues associated with the challenge of growth. This class of markets, of growing importance in the new economy, has forces at work that can make or break a company without its managers even knowing why.[2]

The Rise of the Modern-Day Artisan

January 1986 was marked by the worst space disaster to date with the loss of the Space Shuttle Challenger and its crew. Why did the shuttle fail? The shuttle's O-rings were not designed to seal the boosters against leakage of hot exhaust gases at winter temperatures. The engineers knew this, and so did the people at NASA. Why did they proceed with the launch? Why did the people in charge disregard their own best judgment?

The pressures of the launch schedule took over, combined with the cost overruns of redesigning the boosters, and NASA's desire to get the shuttle up and running as a profitable business venture, supported by revenues from carrying commercial payloads into space. Like a commercial business, NASA was trying to keep costs low and volume up by increasing the number of flights. Management, in effect, wanted to standardize the shuttle operation to gain economies of scale. By resisting costly, time-consuming changes in the O-ring design, NASA was pursuing greater repeatability and efficiency, as most organizations functioning within commercial markets would.

Yet, in terms of renewal, NASA functions more like a Renaissance craft guild than like Ford or Toyota. Space shuttles are built by hand by teams of highly skilled, modern-day artisans who concentrate on their craft; not on efficiency, mass production, cost cutting, and scheduling efficiency. Like their sixteenth-century counterparts, NASA's artisans require a long time to produce one-of-a-kind products that serve a specialized market.

Because of the technical requirements and costs for a project as sophisticated as a space shuttle, it takes years to build the necessary rapport between engineers at NASA and suppliers like Morton Thiokol. The Thiokol/NASA relationship is built upon one-of-a-kind knowledge and specialized skills that are valuable only to each other.

This relationship, a bilateral monopoly (one-buyer, one-seller), creates high switching costs for both. For Thiokol, the company's highly specialized knowledge and investment in plant and equipment, is nearly worthless in any other customer setting. For NASA, the costs of switching to another vendor would be prohibitive. After the Challenger disaster, these mutually binding switching costs were the reason that Thiokol was awarded a $425 million contract to redesign the failed booster O-rings, in the face of criticism that NASA should switch to another supplier. This example is not a criticism of NASA or Morton Thiokol management, but rather an example of the lock-in effects that can tie companies and customers together in slow-cycle markets.

Slow-cycle products naturally dominate their markets. They define their market. They *own* their market. They *are* their market. A slow-cycle company operates within a strategic group of one: itself. Market ownership is localized to a factor of the market that the company owns exclusively.

Localized ownership does not mean localized in the geographical sense. It means competition is confined to the factor of market ownership. The key to gaining slow-cycle advantage lies in securing a naturally shielded property right that is innately unprofitable for competitors to duplicate. What results is an innate, natural, near-automatic resistance to competition. Competitors may wish to imitate the slow-cycle advantages of another company, but they know that the attempt will likely cost them more than the advantage is worth.

Microsoft owns the operating system for personal computers through its Windows software. In the telecommunications industry the market value of the sought-after VHF, UHF, cellular, and narrowband spectrum exceeds $100 billion. These are gateways to the information age, like the right of way on which railroads like James J. Hill's great Pacific Northern were built a century ago.

Is this monopolistic competition? Of course it is. But these monopolistic advantages can be created legally. As we will see, there can be a complex interpretation of monopoly power in slow-cycle markets. But by and large, slow-cycle advantages are earned the old fashioned way: through hard work, smart decisions, careful investment, and foresight into new market opportunities.

Slow-cycle advantage results from something that is naturally difficult or automatically unprofitable for rivals to imitate but must be used by the customer.

Slow-cycle advantages convey noncontested market ownership. Product advantage is localized to and secured within the company. Slow-cycle products gain first-mover advantages that are highly sustainable, and once obtained, are inherently sticky.

The land rush is on again. This time the objective is exclusive product advantage arising from one or more of these sources:

- *The human capital monopoly,* where market ownership is created by the valuable, hard-to-duplicate skills of the modern-day artisan. Examples are found in entertainers and sports heroes (Bill Cosby and Michael Jordan), personal computer industry pioneers (Microsoft's Bill Gates, NEXT's Steve Jobs), consultants (Tom Peters), and healthcare pioneers (Christiaan Barnard). The market value of the world's most profitable biotechnology company, Amgen, in 1995 was $12 billion. By some estimates, Amgen needed only 500 of its 3,400 employees to generate these results. By this measure Amgen was generating $3 million in sales and $24 million in market value per employee.
- *The bilateral monopoly,* found in the defense, consulting, and aerospace industries, where the complexity of the product is the barrier to entry. Rockwell International built the space shuttle. Later, Lockheed Martin took over management of the shuttle. In each case there was only one buyer and one seller in this long-lived multibillion-dollar market.
- *Location, brand, or standards ownership,* where ownership of a central market factor or market gateway, as for Microsoft's Windows95 operating system or USAirways hub control at Pittsburgh, creates barriers to entry. Alfred Kahn, the father of deregulation, describes airline deregulation as "a mess" because regulators did not foresee the onset of hub control. Similar arguments can be made for the information industry, as we will see, where modern-day antitrust law has failed to keep pace with new ways to create competitive advantage.
- *Patents and copyrights.* Merck's leadership in the pharmaceutical industry and Genentech in genetic engineering provide examples. Mevacor's economic half-life, the period during which the drug will generate profits for Merck, is estimated at a decade or more. Capoten, the hy-

pertension product from Bristol-Myers Squibb, generated $1.5 billion in annual revenues worldwide even after Capoten's profit cycle passed ten years in length.

These new business advantages are proliferating. Some are not new, like geography, patents, and copyrights. But they, and other genuinely new slow-cycle advantages, are becoming more widespread and more influential. As a marketplace becomes advanced and more sophisticated, activities shift from basic services like food, shelter, and manufacturing, to activities based on intangible, information-based assets. Increasing demand in wealthy economies for artisan-based activities, combined with their natural resistance to duplication, is the reason for the growing global economic value accounted for by these competitively exclusive activities.

Slow-cycle advantages also can combine and overlap, making the understanding of these markets interesting and challenging. Let's look at some of the more visible examples.

Human Capital Monopolies

Where do we look for authority in the new economy? Increasingly, the source is scientists, consultants, health care specialists, politicians, athletes, entertainers, talk-show hosts, software developers, authors, academics, and inventors. The specialized skills of these talented and gifted individuals play an increasing role in advanced economies.

Look at what has happened to the century-old human capital-based industry, baseball. The advent of free agency, combined with revenue from television rights, caused baseball salaries to rise twentyfold. From 1976 to 1994, the average baseball player salary rose from $52,000 to $1.2 million.

Consider the entertainment industry. More than 450 films are made each year in the United States. But the number of stars who can almost guarantee a film's success worldwide remains fixed. The rule of thumb is that about fifteen well-known actors and actresses alone have the star power to ensure a good audience. Bruce Willis got $5 million in 1986 for the movie *Die Hard,* which was twice his earlier salary and, at the time, the most ever for an action film. Ten years later Mel Gibson, Jim Carrey, Tom Cruise, and Harrison Ford were signing movie contracts for $20 million.

McKinsey's 3,100 consultants' salary averaged $387,000 each in 1992. The 780 professionals at the Boston Consulting Group came in second at

$359,000 each. Senior partners in advice-driven markets on Wall Street routinely earn in excess of $1 million a year.

Nobel laureate Herbert Simon points out that it takes about thirteen years to create a genius. Mozart, who wrote and performed marvelous works of music at age seventeen, had been practicing and learning his trade since he was four. The lives of modern-day artisans are spent forming their trade and developing their markets through their unique talents. This is one reason why the authority of modern-day artisans is difficult to challenge.

Jeffrey Katzenberg, Steven Spielberg, and David Geffen, the team that founded the $2 billion DreamWorks studio, are all college dropouts. Modern-day artisans possess advantages that are innate to the persona of the individual and, as we will see, can be difficult to extend.

Modern-day artisans can act together to create a market that they own collectively. NASA functions more like a Renaissance craft guild than a traditional, modern-day business. In this sense space shuttles are like fine furniture, made by craftsmen operating in ways similar to their forebears in the craft guilds of Europe, hundreds of years ago.

Bilateral Monopolies

Artisans long ago flourished by cultivating complex relationships with their patron-customers. Specialized relationships are now built on technological complexity. It takes years to develop the close rapport between engineers at NASA and suppliers like Morton Thiokol needed to build the shuttle's booster rockets. The Grumman F-14, described by company managers as a flying computer, is designed around complex electronic countermeasure systems that are continually updated by the Defense Department. Once developed by Grumman and Pentagon engineers, the relationship is highly specialized and idiosyncratic, resistant to outside influences. The Sidewinder heat-seeking missile made by Ford Aerospace, Raytheon, and twelve other contractors reflected a thirty-year marriage between the engineering groups of these companies.

Want to become a successful investment banker? You should learn the latest financial instruments, study new product technologies, and polish your sales skills . . . no, it's not enough. It's still a network. A London-based money manager says "we all know the same people" when referring to a group of wealthy individuals who invested in the $1.2 billion Vairocana Ltd. fund run by David de Jongh Weill, who maintained a tony lifestyle in Paris that helped him network with rich clientele.

McKinsey expects its high-level consultants to have the same social and philanthropic interests as executives at their client corporations. As a Bain competitor put it, "The hardest thing about competing with them is that they have these deep relationships with senior management that prompts them to return to McKinsey, unquestioned, time and time again."

Relationship complexity can be reinforced by product complexity. Weill, the fund manager of Vairocana, had woven complex swaps and options into the portfolio to hedge against risk, a common industry practice. This makes fund positions difficult to evaluate. At one point Weill's outside auditor needed five days a month and a staff of ten full-time employees just to determine the fund's value.

In standard-cycle markets customers see a final product, a car for example, but not the automobile assembly line. In these slow-cycle markets the unit of production is the relationship with the customer. Thus, the traditional distinction between product and process, and the ability to divide and conquer each, breaks down. Tightly coupled product/process relationships create strong isolating mechanisms, raising barriers to would-be competitors.

Location

Airline hub control results when a carrier obtains leases on the majority of gates at an airport. This allows carriers to gain supremacy within a geographical region and raise prices with little chance of competitor entry. Examples include USAirways at Pittsburgh, Delta at Atlanta, and Northwest at Detroit. Airline gates and the landing rights associated with them are effectively impossible to duplicate. Further, their function cannot be taken over in some other way. Thus, once hub-control advantage is established, even otherwise skillful competitors cannot gain a foothold with an airline's customers.

Look again at the baseball industry. One of the puzzles of sports is why franchises that lose money continue to rise in value, year after year. In the first seventy years of the twentieth century, the value of professional sports franchises doubled every nine years, approximately staying even with the overall inflation rate. The value of the New York Mets and Texas Rangers, sold twice in the 1980s, doubled in less than three years. Why? The promise of long-lived cash flows, as well as the trophy effect, whereby ownership of the club conveys cachet to its owners by virtue of locational exclusivity.

Another trophy property is premium vineyards. Twenty years ago, there were about sixty wineries in California; now there are more than eight hundred, most of them making small lots of higher-priced wines. Gross margins on premium wines can reach 70 percent. The land on which grapes are grown is so important that family-owned wineries frequently pass down their land through generations. Cabernet Sauvignon grapes can be grown in many geographical regions but will not have the same quality as those grown in California's Napa and Sonoma Valleys. The climate and soil there are ideal for growing this variety of grape. Similarly, Chardonnay grapes tend to grow best in Santa Barbara County, just north of Los Angeles. In both cases, the geography of the land, the soil type, and the proximity to the climate-controlling effects of the Pacific Ocean all have an effect on the quality of the grapes grown there.

The quality of a bottle of wine, additionally, depends on vine maturity and strict quality standards. This is one of the keys to the success of smaller wineries. A winery that owns its own vineyard portrays an image of higher quality, since, through vertical integration of this type, it is in a better position to control the quality of its own grapes, at least in the eyes of consumers. Wineries of this type exhibit an intimate knowledge of the local aspects of the production process (women, reportedly, are better wine tasters then men) and a more guild-like approach to production that connoisseurs swear by. Helen Turley, considered a "vinous goddess" by industry experts, makes no more than 2,500 cases of wine at time, concluding, "that is the upper limit if you want to taste every barrel."

Some well-known wineries have gotten out of the distribution and advertising parts of the wine business entirely by focusing on growth and harvesting. Fetzer of Mendocino County was purchased by Brown-Forman Corporation in one of the largest winery purchases in history. Brown-Forman markets and distributes Jack Daniel's and Korbel Champagne. Although analysts expressed surprise at the sale of the sixth largest premium wine producer, Fetzer managers judged that their future lay in a return to the artisan-like aspects of the business.

Brand Ownership

Why do simple products like McIlhenny Tabasco sauce and Kikkoman soy sauce remain popular, decade after decade? These products were the first of their kind to create near-ownership of their brand category. Most people believe that no comparable product is available. Both products have come to own their product space. Similar advantages came about for products like Arm and Hammer baking soda and Ivory soap.

Other examples are Lego blocks, Swiss Army knives and Barbie dolls. These products don't just dominate customers' perceptions of their brand category, they *are* the brand category. As long as a product defines a brand, advantage is sustainable as long as the brand is in demand. Brand managers experience few competitive pressures. Prices are stable. There is no brand erosion.

With this brief listing we see that there are many ways to create slow-cycle advantage. Although the examples vary, common among them is ownership of a factor necessary for the functioning of a market.

Another common trait of slow-cycle markets is this: advantage, although sustainable, can be especially difficult to replicate on a large scale. Economists might call this the no free lunch theory of advantage. Let's look at the problem in detail.

Standards Ownership

Microsoft's dominance in the software industry at the turn of the century reflects the creation and ownership of the central gateway to the information economy, the de facto standard for personal computer operating systems. By creating what are known as network externalities, common operating systems encourage development of an industry by allowing a common entry point and means of commerce for companies and customers alike. Without central gateways, many information industries simply would not function. An example is the telephone, an open network based on an electrical standard freely available to all.

Network standards that are proprietary allow companies to influence which "vehicles" enter and exit the "data highway." In this way, companies can direct the extension of their advantage over long periods. As we will see, companies like Microsoft and Intuit's Quicken (checkbook software) benefit from gate control in their market. Both have used standards ownership to create a string of profitable, interconnected, naturally isolated advantages.

Patents and Copyrights

The race for property rights includes scientists working to patent the DNA structure of the human body in treating specific diseases. Companies successful in patenting the molecular sequence of human genes in treating diseases could create ownership of a treatment category. These categories could become "pharmaceutical operating systems" on which companies own exclusive treatments for diseases like cancer and aging, applicable anywhere on earth.

Knowing the molecular sequences of human genes is valuable even if companies don't manufacture the drugs. Genetic knowledge, or more precisely its application in a particular clinical setting, is traded between drug manufacturers for large fees. The U.S. marketplace alone supports twenty patent-protected drugs at any one time, with each generating a billion dollars or more in annual sales.

In a patent race of another kind, Harley-Davidson has used a two-cylinder, V-twin engine in its motorcycles since 1909. Harley managers have always claimed that the sound that their motorcycle makes is distinctive. Harley owners also agree that the sound, described as a fast "potato, potato, potato," is one of the things that make their bikes desirable. In recognition of this, Harley-Davidson filed for trademark protection for the sound that its 45 degree V-twin single crankpin motor makes.

A trademark and a patent are not the same thing, although they are both forms of intellectual property. A patent protects a process, machine, or composition from use by other companies and lasts for up to twenty years. A trademark is any word, name, symbol, or device used by a manufacturer or merchant to identify and distinguish his goods, including a unique product, from those manufactured or sold by others. A trademark guarantees that what's inside (or what you hear) is the genuine article. A trademark, unlike a patent, never ends. Therefore a trademark has the potential of being more sustainable than a patent.

Harley managers contend that competitors are trying to copy the potato sound. If Harley is successful, they will strengthen ownership of their product category. As a competitor put it, "If Harley is not contested, if they do acquire the trademark, they back into a patent because none of us will be able to build a motorcycle in this category anymore."

Harley-Davidson protects other trademarks. Harley has a trademark for its winged logo, and the use of the term "hogs." Only Harley can use the term to refer to its motorcycles, although it still can be used to refer to pigs. When Bikers' Dream Inc., which sells parts for Harleys, went public, the NASDAQ ticker symbol it chose was HOGS. Harley sent a warning letter, and the owner backed out and changed the company's symbol.

MIGHTY FORTRESSES

Slow-cycle markets can be attractive. They resist traditional competitive pressures. Airline passengers dissatisfied with their air carrier return, time and again. Pharmaceutical companies charge higher prices and expand their sales. Products, like Windows95, are late to market, yet customers wait.

So you might ask, why doesn't all business seek out slow-cycle markets? In a sense we do. We all strive for that Holy Grail that we call sustainable advantage.

The problem is that, ironically, or perhaps understandably, the factors that make it difficult for competitors to duplicate slow-cycle success can also make it difficult for the slow-cycle company *itself* to duplicate *its own* success. Renewal can be confined to the original source of market ownership.

Think of slow-cycle renewal pathways as highly circumscribed, offering narrow expansion possibilities. Like narrow pathways through thick forests, growth, beyond the original source of market ownership, can be limited by the same forces that keep competitors out. Or put simply: What is difficult to imitate can be difficult to replicate. This is the price for competition-free growth.

Superstars, for example, are difficult to create or replace. Ownership of their image remains with them. One difference between movie stars and television stars is that movie stars are less dependent on a particular script. This is one reason why movie stars are paid more than television stars. There are exceptions such as Bill Cosby and Bob Newhart but, for the most part, television stars tend to come and go with the shows that create their image. Hollywood stars, in contrast, move among many scripts. In this sense they own their character. Actors Sean Connery, Tom Cruise, and Clint Eastwood achieve character ownership to the point that movie scripts are written around them, their particular mannerisms, traits, and styles. In effect, their character *is* their operating system.

At Disney, the same actor recorded the voice for the Goofy character for nearly a decade, singing all of Goofy's songs even though he had no singing voice. Disney's attempts to replace this individual with professional singers were ultimately rejected by Disney management because the results were not true Goofy songs.

The otherwise highly successful Steven Spielberg was unsuccessful in attempts to expand beyond the movie medium. His *Amazing Stories* and

Earth 2 television shows, although well done, did not generate enough of a following. Spielberg was similarly unsuccessful in his attempt to translate his talents in movie making into *We're Back! A Dinosaur's Story,* a children's version of *Jurassic Park.* The craft of television, although seemingly similar to movie making, requires its own, specialized screenwriters, story lines, characters, and distribution arrangements.

Consulting firms rely on personalized relationships with clients for the important processes of lead generation. The one-of-a-kind nature of these relationships, the time-consuming process of generating them, make these businesses slow to grow. Similar growth barriers are experienced in investment banking.

Gardener-style Managers

Often, the style of management in slow-cycle organizations is flexible and informal. The culture is one of internal self-control and autonomy. Examples include Microsoft, McKinsey, Disney, and Merck. Gemini Consulting, for example, had no office for its sixty-plus professionals in Pittsburgh. Most of its meetings were held by teleconferencing. Consultants' business cards had no titles. These kinds of slow-cycle organizations draw strength from informality and flexible reporting relationships. Gardener-style management can be difficult to duplicate and it can make growth difficult.

Imagine approaching your organization as you might a garden. You supply, in effect, all the necessary ingredients for the "planting and growing" of individuals. When novices are trained at Disney, managers reinforce the illusion that Walt Disney himself is still alive, along with all the company's original values. Like a successful garden, the process takes time. Early on, you are not sure which plantings will grow best. But you watch and nurture those that do well and you weed out those that don't.

Gardener-style leaders manage through complex relationships with the organization's individuals. Leaders who don't fit into their organization's culture can find it difficult to change the organization to their liking. It takes time and patience. This is one reason why, in industries like health care, academia, and consulting, leaders are consultative rather than dictatorial in their style. Growth and maturation of "the luminaries in the garden" is overseen through a process of forbearance, encouragement, and negotiation.

Renewal can stop with the loss of the superstars that fuel growth. The rock group The Doors declined after the loss of leader Jim Morrison in 1971. The breakup of Led Zeppelin after the death of drummer John Bonham is another example. The long-lasting success of the Rolling Stones can be attributed to the extraordinary durability of Mick Jagger, the band's leader.

Why is growth difficult? Consider McKinsey. In describing their growth experience in the 1980s, managers reflected that, "We grew too fast. It strained the fabric of the place. There are some very sophisticated things that keep McKinsey together. . . . The big challenge is to evolve without losing our values in spite of the scale and complexity of the organization." Note the challenge: to renew growth *despite increasing scale.*

Restraints on Innovation

Naturally shielded advantage is not easily separated from a resistance to change. USAirways, for example, trailed all other major airlines in instituting a frequent-flyer program. Paradoxically, often resistance comes from customers. Examples include the initially successful Novell NetWare and Lotus 1-2-3 software programs, which were followed by resistance to NetWare and Lotus 123 (Symphony) upgrades. Lucent Technologies had difficulty selling 5ESS switching systems to its customers because they were attached through millions of lines of specialized software code to Bell Labs' thirty-year-old, aging but proven predecessor, the 4ESS. Competitive lock-in works both ways, locking in customers, but locking in the slow-cycle company to its products as well.

With advantage secured to the original source of market ownership, slow-cycle managers can face the challenge of ending up as single-product companies. Polaroid has owned the instant film photography market for decades based on extensions of 1950s patents granted to Edwin Land, the company founder. But when Polaroid has attempted to move beyond instant-film products, results have been disappointing. This has caused Polaroid problems in extending its advantage, which to this day remains centered on extensions of instant photography technology. Grumman faced the same renewal problems with the expiration of their twenty-year contract on the F-14.

Before Glaxo's merger with Wellcome, Glaxo was the world's fourth-largest drug company. Yet it was primarily a one-product company, based on the success of its antiulcer drug Zantac, which in 1993 generated $3.5 billion in sales, more than half of Glaxo's revenue. Before the Wellcome merger, word was that company scientists were struggling with a lack of new products in the pipeline. Or consider the Squibb division of Bristol-Myers Squibb, where the hypertension drug Capoten once accounted for 40 percent of sales. There a scientist asked us rhetorically, "Are we a one-product company?"

The points discussed next can aid in understanding the special growth challenges of slow-cycle companies.

THE SLOW-CYCLE GROWTH PUZZLE

When slow-cycle managers pursue growth, outside of their source of market ownership, the result can be to outstrip the boundaries of advantage. USAirways' decade of annual losses, ending at the turn of the century, resulted in part from an expansion strategy that took the carrier too far beyond its localized advantage based on hub control at Pittsburgh and Washington. This created limits to how much and in what ways advantage can be enlarged. Routing possibilities for flights through Pittsburgh are fully exploited and the airport cannot be expanded. In this sense, this part of USAirways advantage cannot be replicated by anyone, including USAirways itself.

Profitless growth became the fate of Frontier Airlines when it gave up its hub control at Denver. Frontier's strategy called for adding East-West routes across the United States in large numbers. As resources were diverted away from Denver, Frontier's gates at the Denver airport were taken over by competitors. This reduced Frontier's original 60 percent gate control enough to put Frontier in direct competition with other air carriers at its home port of Denver. Having given up gate control, but unable to achieve nationwide economies of scale, Frontier was no longer viable.

Consider also Ashton-Tate, a well-known company in the early days of the personal computer industry. Company managers were unable to expand beyond their initial success with Ashton-Tate's popular dBASE database software. Customers could not be induced to switch to the next generation dBASE IV.

Winner-Take-All Competition

In slow-cycle markets, the size of the company reflects the size of its market. While this can often be said to be true, in slow-cycle markets this relationship has a special meaning. In slow-cycle markets a company can become big—if it owns a market that is large—but not because it achieves economies of scale.

Or equally, a slow-cycle company can be large or small depending on whether the demand for its market ownership is high or low. In neither case are economies of scale in the traditional sense of spreading high fixed costs over high volume the cause of growth. In these "winner-take-all" markets, managers should be careful about how they associate market share and company size with perceived growth opportunities.

One implication of winner-take-all markets is that small companies can capture and hold markets against larger companies. Microsoft provides an example, in its early days, competing against IBM. Later, when Microsoft was much larger, it was not able to displace much smaller Intuit in the checkbook software market. This was true even though Microsoft's products generated 100 times the revenue of all of Intuit's products. In spite of aggressive promotion, Microsoft Money gained a meager 6 percent market share relative to Intuit Quicken's 90 percent market share.

The reason has little to do with organization size. Quicken had established its proprietary checkbook registry and filing system as a de facto industry standard. This was done at a time when Microsoft's attention was directed elsewhere. Once the Quicken standard was established, even a company as large as Microsoft was unable to displace it.

In winner-take-all markets, mobility barriers, the ability to move between market segments in the same industry, are unusually high. Microsoft's high market share in many segments of the software industry (operating system, word processing, spreadsheet, and graphics programs) did not provide leverage for it to gain entry into the electronic checkbook segment. High mobility barriers were the cause of Microsoft's bid to acquire Intuit, at a 100 percent premium over Intuit's market value, a bid that was later withdrawn when it came under question by the Justice Department.

A traditional measure of market advantage is industry concentration; as an industry becomes more concentrated, profitability increases. However, in slow-cycle markets market concentration and profitability are not connected. Market share can range up to 100 percent in the case of a market defined by a single product. Examples are Disney's dominance of children's film entertainment, Polaroid's ownership of the instant film market, and Microsoft's dominance of the personal computer operating system.

But market share can also be low for companies that are highly profitable. Rockwell had a 5 percent market share of the 1980s defense industry. Or consider suppliers to the nuclear weapons industry over the same period, when more than eighty companies were profitable. Thus, with high mobility barriers between companies, slow-cycle industries can range from concentrated to fragmented, while large and small companies operating in them are profitable. This important result expands the traditional view that sees profitability as determined by market share.

Thus, measures of market share may tell you little about the sources and distribution of advantage. The wide range in market shares, and their tendency to swing widely depending on the extent to which a company's ownership of a central market factor defines a whole industry, reflect the naturally isolated, winner-take-all nature of slow-cycle markets.

Tipping

Winner-take-all markets can experience a form of dynamic lock-in that we term *tipping*. Tipping is the tendency of a slow-cycle market to tilt all the way towards the adoption of a single product or service. Another expression of the winner-take-all nature of these markets, tipping is encouraged when a market is aided by the emergence of a common factor, such as gate control in airlines or a common computer operating system. When tipping occurs, a competitor either wins the bulk of the customers or loses them to the winning company. Tipping, or tilting as it is called by economic theorist Brian Arthur, is an important new branch of economics based on the idea of continually increasing returns.[3]

Tipping is accelerated where an element of market ownership is needed to facilitate industry growth. In software, second- and third-party vendors benefit from uniform operating systems. This helped to tip the market toward one standard (Windows95). Intuit's Quicken provides a common protocol around which banks develop on-line financial services. Tipping effects will be stronger when vendors and customers benefit from a uniform standard.

There is an important growth implication associated with tipping that is unique to slow-cycle markets. Figure 4.1 shows how, with tipping, the cost to acquire market share rises to a threshold point then declines as a company moves toward market ownership.

Tipping occurs in traditional markets, as for the VHS dominance over the Beta standard in videotape. How is this different from tipping in slow-cycle

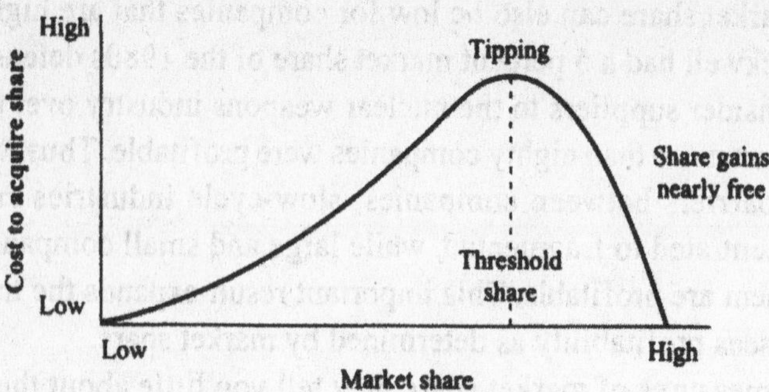

Figure 4.1. Tipping to Market Ownership

markets? After the VHS standard was adopted throughout the industry, the market for VHS remained competitive. The reason was that no single company exercised exclusive rights to the VHS standard. Many companies could produce VHS tapes and equipment. In contrast, in a slow-cycle market, tipping is based on some factor that is proprietary to a single company.

Tipping can occur in many ways. Tipping effects explain how salaries became redistributed in professional baseball. The 1990s saw player salaries skew toward a few superstars with unprecedented salaries. The salaries of baseball superstars came at the expense of other players who saw their salaries remain low. The typical salary structure for a baseball team became a two-sided distribution, with a few multimillion-dollar players on one side, many low paid players on the other side, and very few players in the middle. Salary-tipping effects can be expected in professional organizations where superstars are present.

Tipping can produce an unstable distribution of market share as well. When a company's products compete for an industry standard, its market share can collapse toward zero if the market tips toward a rival's standard.

Thus, even a fiercely loyal customer base may not be enough to counteract tipping effects. When the market share of the Macintosh operating system fell below 10 percent, Apple, in an effort to fight tipping, reduced prices on Macintosh computers. Apple managers correctly reasoned that if sales fell below a minimum threshold level, the market could collapse, and second-party software developers would no longer write software for the Macintosh. Indeed, formerly loyal Macintosh customers, including this author, switched to Windows95 to gain access to new software and hardware and to insure connectivity with the Windows95 community.

When markets tip against companies, their narrow renewal pathways close. If Apple had been in traditional markets, operating under the focus strategy discussed in Chapter 2, low market share would have been sustainable. In contrast, when winner-take-all markets tip against lower-share companies, attempts at sustaining share can become difficult.

Wang in word processing saw its once-safe market tip away as word-processing applications for personal computers came to dominate. As the desktop word-processing market tipped toward PC-based applications, loyal Wang customers, like loyal Macintosh users, were forced to switch. Similar tipping effects put pressure on users of Unix and OS/2 computer operating systems. In the case of OS/2, in particular, note how IBM's large size did not help in stemming the tip toward Windows95. Thus, there is an either-or outcome with tipping that can be independent of organization size, and that is not present in traditional markets.

Managers should be sensitive to the possibilities for tipping in their markets and, in particular, the presence of threshold effects. The amount of market share required to cause tipping, threshold share, may not be evident until it is contested. In 1994 USAirways controlled 55 percent of the Baltimore hub. This was an attractive hub because of its proximity to Washington and southeastern Pennsylvania. When Southwest contested USAirways' dominance by cutting prices, Southwest's Baltimore passenger boardings surged by 30 percent. In retrospect, USAirways' 55 percent control was not enough to lock out rivals. Southwest, with access to six gates, gained competitive entry.

It is important to monitor the extent to which a particular market factor or market standard may be approaching a level of market acceptance that could bring on tipping. When competitors become aware of tipping effects as the market nears the point of tipping, competition is likely to increase. Aggressive actions like price cutting, special product promotions, and free product upgrades can be expected. As competitors struggle to prevent or encourage tipping, companies may turn to strategic alliances as a way to keep their renewal pathways open. Markets experiencing threshold effects are unstable. Successful actions by any competitor at this point are likely to have significant and irreversible consequences for competitors and customers alike.

How Slow Cycle Is Different from Focus

Notice the difference between a growth strategy in slow-cycle markets and a growth strategy in standard-cycle, focused markets, discussed in Chapter 2.

For a slow-cycle organization facing the benefits of tipping, growth is good; indeed, it is necessary to bring on market tipping. At the point of tipping the winning slow-cycle organization benefits further from additional growth, even though growth does not rely on economies of scale.

However, for a focused organization market growth can be problematic. Renewal opportunities depend on market growth remaining below the minimum efficient scale of larger companies, or if the market does grow, on restructuring to grow through economies of scale, a process that is difficult.

Simply put, the renewal opportunities for slow-cycle and focused organizations are different. At some point, both types of organizations can find that growth is difficult, but this will happen for very different reasons. For the slow-cycle organization, renewal will stop because the market has aged; few growth opportunities remain. For the focused organization, the market can be vibrant; the problem is that the organization cannot keep up with larger competitors who are able to grow faster and more efficiently. These growth distinctions, useful for market planning, trace their roots to the different ways that growth operates in economic time.

STAIRCASE STRATEGIES

Tipping can create market ownership. On the other hand, sustaining long-run growth, beyond the original source of market ownership, can be problematic. Yet companies like Microsoft, McKinsey, and Disney provide examples of slow-cycle companies that have achieved steady growth, for extended periods. These companies have been able to grow while sustaining their strong isolating mechanisms. In effect, by expanding their fortress walls each has built a series of strong, unbroken linkages from their original sources of market ownership.

Central to the idea of extending market ownership is the use of what we call *staircase strategies*. This approach consists of extending advantage while maintaining customer lock-in. The advantage of staircase strategies is that they allow a slow-cycle company to extend its advantage beyond its original source of ownership, while extending profit cycles as well. Novell used a staircase strategy to extend its dominance of the early market for networked computers. The central feature of Novell's NetWare was a feature called Directory Services that gave users access to files from anywhere on a corporate network. Company strategy focused on making Net-

Ware Directory Services the backbone, or bridge to a larger suite of NetWare software, in spite of calls by competitors to unbundle Directory Services so that competitors could use it with their products.

Disney has been adept at staircasing its character properties toward new uses. Ubiquitous mouse's ears and three-dimensional cartoon characters from Disney's animated films direct tourists through Disney's fantasy villages and gift shops. A firehouse at Walt Disney World features Dalmatians' spots on its walls. Nineteen-foot-high dwarfs support the pediment of the Team Disney headquarters in Burbank. Disney management is determined to protect its exclusive right to its character properties. The company once sued a day-care center, forcing it to remove the likeness of Mickey Mouse from a wall of the facility.

The staircase strategy can describe the success of Microsoft. Although MS-DOS was only one of three operating systems initially offered by IBM, Microsoft priced MS-DOS lower than its competitors. MS-DOS quickly became the de facto operating system on the IBM PC. Subsequent decisions by Microsoft treated MS-DOS as part of a platform of functions tied to the original MS-DOS.

The second step up the renewal staircase for Microsoft came with the commercialization of Windows 3.0. Windows maintained the MS-DOS operating system but developed a proprietary Graphical User Interface that emulated the look and feel of the popular Macintosh computer (Apple sued Microsoft, claiming copyright infringement, but the court ruled that the look and feel of the Macintosh had been in previous use by Xerox with no proprietary claims; therefore no company could claim exclusive ownership of the Macintosh look and feel). Microsoft used the Graphical User Interface to encourage existing customers to stay with MS-DOS and MS-DOS-based applications as the MS-DOS operating system was upgraded. As customers were persuaded to adopt newer products, the installed base was nurtured and protected. The strategy was always to provide a strong bridge between early and later product releases. See Figure 4.2.

The third step of Microsoft's renewal staircase was built on applications. Early on, competitors like WordPerfect dominated word processing, Lotus 1-2-3 dominated spreadsheets and Harvard Graphics dominated presentation software. But through the linkage of the Graphical User Interface and other software protocols, the company made its word processing (Microsoft Word), spreadsheet (Microsoft Excel), and presentation software

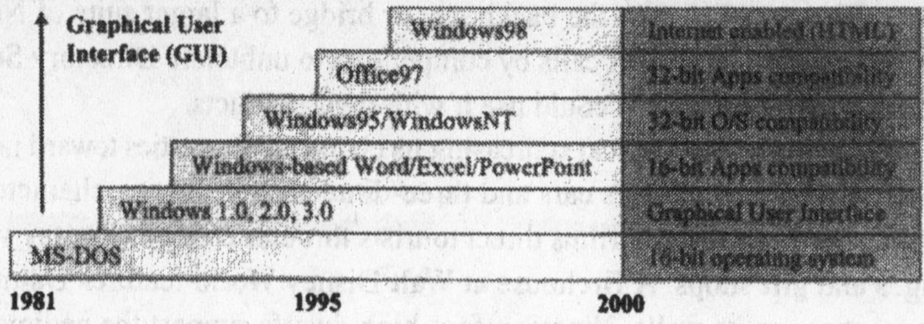

Figure 4.2. Microsoft's Renewal Staircase

(Microsoft PowerPoint) attractively compatible with each other and with the Windows operating environment.

By emphasizing the ease at which customers could move from one application to the other, cutting and pasting a spreadsheet into a document, for example, customers were encouraged to purchase the entire suite of Microsoft applications. Microsoft did license the software necessary to make the Windows operating environment and Graphical User Interface available to competitors. But often, competitor products appeared later than Microsoft applications and without attractive links to other applications.

The fourth step up the staircase was the advent of Windows95, a 32-bit operating system. Windows95 represented the first major technological innovation for Microsoft, coming fourteen years after the introduction of MS-DOS. Windows95 moved customers to a vastly improved operating system while maintaining backward compatibility with the early-generation MS-DOS operating system and applications. The task was formidable. Originally slated for introduction in 1994, delays in development led some to informally tag the product "Windows96" before successful commercialization in the fall of 1995. Although Windows95 was delayed, customers were willing to wait, a consequence common to slow-cycle markets.

A strategic feature of Windows95 was that it was designed to lay the groundwork for steps further up the staircase, in particular, to be cross-platform compatible with WindowsNT, a 32-bit operating system that Microsoft had introduced to the office market. With Windows95 and WindowsNT compatibility, Microsoft became the first company to offer high-performance, cross-platform connectivity between the home and office markets. As before, Windows95 and WindowsNT relied on the Microsoft Graphical User Interface to bring customers from the two markets together.

The fifth step up the staircase solidified the bridge between the home and office markets by promoting third-party applications that worked on both Windows95 and WindowsNT. In order to get the coveted Windows95 compatible seal of approval, third-party developers were required, in advance of the release of Windows95, to write applications that would work on both Windows95 and WindowsNT.

The advent of the Internet represented a paradigm shift for Microsoft. The Internet's HTML (hypertext markup language), in combination with Java software offered by Sun Microsystems, had the potential of becoming an alternative operating system for personal computers that communicated with one another. Microsoft's initial response was to provide Internet access through Microsoft Explorer, Internet browser software that was similar to Netscape's Navigator.

The sixth and highly strategic step up the staircase was to introduce Windows98. This operating system embedded the Internet browser (HTML) functions into the Microsoft operating system, as well as into the Microsoft suite of applications, and third-party software. This was possible because, like the graphical interface from Apple, the HTML software needed for browsing the Internet was an open standard (it had been developed at the University of Illinois).

The strategy was designed to make the need for stand-alone browser software, like Netscape's Browser, irrelevant. Browser functions would be absorbed into the Microsoft staircase and disappear from sight. A customer using the Windows98 system would continue to see and work with the Microsoft Graphical User Interface, while beneath the surface, the HTML operating system would link the growing family of Microsoft products to the Internet automatically.

Microsoft's staircase strategy is reflected in the company's internal slogan, "We embrace and we extend," which is sung within the company to the tune of the "Battle Hymn of the Republic."

This example illustrates how staircase strategies require long-term vision, foresight, and a willingness to commit significant resources to an outcome that is far from certain. Each step up the staircase is part of a carefully considered, long-term vision of how past and present products can be linked to the future. Staircase strategies keep renewal pathways open by encouraging attractive upgrade paths forward, and by maintaining backward lock-in with past products. Staircase strategies treat product extension as part of a carefully evolving platform of customer experiences, continually linked to a company's original source of market ownership.

Master Artisan Disney

Walt Disney and his brother Roy founded the Walt Disney Company in 1923. Walt, as he asked to be called, was innovative in terms of using new techniques and technologies whereas Roy was business oriented. After mortgaging his home, Walt worked for several weeks without pay, and by taking on loans of $1,000, the first animation with sound effects was released. Mickey Mouse premiered in the famous film *Steamboat Willie* at the Colony Theater in New York in 1928. The seven-and-a-half-minute cartoon drew better reviews than the full-length movies released that week. Pluto in 1930 and Goofy and Donald Duck in 1932 provided the base for the Disney staircase that would later emerge. Walt Disney Company was a success early on, but Disney's fortress castle would take decades to create.

In 1932 Walt Disney heard about a coloring technology developed by Technicolor and was fascinated with its potential. *Flowers and Trees,* the first animation with color, won the Oscar for best cartoon made in 1932. From 1935 to 1941 Disney Studios won six Academy Awards for animation. Films provide the base of the Disney renewal staircase. See Figure 4.3.

The Disney's image can be thought of as serving the same function as Microsoft's Graphical User Interface. It provides a link between successive layers of products, which are seen by the customer as an extension of similar experiences. The Disney renewal staircase has several carefully linked steps.

↑ Disney Image	
Re-release films 5-10 yrs.	Renew annuity
Add spinoff characters	Extend complementary assets
Develop theme parks	Add complementary assets
Protect intellectual property	Strengthen isolating mechanisms
Develop characters (Simba, Aladdin)	Establish trophy assets
Produce a film (Lion King)	Create intellectual property
Add Disney magic (Imagineering)	Initiate operating system
Find a fable, e.g., Beauty and the Beast	Public property

Figure 4.3. Disney's Renewal Staircase

Motion Pictures

Disney Chairman Michael Eisner puts it this way, "There is nothing more important for this company than creating another character. Those characters become the pump that kind of feeds the rest of the body." In 1986 *Who Framed Roger Rabbit* became the most expensive film Disney had ever created ($58 million to produce, $32 million to promote and distribute). Within two years, thirty-four licensee agreements for five hundred products were signed. Toys, dolls, brooches, leather bomber jackets, videocassettes, computer games, joint ventures with McDonald's and Coca-Cola, and cover stories in *Newsweek* and *Time* led to $154 million in U.S. box office tickets and $174 million from overseas sales, contributing to profits in excess of $100 million for this single film. Eisner again: "The theme parks may be the heart of this company, but the movie business is its soul."

Cinderella and *Pinocchio* have as much appeal today as when they were released over fifty years ago. The timeless appeal of Disney movies is without equal in the film industry. *The Little Mermaid (1989), Beauty and the Beast (1991),* and *Aladdin* (1992) each yielded profits for Disney of $100 million or more. *The Lion King* broke all previous records, the first cartoon to gross $1 billion in sales and related merchandise worldwide.

The Disney staircase benefits from what Microsoft CEO Bill Gates terms "the positive spiral effect." Success breeds success. The success of Disney's animated features allowed Disney to recruit the best animators in the business. In return, the film's animation improved and so did their reputation for quality. As the Disney name became synonymous with success, popular film stars began to supply the voices for the characters. Films have included the voices of stars such as Robin Williams, Robbie Benson, and Whoopie Goldberg. Tom Hanks, winner of two best actor Oscar awards, supplied the voice for the character Buzz Lightyear in Disney's film *Toy Story.*

The Little Mermaid, Beauty and the Beast, and *Aladdin* each won the Oscar for best song. Elton John composed songs for *The Lion King,* a blockbuster, whose soundtrack sold millions. The positive spiral effect also aids other slow-cycle companies like McKinsey, whereby close-knit relationships between artisans reinforces their association with one another, creating barriers to entry for competitors.

Disney created Touchstone Pictures and Hollywood Pictures as separate entities to produce trendy films to attract teenagers and adults, without affecting the company's image of wholesome family entertainment. They also made better use of the Disney studios by utilizing them at full capacity, allowing Disney to make several movies in a short time span at a low incremental cost. Touchstone and Hollywood studios produce faster-cycle movies for which a significant portion of potential earnings are realized in a few weeks or months after release.

Early Disney management kept film classics off the re-release market out of concern for character saturation. Later, Eisner argued for the opposite effect: that managed right, character properties would perpetuate themselves, expanding demand, to the point where the property would become an industry standard. Disney first released its classics on cassette in 1986 when it sold one million copies of *Sleeping Beauty,* a sales record that surprised even Disney management, while it proved that slow-cycle character properties can have profit cycles of fifty years or more.

Disney releases new films on videocassette, often within six months after they appear in theaters. Home video revenues for Disney films in 1994 totaled $8 billion. Classics such as *101 Dalmatians* and *Snow White and the Seven Dwarfs* are re-released on the big screen while the Disney Channel carries second-tier classics such as *The Love Bug* and *The Absent-Minded Professor.*

The Little Mermaid, Beauty and the Beast, and *Aladdin* are not ordinary movies that come and go. They create long-lived character properties on which associated merchandise, theme park rides, and multiple re-releases can be based, over extended periods of time. Disney has elevated character properties to the status of trophy properties that are an integral part of American and world culture. (We remember a trip to Spain and an evening out to see the local culture of Granada, during which "authentic" Gypsy dancers in a back street cabaret emerged from behind a curtain—dressed in Mickey Mouse T-shirts.)

Few companies have been as successful as Disney in systematically creating long-lived character properties with global appeal. Popular Disney character properties outside the United States are shown in Table 4.1.

In Latin America, the Brazilian parrot Ze Carioca, who appeared in a 1940s Disney animated film *Los Tres Amigos,* outsells Mickey Mouse on associated character merchandise.

The Disney legal team protects Disney character assets, prosecuting those who attempt to infringe their copyrights. Walt learned the value of

Table 4.1. Disney Global Characters

COUNTRY	CHARACTER
England	Winnie the Pooh
France	Bambi & Thumper
Germany	Scrooge McDuck
Japan	Mickey Mouse
Brazil	Ze Carioca

protecting character properties when a business partner won the rights to Disney's first animated character, Oswald the Lucky Rabbit. A staff of dedicated lawyers protects the overall image of Disney. Through 1987 Disney had filed seventeen lawsuits with seven hundred defendants in the United States and seventy-eight defendants overseas. Defendants included manufacturers of toys, T-shirt vendors, other film studios, and the day care center that had painted Disney characters on its walls. The editor of *Show Biz News* considered publishing a special issue that focused on Hollywood legal fights until it became clear that the Walt Disney Company was in one way or another connected to all of the battles.

Theme Parks

Disneyland's first operational year in 1955 took in $10 million. This success was possible because of the unique rides that were linked to Disney's animated films. Disney's biggest financial backer at the time was the ABC network, to which in repayment of a loan, Disney committed to produce a weekly television show called *Disneyland.* Each week the Disneyland theme park and Disney character properties were brought to the attention of the public. In retrospect, this was the first coordinated step in creating the Disney "operating system."

Like the early software industry, Disneyland was beleaguered by an undisciplined periphery. The success of the park prompted developers to buy up miles of surrounding countryside, which was converted into a tangle of hotels and low-end commerce. Disney lost millions to others who were housing its visitors. In the first ten years, Disneyland took in $278 million and the peripherals $555 million. Moreover, the disorder of the surroundings took away from the experience of the park.

In effect, the first Disneyland was an open operating system, allowing vendors to freely attach applications (hotels and restaurants) at Disney's expense and with no guarantee of compatibility with the Disney image. Disney would not repeat this mistake.

Disney purchased 287,000 acres of land near Orlando, Florida for what would become Disney World and the Epcot World Showcase. The new park had ample land to build hotels, restaurants, shops, and virtually any other amenities that visitors might want. Disney gained concessions from the state of Florida, assuring sovereignty over its domain, including rights of policing, taxation, and administration. Disney World draws 100,000 people to its Florida gates each day and thirty million visitors a year.

There is little price competition at the parks: Disney increased prices throughout the 1980s without affecting attendance.

Disney controls every aspect of the customer's experience. Attractions—the scenery and location of a particular fantasy, like *Treasure Island*—are set into their own engineered environmental settings so that customers can immerse themselves without distraction in the details at a particular location, its theme and story line.

Once registered at Disney hotels, guests are captive customers. Few can pass up the Disney merchandise in the gift shops. With free monorail and bus service to take them to parks, few venture to competing parks outside the company property. Staying at the Disney hotels and going to character meals is part of the Disney experience. This author remembers standing in a long line one morning at Disney's Grand Floridian hotel with two eager children in tow, to pay $60 for a simple buffet breakfast, punctuated by visits from Darth Vader and Sleeping Beauty (our table was one of many dozens of tables.)

Disney acquired the Arvida Corporation to build hotels on property owned by Disney. (Arvida was in the business of developing vast chunks of land into planned cities.) After the development of the hotels, Disney affirmed that Disney operates as an entertainment company that plays out its stories in real estate: Disney did not need an in-house construction company to achieve this goal, so Disney divested of Arvida.

The strategy is to attract customers to Disney properties through unique and enjoyable experiences, then build other establishments to capitalize on the land values, thus expanding the Disney operating system.

Disney University was established to train park employees to deliver a uniform Disney experience to its "character property users" (our term). Disney's new hires are told that they are not just employees but pivotal cast members in a show. From street sweepers to monorail pilots, cast members make the resort an integral part of the Disney experience. The approach has been so successful that Disney runs a three-day seminar, *Disney's Approach to People Management,* for which corporate executives pay $2,400 to attend.

In 1987 Disney opened the first company-owned retail store outside of Disney parks. Disney movies bring customers into the stores, where they are exposed to products and videos that recycle customers back to the parks and theaters. At the stores customers learn about upcoming animated features, buy tickets for the theme parks, and watch the Disney channel. By 1994, Disney had 268 stores located in malls throughout the United States and around the world that took in $465 million (54 percent of Disney's domestic box office take). Disney stores averaged $700 in annual sales per square foot, three times the norm for specialized retailing.

Sixty years after Walt Disney introduced the Mickey Mouse watch the company had perfected Walt's theory that "everything sells everything else." Although development of Disney properties is expensive, like many slow-cycle properties, after the initial investment is made, reinvestment rate are low. Storing and re-releasing movies entails a low expense. Although theme rides require maintenance and renovation, their upkeep amounts to a fraction of the original development and construction costs. In this way, the economic half-life of Disney's advantage is inherently long because Disney properties are naturally shielded from competitive aging.

In 1984, the Walt Disney Company was valued at $2.62 billion, $1.35 of that amount for theme parks and intellectual property rights. Ten years later, in 1994, Merrill Lynch valued Disney at $35 billion. The value of Disney increased twentyfold. Disney stockholders realized an annualized return of 27 percent over the period.

The Disney story shows that it is possible to overcome the growth constraints associated with slow-cycle markets. It illustrates similarities to the renewal strategies used by another slow-cycle artisan, Microsoft. It shows how, during a time when it is fashionable to declare that advantage is short-lived, some companies are creating long-lived advantages. Towards the end of this period, an issue of one-hundred-year notes allowed Disney to lock in low interest rates for the twenty-first century.

The New Artisans and Public Policy

In the rush to formulate traditional strategy, slow-cycle markets have been overlooked, underestimated, or lumped into the category of monopolistic competition. Yet as we see, slow-cycle markets are increasing in scope, importance and variety. Consequently, managers and policymakers should be encouraged to rethink some long-held views.

Traditional thinking on monopolies—single seller, restricted output, and high prices—begins and ends with the belief that we cannot even get started with the competitive process. Entry is blocked, prices are higher, and consumption is lower than in competitive markets. The traditional view of monopoly casts a shadow over the behavior of some companies in slow-cycle markets.

The problem with the traditional view is that the new business opportunities put pursuit of shielded property rights at the center of competitive strategy.

One side of the debate over Microsoft's dominance focuses on its increasing power in the information economy. The price of some Microsoft products has increased. On the other hand, even critics of Microsoft acknowledge the benefits of uniform market standards and the compatibility of applications that Microsoft has brought about.

Recall that the emergence of gate control in airlines was not foreseen, causing Alfred Kahn, of the Civil Aeronautics Board, to label airline deregulation a mess. The advent of airport hub control, by carriers like USAirways in Pittsburgh, caused prices of airfares to increase. But the problem in condemning monopoly power in these cases is that we have nothing to compare it with. Because there are few competitive alternatives, it is difficult to compare benefits and costs against alternatives. The hub-and-spoke strategy in airlines and in software yields attractive, system-wide benefits seemingly unavailable in any other way.

Many slow-cycle markets, and the competitive rules under which they operate, simply would not exist without the companies that created them. Consider that:

- In questioning Microsoft's hoped-for acquisition of Intuit, the maker of Quicken, the Justice Department relied on economic reasoning so new (increasing returns economics mentioned earlier) that it had not yet been published in a peer-review journal of legal and economic scholars.
- The current structure of the airline industry can be likened to a collection of fortress castles, with each launching flights from its protected hub into the national airline system. Are we better off with an industry

characterized by a collection of fortress hub companies (USAirways, American, Delta, and United)? Or are we better off with an industry characterized by one giant hub (Microsoft)?

- Pharmaceutical companies, as they are criticized for generating above-average profits,[4] develop drug treatments that offer incomparable benefits. Whether the high earnings of life-saving pharmaceutical products are justified, where consumers are in a position of no bargaining power, is an unsolvable question. How do we judge that the cost of a life-saving drug is too high when no alternative treatment exists? The question will not go away; copyrighting of human gene sequences for specific treatments will bring about unprecedented benefits to customers as they convey unprecedented market power to companies.
- Entertainment companies are not precluded from locking up libraries of films, such as Turner's ownership of classic movies, or Bill Gates's purchase of electronic copyrights to classic artworks (the directors of the Louvre refused the offer). Like software, these intellectual properties provide benefits that are important to society. At some point, the proliferation of information-based advantages will make monopolistic competition commonplace.

These examples multiply with seemingly limitless variations. Inability to separate costs and benefits arises because, as pointed out earlier, slow-cycle products are at the *center* of their market; they *are* their market. In one sense, little is new. Growth and decline of monopoly power has taken place for centuries. What is new is the scope and sophistication of world markets, combined with the shift to information-based products and services. This has increased the possibilities that slow-cycle advantage can emerge anywhere.

The purpose of strategy is to create value by legal means. Any company that is making money has profit-generating power. If managers were prohibited from seeking some kind of monopoly advantage, if only temporarily, there would be little meaning to competitive advantage.

But imagine that Microsoft was the only software company, Merck the only pharmaceutical company, USAirways the only airline, and Disney the only entertainment company. These companies might innovate, but they just as well might overpower the competitive process, which is like the position some say Microsoft is in now.

But there is innovation—and lots of it. The best argument for giving modern-day artisans a lot of maneuvering room, even when they build mighty fortresses, is the inevitability of change. Nothing lasts forever. As long as the gale of creative destruction powers markets, even mighty fortresses are built on shifting ground.

What does this mean for managers? Slow-cycle entrepreneurs will carve out territory and draw competitive maps of the new business landscape, just as entrepreneurs did in the emerging industrial economy. By experimenting with unconventional strategies and in pursuing out-of-the-box ideas, entrepreneurs determine what is possible and what is not. In the process they power and shape our economic growth.

RECAP: NEW ARTISANS

Slow-cycle organizations dominate their markets through exclusive ownership of some factor that is essential for the functioning of their market. In this way, slow-cycle organizations define their market. They own their market. They and their customers are inseparable. Managers who wish to consider the opportunities of slow-cycle markets can keep the following points in mind.

LOOK FOR NATURALLY SHIELDED SOURCES OF MARKET OWNERSHIP

Managers operating in or entering slow-cycle markets should look for aspects or features that are necessary for the functioning of the market. The main sources of slow-cycle advantage are human capital, product or relationship complexity, standards ownership, location, patents and copyrights. Products and services in slow-cycle companies naturally dominate their markets. A slow-cycle company operates within a strategic group of one: itself.

INTERPRET MARKET SHARE CAREFULLY

Market share can range from low to high, depending on whether the source of market ownership appeals to a small or large number of customers. In both cases, market power is high. Thus, market share should be defined carefully. Similarly, the size of a slow-cycle company reflects the size of its market, rather than economies of scale. One implication is that small companies can easily capture and hold slow-cycle markets in the face of competition from larger companies.

LOOK FOR TIPPING EFFECTS

Tipping conveys near-total market ownership or winner-take-all status to the company. Tipping effects are accelerated where the source of market ownership is needed by other, noncompeting companies. Pay particular attention to the emergence of factors that bring on market tipping, such as geography or uniform product standards.

The first stage of market share growth may be relatively easy, followed by intense competition as market share grows toward threshold levels. After tipping takes place, competitiveness will decline. Be particularly sensitive to the possibility that market share is reaching threshold levels needed for tipping. Actions to prevent or insure tipping at this point can have irreversible effects on both companies and customers.

UNDERSTAND THE GROWTH CONUNDRUM

The factors that make it difficult for competitors to duplicate the success of a slow-cycle company also make it difficult for a slow-cycle company to extend its own success beyond its original source of market ownership. Pay special attention to the emergence of growth barriers when setting growth objectives.

EMPLOY STAIRCASE STRATEGIES

Seek to extend products and services based on strong, unbroken links to original sources of market ownership. Encourage an ownership-based mind-set and the discipline to develop products based on staircase links. The goal is to maintain customer lock-in while expanding market ownership to encompass new uses. Remember that the renewal challenge in slow-cycle markets is to expand your fortress walls while keeping them high.

SEEK AND YE SHALL FIND

Antitrust policy is evolving as ideas like tipping are being tested alongside traditional ways of thinking. During this time there is an opportunity for managers to help redefine the boundaries of traditional monopoly thinking. As we look back on twentieth-century markets, one distinguishing feature will be the generalized emergence of slow-cycle markets. Managers who understand the special features of these markets will be among the first to capitalize on their opportunities and influence the policy agenda for the new economy.

At this point our introduction to the cycles of economic time is complete. The first step in your journey through economic time has been to develop a high-level map of the new, emerging multicycle markets. The second step is to take steps, by mapping these opportunities against what your organization is capable of doing. This requires specific tools and principles. Next, we look at what we have come to think of as the three laws of renewal: convergence, alignment, and renewal. Operating by these principles, managers can understand how economic time operates for their companies.

CHAPTER 5

THE THREE LAWS OF RENEWAL

Look at Figure 5.1. It shows the long-run profitability of companies. There are ten groups of companies, grouped from the highest to the lowest ten percent.[1] Notice that the top group did not sustain their advantage. They moved toward the market average. But also look at the lowest-performing group. Companies that began with the poorest profitability improved; they ended the decade close to the industry average. Nothing lasts forever: success *or* failure.

Profitable companies come under attack as competitors are attracted by their success. This initiates the process of convergence. Through convergence, the least profitable companies come under attack also, not by competitors but by the capital markets. Investors withdraw support of underperforming companies, forcing them to improve or go under. This process of convergence, realignment, and renewal is the basis of all com-

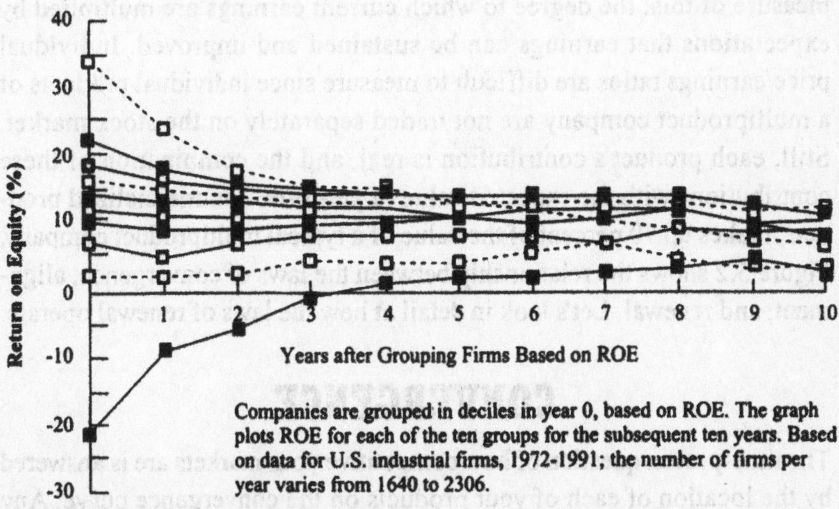

Figure 5.1. Endurance of Advantage

petitive renewal. Briefly stated, the three laws of renewal as we observe them are:

Convergence. Thirty percent of a typical company's value is set by where its products are located on the convergence curve. For a multiproduct company, the aggregate location of all of its products on the convergence curve shows up as total current profits. Significant also is the speed at which a company's markets are becoming more competitive. This shows up as the rate of movement of products along the convergence curve toward zero profits. While rate of movement along the convergence curve will not affect current profits, rate of movement affects sustainability of profits.

Alignment. The quality of fit between a company's products and its customers determines its alignment. When product alignment is good, the company is capturing the full profits possible at any point on the convergence curve. This is why alignment can be good and current profits poor if the company is positioned far down the convergence curve, in a market that is highly competitive. When product alignment is poor, profits are less than they could be for products positioned at any point on the convergence curve. What does this mean? High profits require *both* good alignment *and* products that are positioned high up on the convergence curve.

Renewal. Seventy percent of a company's value is determined by efforts in place to refresh aging products. The company's price/earnings ratio is a measure of this: the degree to which current earnings are multiplied by expectations that earnings can be sustained and improved. Individual price/earnings ratios are difficult to measure since individual products of a multiproduct company are not traded separately on the stock market. Still, each product's contribution is real, and the combination of these contributions with the expected value of yet-to-be-commercialized products, makes up 70 percent of the value of a typical multiproduct company. Figure 5.2 shows the relationship between the laws of convergence, alignment, and renewal. Let's look in detail at how the laws of renewal operate.

CONVERGENCE

The time-proven question of how competitive your markets are is answered by the location of each of your products on the convergence curve. Any

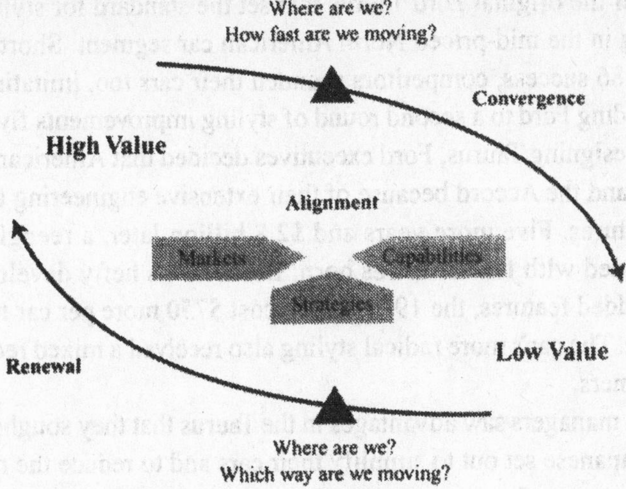

Figure 5.2. The Three Laws of Renewal

given product, depending on market conditions, can be positioned anywhere on the convergence curve—between highly profitable, noncompetitive markets on the higher end of the curve and fully competitive, unprofitable markets on the lower end of the curve. Product value is highest up the curve where there is little or no competition. Profits are zero or near zero at the lower end of the convergence curve because at this point markets are highly competitive.

Competitive markets are like the "black hole" from which profits cannot emerge. A fully competitive market results when at least two companies with the same capabilities and similar strategies pursue the same customers. Two equally matched and aggressive competitors on a competitive playing field wear each other out; this is true in sports, military combat, and in economic competition where the result is profitability so low that it is not sustainable.

Now move back up the convergence curve. The high profits that come with successful innovation attract competitors. Profits are sustained for a while; then profits decline as competitors learn how to imitate innovations at lower cost or to offer improved products. Competitive crowding, or the entry of competitors into your once-profitable markets, is the result of convergence. Even the most successful products are predestined to fail through inevitable movement down the convergence curve into highly competitive markets.

Consider the original Ford Taurus that set the standard for styling and engineering in the mid-priced North American car segment. Shortly after Taurus's 1986 success, competitors rounded their cars too, imitating Taurus, and leading Ford to a second round of styling improvements five years later. In redesigning Taurus, Ford executives decided that Americans liked the Camry and the Accord because of their extensive engineering and numerous features. Five more years and $2.8 billion later, a reengineered Taurus, loaded with features, was born. But with its hefty development costs and added features, the 1997 Taurus cost $750 more per car to build than the old. The car's more radical styling also received a mixed reception from customers.

Toyota's managers saw advantages in the Taurus that they sought to imitate. The Japanese set out to simplify their cars and to reduce the number of parts to cut costs. Toyota engineers disassembled a 1992 Taurus and saw its relatively simple mechanics; the Taurus front bumper had far fewer parts than the Camry's. In response, the complex array of 24 parts and 53 fasteners got reduced down to 4 pieces and 15 fasteners. By 1996, the redesigned Camry had reduced costs by $1,000. Thus by the late 1990s, through action-reaction cycles typical of standard-cycle markets, Ford and Toyota had converged on the best features of each other's automobiles.

Convergence expresses *how fast* products displace each other. Sustainability of advantage is dependent on the relative speed of convergence, that is, how fast your markets become competitive. This is where economic time comes in.

Think about the different products and services that you sell. Products with similar profits typically see profit levels decline at different speeds. When profit levels are declining slowly, chances are that you are operating in slow economic time. As profit levels decline more quickly, products operate in faster economic time. Compaq, with weak isolating mechanisms, faces many rivals, each months or less away from imitating Compaq's products at lower prices. In contrast, Intuit with its Quicken program, because of strong isolating mechanisms, sees few convergence pressures. Thus, if we measured products offered by Compaq and Quicken at some point in time they could easily show the same profit levels; but when we measured the same products later, profit levels for Quicken would be higher than for Compaq.

In this way, managers making different products that show similar levels of profit face vastly different competitive pressures and renewal opportunities. This is why the value for two companies or two business units within a company that have similar profit levels can be different, depending on where they operate in economic time. Variance in the capitalized value of businesses with similar profit levels reflects differences in the speed at which profits are growing or shrinking.

Joseph Schumpeter pointed out that the way to understand business is to assume that all advantage is temporary. The principle of convergence affirms this way of thinking. This is also why traditional strategy, which does not start with the central assumption of convergence, is static, or anti-Schumpeterian—frozen in time. It is no wonder that traditional methods can fail to assist managers in the ongoing search for renewal.

Convergence thinking encourages—actually forces—us to move away from implicit notions that advantage is sustainable unless it is lost, and toward the transforming assumption that *advantage will be lost unless it is renewed.* Once managers become comfortable with the idea that, through convergence, all advantage is temporary, they ask questions of themselves and their companies that take on a greater responsibility for creating the future. By making the reality of convergence central at the onset, leadership becomes focused on reformation and rebirth.

ALIGNMENT

The capabilities of your company and the needs of your customers have evolved together. Each has been shaped by the expectations placed on it by the other. The behavior of each is influenced by, indeed defined by, and ultimately limited by the other. The second law of renewal, alignment, is based on the simple idea that customers and companies gain their meaning from each other. Organizations and markets are aligned to each other and evolve together only as long as benefits accrue to both.

IBM convinced customers that they needed computer mainframes. As customers' experiences with mainframes grew, so did IBM's ability to supply a no-surprises mainframe environment. Intel convinced customers that they needed increasing microprocessor performance; as customers became familiar with microprocessor-intensive applications they encouraged Intel to develop ever-faster microprocessors. The demand created by McDonald's for fast food encouraged McDonald's and its competitors to orchestrate larger organizations and develop more efficient control systems by which to satisfy worldwide demand. This, in turn, expanded the demand for fast food. And so on it goes; markets are developed by companies that are, in turn, shaped by demand for their products.

Alignment has another, more common meaning. It is expressed through your strategy. Alignment reflects your actions, how you behave toward customers. Strategy, or how market alignment is pursued from day to day, is the pattern of activities by which a company selects which customers to serve, how to maintain favorable relationships with them, and how to hold competitors at bay. Strategy is the set of mutually beneficial actions that brings companies and customers together.

All organizations have strategies. This is true regardless of whether they articulate them. Strategy is repeated behavior. Some of the most purposeful strategies a company has can be embedded deep within the organization, based on past behavior that has worked but never has been written down. Procedures are understood to be "the way we do things around here." Key individuals may not even be aware of, or even be able to articulate, how their behavior contributes to success.

We know of one safety equipment company whose managers had developed a pattern of putting their highest-level executives to work immediately on quality control problems. This was true, even when their behavior drew resources away from long-term development. In reality, the attention to fighting fires that the managers pointed to so proudly was hindering much-needed renewal efforts. Although each manager saw himself as a fire fighter, the group as a whole did not know the extent to which fire-fighting behavior had become the central expression of the company's strategy.

Thus, we advise managers that, to understand day-to-day strategy, they should look for what an organization actually does on a day-to-day basis rather than relying on formal statements of what they claim to do. Or put simply: "Watch what I do, not what I say."

Try this test: Ask your people to describe what they actually do day-to-day. We predict that you get answers that are different from what you expect. Ask yourself: Who *is* running your company?

Short Term Is Different from Long Term

Through strategy, your company and your customers are tied together in the short run and in the long run. But strategy takes on a different role in the two planning horizons. Consider short-run strategy. Estimates of corporate culture suggest that it takes no less than three years to create a new capability. Since strategy is responsible for alignment, strategy in the short run must take your capabilities more or less for what they are. The best you can do in the short run is to align what you already do well with what customers are willing to pay for.

Short-term strategy is, in a sense, reactive. Being reactive is not bad; in fact, it is necessary. It is consistent with the idea of sticking close to customers. Day-to-day policies, tactics, and operating procedures are continually refined in search of better alignment with what customers currently want.

This is also why, in good planning efforts, development of short-run strategies comes last, and not first, as we have seen in so many failed planning efforts. Only by purposely aligning current market conditions and current capabilities can strategy carry out its responsibility of bringing companies and customers together.

In the long term, the process of building new relationships with new customers can take years. Part of the reason is that customers may not know what they want until a company supplies it and starts the parallel, customer/company learning experience discussed earlier. In this way, companies create demand. To be sure, demand can arise without prompting by companies, as in the building of the American western railroad empires in response to burgeoning demand for transcontinental transportation. Whether in creating demand or by building new capabilities, long-run strategy is the process of making a long-term, and therefore sometimes risky, commitment to the future, to renewal. And this is why, in the long run, strategy, both its development and the commitment to it, comes first.

Leadership creates new customer relationships, that is, new terms of alignment with customers. In the long run, strategy shifts from being reactive to proactive, to shaping new capabilities and seeking out or creating new customers. As a planning horizon moves farther out, managers should shift their thinking from a reactive mindset to a proactive orientation, where they seek to create the future.

Simply put, in the short run strategy follows structure. In the long run, structure follows strategy.

Why should you care? Because, like most managers, your managers probably spend most of their time reacting to current problems. Yet it is normally difficult to initiate renewal in a meaningful way unless managers take a proactive stance. The problem in long-run planning is that when put into a planning mode, many day-to-day managers will make the mistake of applying their reactive approach to the long run. One result is that you will always be at the mercy of market events that seem outside of your control.

Ask yourself: Does my organization think of strategy as responsible for reacting to market changes, or do we see strategy as initiating market changes that can favor us? Do we even make this distinction in our planning processes?

Long-run strategic thinking also should take into account the amount of time required to renew various capabilities. Estimates of how economic time operates, of the speed at which a market is converging, can provide guidelines as to whether an aging business will have time to acquire the new skills to renew itself. Where economic time is moving faster than the ability of a company to transform itself, restructuring through mergers, acquisitions, divestment, or alliances can accelerate renewal. In other cases, it may be possible to slow down economic time for a while, giving managers more time to institute change. In extreme cases, market exit may be the only alternative.

How Markets Are Created

Demand doesn't exist "out there." It is created. When McDonald's introduced the Egg McMuffin as the first item on its breakfast menu in the early 1970s, English muffins were popular only in a few regions of America. By popularizing the muffin nationwide, McDonald's helped create a market segment that has since grown twice as fast as the baking industry as a whole. The company's Chicken McNuggets had much the same impact when they were introduced in 1982. Now, chicken nuggets are widely emulated by the company's competitors. McDonald's, the hamburger king, became the second largest purchaser of chicken in the United States behind Kentucky Fried Chicken.

Fast food has the characteristics it does—uniformity, low price, and quick service—because of the organizational processes pioneered by McDonald's. Sony not only prevails against Schumpeter's gale of creative destruction, Sony helped to create it. Microsoft wrote the book on how to create demand in the software industry.

Thus, the various possible ways to create markets are often not clear until entrepreneurs bring them into being through experimentation. The timeless story of how Heublein responded to a loss in market share for its premium Smirnoff brand by raising its price is one example. (Market share should have fallen. Instead, it rose; when the quality of goods is not easily compared, high price signals quality.) Or consider Intel. Like Heublein, Intel established a new but very different role for pricing in the renewal of advantage.

Understanding does not have to precede action. Sometimes it is useful to just *do something.* Careful analysis, thoughtful experimentation, done with an eye toward bridging the past with the future, is the goal: to gain knowledge of what might be possible. Through market research, and superior ability to select and reject projects, managers learn to place intelligent bets on the future. Willingness to experiment combined with the ability to learn quickly from what you find are increasingly valuable, indeed critical, renewable skills.

How Organizations Are Renewed

Leaders are explorers. But they are also genetic engineers. Strategy can be thought of as organizational DNA, or the code by which your organization replicates itself. DNA, of course, is the genetic blueprint that guides how an organism reproduces itself, how it interacts to maintain alignment with its environment. DNA determines the growth of the organism, its shape, its life span, and what resources it must consume, and in which environment it must exist in order to sustain itself.

How do you change your organization's DNA? In biology, species cannot change their genetic makeup. Most species die out when they cannot adapt their DNA to their changing environments.

Strategy is difficult to change for the same reason. It requires a change in the basic blueprint by which a company operates. Like in biology, the natural tendency is towards inertia. However, this is where the biological analogy breaks down. Because unlike in biology, organizations, or more precisely, leaders, have the capability to change their organization's DNA.

This is also why, once you understand a competitor's DNA, its capabilities, its strategies, and its leadership, or lack of leadership, you can predict your competitor's limits with a useful degree of accuracy. This is an important step in building an understanding of what can and cannot be done.

Strategies Are Like Fashions

Strategy has a fashionable nature to it. This simply reflects the fact that popular competitive ideas come and go, like fashions. The drive for market share popular in the 1970s was followed a decade later by an emphasis on profitable, smaller market niches. The early emphasis on centralized planning gave way to a widespread interest in decentralization, and still later to interest in the benefits of core competencies. These changes, although sometimes criticized as signs of weakness, are actually deeper signs of convergence and alignment at work.

Like new products, new strategies can evolve to become commodity-like, adopted by many, and thus commonplace. TQM is one example. Does the stylish nature of strategy mean that new strategies are not important? Or that strategy somehow doesn't matter? Far from it. In a dynamic economy, strategy ideas come and go, and sometimes come back, and with them so do the opportunities for renewal.

Being sensitive to the fashionable nature of strategy is part of the process of renewal. New strategies can be as innovative as new products. A new way of competing, some approach to customers that has never been tried before, can convey great advantage to an innovator. Examples include the innovative use of staircase strategies (Disney, Microsoft); a pioneering approach to building a no-surprises approach to customers (Toyota, Southwest Airlines); and the heretofore unheard of willingness to eat their children (Sony, Intel).

Innovative strategies can slow down the action-reaction cycles of competitors, thereby increasing the time before they can respond to a market leader's innovation. A new strategy may not be fully understood by competitors until far into the future, at which time potential imitators will likely lag behind in the race to access the needed capabilities to imitate the strategy. Innovative strategies slow down action-reaction cycles because they force competitors back to ground zero, the initial observation and orientation stages, in their action-reaction cycles.

In order to imitate the innovator, competitors must *first* uncover the new strategy and understand it, and only *later* potentially respond to it. Slower reaction times on the part of competitors translate into longer profit cycles for innovators.

Look at the strategy of Kanban, just-in-time production, commercialized in Japan. The idea of zero inventories was so unorthodox that more than a decade passed before Kanban drew the attention of American managers. Another ten years passed before its adoption in American factories was widespread.

As Kanban was copied throughout the U.S. automobile industry, its ability to convey a distinctive advantage to any one company declined. Twenty years after its introduction, Kanban, with its ability to reduce inventory costs, speed delivery, and increase quality, finally became widespread. At this point the Kanban strategy was not obsolete, of course, because it was still needed. But in another, perhaps more important sense, the context of renewal, Kanban strategies had run their course: Kanban offered less of an opportunity, or a means of achieving sustainable growth, and above average returns, in the automobile industry.

Another implication of the fashions of strategy is that the obsolescence of a particular strategy should not be seen as a failure. The ebb and flow of any particular competitive idea is a natural part of the larger, evolving competitive process.

Think back in time. The simple economies of the past limited the ways to compete. In contrast, the markets of the new economy see continually expanding global demand, seemingly limitless ways to make products, and extremely efficient ways to bring customers and suppliers together. With potentially endless commercial combinations possible, innovative strategies are needed to distinguish one company from another, as are innovative products. The increasing variety of competitive styles that result is one reason for economic time.

You likely encourage your managers to develop new customers and new products, but do you encourage your managers to develop new strategies? Are proposals for doing things in a new way received with the same openness as new product proposals? Or do you assume that growth can be sustained against a backdrop of unchanging behavior? New strategies may require the development of new skills, to be sure, and in this way new strategies require more basic changes in an organization than the development of new products. Yet, if you treat your time-honored strategies as somehow more sacred than your products, you may limit your opportunities for renewal.

A renewal-oriented culture encourages managers to question "the way we do things around here" on an ongoing, systematic basis. In the new economy, willingness to explore, test, and expand the rules of the game should be in the formal job description of managers.

Why Some Strategies Are Copied Faster Than Others

Some strategies are copied quickly while others are copied slowly. Why is this? The answer is found in economic time. How fast a strategy can be imitated is determined by the ease of imitation of the underlying capabilities that support that strategy.

As we continually point out, a strategy is only as good as its ability to achieve profitable alignment; and you cannot achieve alignment with something that does not exist. You may talk about alignment, but you will not be in a position to influence results until you have, or are seen as having, the associated, underlying capability.

When a strategy is imitated, what is actually copied is alignment, the way that capabilities are directed to serve customers. You cannot imitate a strategy unless you have access to the underlying capabilities needed to execute it. You may announce that you are pursuing an innovative strategy. But until you actually acquire the skills to implement it effectively, customers and competitors won't see a change. Here is where considerations of economic time can be helpful.

Where your isolating mechanisms are weak, economic time moves fast, so strategies can be imitated quickly. This is another reason why strategy in fast-cycle markets needs to be quick and adaptive. Where isolating power is strong, and economic time moves more slowly, strategies will be more difficult to imitate. In this way the speed at which a strategy can be copied mirrors underlying capabilities and the economic cycle time of a market.

Or put simply: think about the half-life of your strategy. It's part of the calculus of economic time.

Finally, does your strategy need to be unique? No. It is enough that effectiveness of execution distinguishes you. Your actual, realized alignment is all that customers care about.

RENEWAL

The purpose of renewal is to recapitalize aging products and services. Renewal is based on the assumption that what is worthwhile today will be obsolete tomorrow. Its goal is the removal of the company from competitive markets brought on by convergence. Renewal emphasizes the need to refresh advantage on an ongoing basis.

The renewability of any capability is relative to the rate of progress of competitors along the same dimension. Advantage is relative, measured against its closest alternative. So is renewal. Huge sums may be invested in developing a product, but if customers believe they can get the product from a competitor for less money, then there is little value creation. This is why the success of renewal efforts is measured against the nearest alternative readily available to customers. Absolute renewal, in isolation from competitors, is rare.

Capabilities may generate several types of advantage, or several generations of advantage, but, like products, capabilities grow and fade in importance. As more companies acquire a capability, or are able to access a capability, its value diminishes. Thus the capabilities that matter are often rare, expensive, and difficult to acquire. If capabilities are valuable and easy to acquire, competing companies will acquire them, or render them obsolete through product substitutes. This is why the question of how long a capability remains viable is central to renewal.

Thus, we find that it is important to distinguish between capabilities that can be renewed and those that cannot. A capability may convey an advantage, such as airport hub control, yet not be renewable in the sense of providing a basis for growth because it cannot be duplicated by the hub-controlling company itself.

And thus, in determining the extent to which a capability is renewable, it can be helpful to distinguish how capabilities arise. Generally, capabilities can arise from any of three sources: skills (hard work and investments), endowments (something that is handed to you), or good fortune (luck). While each of these sources can be a source of renewal, the leverage associated with each and the renewal opportunities that they present for managers are different.

Skills

Skills are the result of systematic steps taken to renew advantage. These steps can be conscious or unwitting. Groups of people and individuals may have achieved success through past actions that they do not fully understand. Or, knowledge of how to replicate success may be buried deep within your company or shared among individuals who may not be able to articulate it. In these very real cases, people may be able to replicate their successful behavior but not be able to describe what they do.[2]

An organization's inability to articulate the basis of success can be acceptable as long as market conditions do not change. When markets are stable, informal patterns of behavior, casual operating procedures, and relaxed ways of dealing with customers work; they can be reinforced with little thought given to explicit understanding of their detail or scope. Renewal in stable environments usually does not require as deep an understanding of the workings of your organization.

However, if your market is changing, hidden knowledge can be a problem. Poor understanding of past success handicaps an organization in crafting a renewal strategy. It becomes difficult to know to what extent your company needs to change to move from "A" to "B" because you don't know what "A" *is*. Not understanding the source of past successes adds another layer of complexity in dealing with change. You must first decide who you are, with an unaccustomed level of precision. (You must go back to ground zero in observing and orienting yourself to your own organization.) In this way, uncertain skills can be difficult to extend forward.

For example, members in slow-cycle organizations may not recognize the extent to which past success was based on the special talents of a few individuals. We have seen this happen in professional companies, consulting firms, or entertainment companies. Managers in these companies may not understand why growth stalls when they try to extend their reach beyond the part of the business served by their artisans. Questions were raised when Jeffrey Katzenberg left Disney to join DreamWorks. Would Disney's powerful animation division, originator of blockbuster movies *The Little Mermaid, Aladdin, Beauty and the Beast,* and *The Lion King* under Katzenberg's leadership, suffer greatly the loss of this one individual?

Organizations with a stronger sense of who they are have an advantage in positioning themselves for important, make-or-break decisions that come with change. Renewal strategies are more likely to be realized when management shares in the knowledge and origin of the company's past successes and failures. For this reason it can be helpful in the strategy-setting process to insure that all members of the strategy-setting team share an understanding of your company's history.

Endowments

Endowments can be the basis for success but they are not based on systematic steps taken to renew advantage. Endowments are not created through an organization's systematic actions. Instead, endowment-based capabilities are handed down by virtue of some market factor or consequence outside of managers' control. Although managers are not capable of creating endowments they *are* responsible for recognizing and acting on them.

Mellon Bank had an advantage in back-room check processing through access to a stable Pittsburgh labor force. This endowment helped when competing against Citibank in New York, where the labor force is more expensive and less stable. This advantage influenced an attempted merger between Mellon Bank and the Bank of New York that could have moved check processing from New York to Pittsburgh. So we see that endowments are not assets that managers can cause to come into existence, nor can they take credit for them. But endowments can be exploited to the extent that managers recognize them and competitors cannot gain access to them.

The distinction between skills and endowments matters importantly for renewal opportunities. Advantage based on endowments, because it is outside the control of the organization, is generally difficult to replicate. Thus, endowments are harder to extend forward, beyond the region of past success. The reason, again, is that endowments cannot be replaced at the will of managers. Thus, insofar as this is true in a particular case, managers should be alert to the extent to which renewal plans are based on endowment-based strategies that may have hidden growth barriers associated with them.

To what extent is your success based on endowments? Are you relying on advantages that can or can not be extended forward? Can they be built upon to sustain growth or will success be limited to your current customers?

Luck

Success, of course, can come about through chance. Product development, for example, can be a process of "throwing products against the wall" to see which ones "stick." In these and related cases, random outcomes can be an important contributor to the evolution of advantage. More often, as you can imagine, luck-based success is a one-time event, or at best repeated a few times.

Common sense tells us that luck is difficult to replicate. Of less sustainable value than endowments, luck provides temporary and uncertain advantage. Obvious? Ask yourself: To what degree has your company's success been based on luck? Then ask your key managers. We think that you may be surprised at the high fraction of renewal that some managers attribute to luck. Now ask yourself: What is their attitude toward renewal?

We have asked thousands of managers to estimate the percentage of their companies' success that has come from skills, endowments, and luck. The answer differs by industry and experience, but on average, we found they believe that 10 percent of renewal comes through luck; 15 percent is based on extending endowments; and 75 *percent of renewal comes through superior skills* (the answer becomes more uniform as we ask the question higher up in organizations and when we ask managers how their *competitors* became successful).

We think that the implications are clear. Perhaps like yourself, top managers believe that three-quarters of long-run success comes from purposeful, controllable efforts—actions over which managers, collectively, have ultimate responsibility. Senior managers believe that companies earn the right to stay in business the old-fashioned way, through hard work and smart investments. But, does the rest of your organization?

If your managers disagree about where your success has come from, they may see their roles and responsibilities differently than they would with a shared view of the past. Similarly, they may see your renewal options differently, even if they otherwise appear to be similar in attitude and experience. For example, managers who believe that past success is based on endowments or luck will approach their renewal opportunities less proactively than those who believe that they have earned—that is, in the old-fashioned way—their success. The differences in beliefs that can arise from these three perspectives can be subtle, but a lack of understanding of them in the collective mind-set of your company can harm your renewal prospects.

Ask your managers where your past success has come from. If you find that shared views do not exist, a useful step in the strategy-setting process is to review the reasons for disagreement. They are often deeply rooted in basic personality styles. Work toward a more accurate consensus of your competitive history as well as your competitive strengths and weaknesses.

Ultimately, the benefit of understanding the relative contribution of skills, endowments, and luck is to distinguish renewable capabilities from limiting capabilities. This helps to uncover strengths that have contributed to past success that may be extended forward. Gaining common understanding is an essential step in equipping your management team to make good choices about how much change is expected, and how much can be realistically accomplished as you head into unfamiliar territory.

Renewal Cycles

How do the ideas in this chapter help us trace back to economic time? Recall our earlier discussion about your organization's DNA. Unlike biology, where genetic change can not be controlled, managers—or leaders—can create a change in behavior. But like biology, companies go through a period of instability when this happens. As an organization's members experience the decline of practices and the loss of relationships that were previously important, alignment begins to change. The instability associated with this is necessary. Indeed, it is needed to open the way for forgetting.

Recall that renewable advantage is based on the transforming assumption that what all of us are doing today *will* become obsolete tomorrow. The laws of renewal encourage forgetting, removing old patterns of behavior to make way for new. Discarding old ideas on an ongoing basis becomes normal. The burden in managing shifts from assuming that change is unusual to knowing that lack of change is rare. Try this transforming assumption on your organization and you will identify your future leaders.

And so, like products, renewal strategies have a half-life. They come and go. Only in a world with no anticipated change should short- and long-term strategies be the same. The forced stability of the Eastern Bloc countries discouraged innovation and preserved historical practices long after they were obsolete. Alignment remained strong, but it was expressed in stagnation and decline.

In a dynamic situation, your short- and long-term strategy must be different. This is the only way that purposeful change can occur. This is also why a change in strategy, regardless of where it takes place in economic time, should not be seen as a sign of failure. Just the opposite. Guided change, by encouraging managers to let go of aging products and practices, is a source of sustainable advantage. This brings us to a final point about renewal.

The length of an organization's *renewal cycle,* the amount of time required to recapitalize itself, is influenced by where the organization operates in economic time. This is because economic time provides a guide to the amount of time over which market alignment is likely to remain viable. To the degree that a company's environment is changing, or is transforming in economic time, the renewal cycle must keep pace. When an organization's renewal cycle falls behind the speed of realignment, the rate of capitalization of the company will fall. This is just another way of saying that the company's capabilities are aging faster than they need to be renewed.

When your renewal cycle keeps pace or moves ahead of the pace of strategic realignment taking place in your industry, the capitalization of your assets should increase. Thus, companies that remain viable over decades maintain their renewal cycles at the same pace or faster than their markets. Intel's Andy Grove has spoken of Intel not having a strategy. Intel, of course, has a strategy and a very proactive one. What Grove's comment points out is that in the turbulent environment of microelectronics, renewal cycles require extremely responsive, adaptive leadership. Fast-cycle leadership, for example, can *appear* chaotic; in reality, it operates in the *70 percent zone,* as we would call it, that region of management where 70 percent of value comes from what is expected to happen in the future.

Renewable advantage is not based on endowments, handed down from outside, over which you have little control. Neither is it based on luck, outcomes you did not create, don't control, or do not understand. Renewal is not a crapshoot. Nor is it a game of narrow-mindedly extending past behavior forward. For successful companies, leadership—the management of guided obsolescence through economic time—matters and it matters a lot.

What are the renewal cycles in your industry? What are they for the various groups in your company? Answer these questions and you may be able to trace why the value of your organization has moved up (or down) relative to your competitors.

RECAP: THE THREE LAWS WORKSHEET

The first law of renewal is convergence, the principle that products become less profitable over time as they are duplicated or rendered obsolete. Accounting for about 30 percent of a company's value, convergence reflects the distance from and movement of products toward competitive markets. The second law of renewal is alignment, which accounts for the relationships that exist between a company and its customers. The third law, renewal, which accounts for 70 percent of a company's value, is responsible for those activities that recapitalize aging capabilities. This is done through improvement of existing products, betterment of processes, or introduction of better products.

The following summarizes the use of the laws of convergence, alignment, and renewal in setting strategy.

DETERMINE YOUR POSITION ON THE CONVERGENCE CURVE

The convergence curve is bounded by the maximum profit potential of a product on the upper left side and by no profit on the lower right side. The location of each product on the convergence curve can be estimated by the per-unit profit margin for the each product under consideration.

Determine the speed of movement, or economic cycle time of each product. The speed of movement, or the rate of profit erosion, can be determined by how fast the product profit margin is eroding. A separate analysis should be done for each product, as products occupy different positions on the convergence curve and, depending on the strength of their isolating mechanisms, may be moving toward competitive markets at different rates of speed.

Estimate the extent to which economic time for each product is shifting. This will show up as a noticeable change in the rate of profit erosion. Judge whether shifts in economic time are significant enough to place the product in another category of economic time, currently or in the near future.

DETERMINE YOUR ALIGNMENT

The elements of alignment are your markets (what customers want and the rules of the game), your strategies (your patterns of actual behavior or how you play the game), and your capabilities (what makes you special, different from competitors). When markets, strategies, and capabilities are closely aligned with each other, profits are as high as possible for any product's location on the convergence curve.

Determine how well each product is aligned with customer needs. For short-term strategies, attention should be directed toward identifying ways in which better fit between the company and its customers can be achieved quickly. As the planning horizon moves forward, the analysis should become more proactive, shifting to strategies for creating new market demand and new corporate capabilities. Where products are poorly aligned, and therefore undervalued, identify which changes in strategy will restore value.

Work to gain consensus as to the degree to which past success has been based on skills, endowments, or luck. Press for a distinction as to what degree capabilities are renewable, or instead are in some way limited in their ability to be replicated. Pay particular attention to the speed at which changes in alignment will force changes in strategy or be forced by changes in strategy. See the rise and fall of once-successful strategies as normal. Encourage managers to propose new strategies as a regular part of the planning process.

DETERMINE YOUR POSITION ON THE RENEWAL CURVE

The location of products on the renewal curve determines how well your company is capitalized. The location of each product on the renewal curve reflects an imaginary price/earnings ratio that would exist for that product if it were produced by a single-product company traded as a stock. It follows that the multiproduct company's price/earnings ratio is the average of the renewal contribution of each of its products.

Determine where each product is located on the renewal curve and what actions are being taken to move products up the renewal curve, to a higher rate of capitalization. Because price/earnings ratios are difficult to estimate for individual products, simply judge whether the product in question is being capitalized at a greater or lesser rate than for company products as a whole. As an approximation of this, ask whether each product is ahead or behind the expected average profit growth for all company products.

Think about your various renewal cycles. Question whether the rate of renewal, or extent of recapitalization, is changing. This is similar to estimating how the portfolio of company products is shifting up or down the renewal curve. Depending on whether your company's renewal cycle leads or lags your industry, your products are likely being repositioned on the renewal curve upward toward a higher P/E or downward toward a lower P/E.

Considerations of economic time can help you to know: (1) specific types of investments that can bring on patterns of cash flow; (2) how fast market conditions will change and how stable cash flows associated with change are likely to be; and (3) whether there is sufficient time to acquire new capabilities.

Where products are mixed or shifting in economic time, it may be difficult to judge the reactions of investors. Mixed and shifting economic time makes it more difficult to separate short-term strategy from long-term strategy. In these cases it is important to agree on the appropriate planning horizon over which to expect results and to pinpoint responsibility for change through measurable results, linked to specific timelines.

Ultimately, of course, the choice of where to take your company will be based on your vision of what is needed and what is possible. Taking economic time into account will help, although the final choice is yours. How does economic time help? It shows what you can and cannot become.

Next, we look at ways of reinforcing the principles of renewal with investors.

CHAPTER 6

ALIGNING STRATEGY WITH INVESTORS

Imagine that you have invested millions of dollars and countless hours in pursuing a strategy central to creating some advantage. But imagine that your alignment is bad, that you are not crafting your strategy in ways that make best use of your market opportunities or what sets you apart.

Consider how bad fit could happen. There are lots of possibilities. Your company could have a potentially valuable product, but if it has not advertised it effectively, customers will not be aware of it. General Motors in the 1980s had the best engine technology of North American automakers, but did not stress engine technology in advertising, thus short-changing the value of the company's superior technology. Choosing a bad fit for a strategic alliance, the wrong outsourcing strategy, an ineffective distribution outlet, or a decision to take technology to market too late, or too soon, are but a few of the many mistakes in strategy that can have the same, unfortunate effects. There are countless ways to depress the value of your company.

The unfortunate consequence of bad strategy is undervalued assets. The idea of undervalued assets emphasizes that capabilities are suppressed when not deployed in the best possible way. Investors seek companies that achieve the best alignment, where capabilities are leveraged to yield the highest returns.[1]

When bad fit and the loss in value become apparent, forces are set into motion to establish better alignment. Suppliers of capital reward managers who look for better alignment, for strategies that renew value. That's why companies with chronically undervalued assets become targets for restructuring.

That is also why, to maintain control over your businesses, you should craft strategy by the laws of renewal. These laws apply in many competitive games.

Assume that it is Monday and imagine that you are on a tennis court. Let's look at the rules of the game. Most are familiar and unchanging; the net is a certain height; the ball is a fixed size, composition, and weight. Tennis rackets? They, of course, represent fast-changing technology that is developed and copied quickly. So some parts of the game are stable while others are changing rapidly. This is a critical distinction to begin with whenever you are operating in economic time. For our purposes, let's focus on the more stable parts of the game, in particular, one more part—player height.

Capabilities Are Relative. Let's make you tall—six feet, six inches tall. Does that suggest an advantage? You are taller than just about everybody. Is that a skill? No, it's an endowment, something you can't take credit for. You are tall relative to the rest of the population, and the population does not change quickly. Height is difficult to duplicate. You can recognize this and act upon it; in fact, you must to do your best at any sport, including tennis.

Let's make predictions. How should you play tennis? What will be your strategy, your style of play? You will concentrate on your service because you are tall. You can hit the ball at a high angle onto your opponent's court, which makes it difficult for him or her to return. A net game suits you well too. If you concentrate on your service and net game, both of which involve relatively low energy expenditures, you achieve good competitive fit. You do not win all your games, but you maximize your odds of winning.

Strategy keeps you from playing wrong. What style of play should you avoid as a tall tennis player? The baseline game is one of speed and endurance. The tall player cannot play a baseline game particularly well because with height comes momentum, which slows down the tall player.

But what if you enjoy the fast game, the baseline game, and running around the court. What this means is that if left to your inclination, you are going to play a baseline game. You are not bad at baseline, but you are only good at it for about five minutes. By then you become so tired that your shorter opponent can prevail over you. You will have turned yourself into an undervalued asset.

What does strategy do for you? It reminds you to do things that may not come naturally, to stretch toward a better competitive style, one that improves the value in use of your capabilities. If we all did what comes naturally, we wouldn't need to go through the process of crafting strategy.

Strategy keeps your managers focused on a style of play that leverages their unique capabilities and avoids their weaknesses.

Natural vs. Unnatural Competitors. Strategy also says, "Find a tall opponent, one who lets me play the style that I like best." Managers prefer to play against opponents that are like them. IBM would rather compete against Amdahl in computers, a company like IBM, than against Microsoft or Compaq, companies with very different styles of play. Companies face less need for change when they play against their rivals along similar dimensions. This leads us to the next point.

Let's change capabilities. Assume now that it is Tuesday morning. You step onto the court and your competitor is seven feet tall. That is unlikely, of course, but bear with us. What has changed? You are now the shorter player.

Have your capabilities changed? Yes, in the important, competitive sense, even though you are the same in absolute terms. The point? Capabilities should not be defined in isolation. They must be defined comparatively against whoever steps onto your court. You say, "I am good at X." But how do you know that you are *best* at X? The answer is found only by measuring yourself against your strongest competitors on dimensions of X.

Now that you are shorter, what should your style of play be? Now it is the baseline style. Are you still going to get tired in five minutes? Yes. But how fast will your seven-foot-tall opponent get tired? Three minutes. You win.

When you see the strength of your capabilities and the value of your strategies relative to those of your competitors you increase your chances of winning. This is because you emulate the logic used by customers and by investors. Customers shop around and compare. So do investors. Both choose organizations that pursue what they do best, relative to their competitors.

Now let's change the game. Assume that it is Wednesday and you step out onto the tennis court and the net is missing. In its place is a table with two chairs and a chessboard. You are holding your tennis racket and your opponent says, "Do you want to compete today?" You say, "I'm ready!" Your opponent motions you to take a seat at the chessboard.

What has happened is that the rules of the game have changed. Now how important is your height advantage? For chess height is irrelevant. When the rules of the game shift, you should rethink basic ideas about the capabilities that matter. It may mean that height, or, in the case of what happened to IBM's mainframe computer business, economies of scale, are less relevant.

Managers may have all kinds of intelligence systems in place to gauge opponents' height, or market share, but with paradigm shifts the information may become not wrong, but irrelevant. Old information, attitudes, and values become dangerous. They draw attention away from what matters in the new game. Now you need to forget before you can begin the new learning process.

When markets of any kind are changing, be it in sports, military combat, or business competition, one of the most difficult tasks is to maintain the links that keep the organization viable. One aid in this direction is the idea of renewable success factors.

RENEWABLE SUCCESS FACTORS

We have been focusing on how advantages come and go, and with them the practices that must be mastered to sustain growth. Microprocessor speed became a critical success factor, indeed an industry driver, in the personal computer industry. Japanese automakers demonstrated in the 1980s that quality improvements could be used as a success factor to differentiate automobiles. Common operating systems determined the success and failure of software companies early in the information industry. For a time these critical success factors were a basis for renewal.

Yet each of these success factors was eventually copied, became commonplace, or became less important. Microprocessor performance became so fast that many user needs could be met with commodity-level technology. As Total Quality Management became the focus of competition, quality differences between Japanese and American automakers narrowed to the point where customers could scarcely detect differences in quality among automobile brands. The advent of the Internet and Java programming language reduced the power of Windows95 because it made applications operate independently of operating systems.

As convergence erodes success factors, the profitability to be had by focusing on them declines. Indeed, it may be necessary to sustain the activity, as it becomes the price of entry into an industry, but the activity will no longer generate attractive profits. Quality, discussed earlier, became less of a basis for distinction in the auto industry, but attention to quality remained as a price of staying in business.

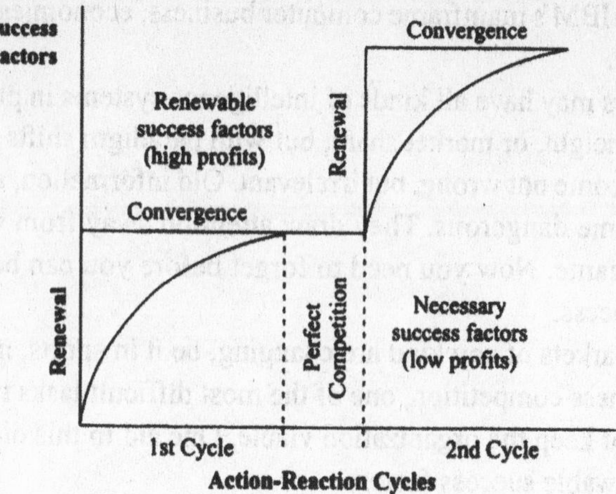

Figure 6.1. Renewable Success Factors

In this case we can say that a success factor has evolved from a *renewable* success factor to a *necessary* success factor. Mastery of a necessary success factor is needed for entry and survival, but it does not generate attractive profits. In order for an industry to remain attractive, newer success factors must arise that become the focus of renewal. The pattern of decline and renewal of success factors is shown in Figure 6.1.

Renewable success factors decline to the status of required success factors when they no longer provide a point of distinction, or renewal. When success factors are imitated or rendered commonplace they disappear altogether or add to the inventory of requirements that need to be mastered. Their usefulness in maintaining the company's products up on the convergence curve declines.

The downgrading of critical success factors to required success factors is a way of understanding how an industry can mature to the point where once-profitable companies lose their vitality. These companies still may be very good at what they do, the problem is that what they do no longer matters to customers.

Predicting the speed and degree by which success factors change can be aided by knowledge of the economic time in which a company operates. In slow-cycle markets, success factors tend to be stable, changing little over the life of products. Examples include geography, reputation, highly skilled human capital, or patents and copyrights. In standard-cycle markets, success factors change gradually, as the orchestration of learning processes gradually transforms products into commodities or draws away demand. Examples include the quality movement in automobiles and the shift in demand away from passenger cars toward four-wheel-drive vehicles. In fast-cycle markets, success factors are unstable. Examples include the constellation of changing technologies and usage patterns that displaced bulky PC boxes and cathode ray tubes with flat screen, laptop PCs.

This is why renewable success factors are closely related to renewal cycles, discussed earlier. The rise and fall of success factors causes the patterns of alignment for organizations to change. As success factors evolve, such as from mainframe-based operating systems to personal computer–based operating systems, nontraditional companies (like Microsoft) can enter an industry (such as office computing) and become dominant. Part of the reason why nontraditional companies do well in these settings is that their renewal cycles are faster. Their managers, not burdened by perceptions of how things operated in the past, are more likely to embrace new success factors. Thus, in these, as well as less radical cases, it is often necessary to plan years ahead for change, and to put programs in place to restructure a company's capabilities ahead of changes in demand.

In any case, managers should monitor the evolution of success factors in their industry as a normal part of doing business. Identification of changing success factors needs to take place on a regular basis, before current success factors are downgraded to necessary success factors or disappear altogether. Emphasizing how success factors rise and fall as a normal part of planning makes it easier to convince managers of the need for managing change as normal.

Another benefit of thinking about the evolution of success factors is to unfreeze managers' thinking, giving them another reason to become responsible for change. In company after company that we studied, the best managers had created a culture whereby long-held assumptions were continually under question; about what is important in their industry, whether the rules of the game are changing and, if so, what the new success drivers would be. Renewable success factors orient your managers toward the future, treating change, as we continually emphasize, as a normal part of management.

HIGH-ENERGY MARKETS

For most companies, there is a tenuous relationship between the balance sheet and economic value. Recall what happened to IBM as mainframe capabilities were duplicated by microprocessors. IBM's balance sheet remained unaffected while IBM's stock price plummeted. How can your managers predict which capabilities are at risk of becoming misaligned with changing markets and which capabilities are safe? Since alignment is always changing to some degree, how can you focus your attention on the most important changes in your markets?

One way to focus on long-term renewal is to look for what we think of as high-energy markets. Where significant change is possible, markets receive more attention. A high-energy market is one where a watershed event is likely to occur that can radically alter how value is created. The benefit of being sensitive to the onset of high-energy markets is to direct attention away from today's profits, and to think through paradigm shifts in how value will be created in the future.

We can understand, for example, how Microsoft can be classified as a slow-cycle company, and yet face the need for constant, intense planning: Microsoft faces the possibility of transformations in economic time by competitors attempting to change the rules of the game for Microsoft.

In a high-energy market the consequences of a wrong strategy or a poorly conceived tactic can be particularly harmful. An example is the personal computer industry in the 1980s when Apple Computer failed to license the Macintosh operating system, only to see its renewal pathway blocked later as the market tipped toward Microsoft Windows. Understanding energy levels in a market can be helpful in managing renewal because energy levels provide one gauge of a market's expected stability. In high-energy markets, steps are being taken today, or environmental changes are taking place, that are likely to make a major difference tomorrow. High energy levels in a market both reflect and direct managers' attention, away from the present and toward the future.

High-energy markets arise where major changes are anticipated in the level of competitiveness, higher or lower. This correlates with changes in where products in an industry are expected to be repositioned on the convergence line. High-energy markets arise also where the speed of convergence of products on the convergence line is expected to change, to speed up or to slow down. This is why traditional, snapshot measures of profitability are an unreliable guide to how a company's advantages are changing, as was true for telecommunications and software companies in the 1990s. Energy levels can vary enormously in markets where competitors have similar profits. This is how price/earnings ratios can vary for companies with similar profits. Where energy levels are high, the market's capitalization potential is ripe for change.

When profit levels are expected to change, up or down, the level of management attention and energy directed to the business increases. Attention to forward-looking strategy grows. Energy levels can be high in markets operating anywhere in economic time. What gives markets and the companies operating in them a rise in energy levels is belief by managers of the potential of radically altering the nature and makeup of historical competitive processes. In contrast, market energy levels decline when there is little opportunity for changing the way that profits are made.

A low-energy market can be profitable or unprofitable; but in either case no change is believed possible in how profits are made. The lobster industry is a low-energy market, a classically competitive market comprised of numerous small fishing boat operators who troll the ocean floor in ways unchanged for decades. The lobster industry has fierce day-to-day competition among small fishing boats; yet the structure of that competition is stable and predictable. Profits are low and there is little opportunity for changing profit levels through transforming effects like technological change, change in regulation, or management innovation.

Where the potential for change in profitability is low, the long-run payoff from strategic behavior is low. Little attention is paid to the potential for a change to make a difference. This is why the lobster fisherman lives life in a more relaxed fashion than the personal computer salesman does, even though both are in competitive markets by traditional standards.

The early days of personal computers saw software writers and PC sales representatives working feverishly. Their energy came about not because profits were high (many companies lost money), but because of the expectation profits could *become* high. In high-energy markets basic changes are believed to be at work, as a result of regulatory or technological change or the actions of companies, in how value is created and renewed.

Through the early 1990s, the U.S. domestic markets for local telephone service were low-energy in nature. The Baby Bells, with a profitable monopoly over service in their markets, faced little competition and as an industry group turned in above-average profits. With the passage of the Telecommunications Act in 1996, energy levels in the telecommunications industry increased even as profits remained little changed. Numerous competitors were expected to try to bypass copper wire service with fiber, cable, or wireless services. By traditional standards, these markets were noncompetitive, still profitable. Indeed, they remained profitable well into the 1990s. But in terms of renewal, they had become highly energetic from the standpoint of the possibility of *changes* in how economic time operates.

Like other aspects of renewal, energy levels in markets rise and fall. In 1995, when Apple management eventually licensed the MAC operating system, the energy level in the market for personal computer operating systems had declined. Microsoft's near dominance of personal computer operating systems created little interest in the decision to license the Mac operating system, slight response on the part of computer makers or customers, and virtually no reaction by the capital markets in their valuation of Apple. The energy had gone out of the battle for desktop computer operating systems.

High-energy markets are the focus of intense managerial attention and commitment. Potentially irreversible investments lead to the unavoidable you-bet-your-company investments directed toward a changed future. In high-energy markets, the manager asks, "What actions can be taken today, by us or by our competitors, that hold the promise of fundamentally *transforming* the way that value is created tomorrow?"

OPTIONS-RICH MANAGING

Recall that it can take from three to fifteen years to build the core competencies of a business. Payback comes over a long and uncertain horizon, especially relative to results from more localized, shorter-term investments. The well-known result of uncertain, lagged payback periods for companies that are bottom line–oriented is that long-term investments can be shortchanged in favor of near-term results. While this problem is well known, it can be particularly problematic to renewal-oriented managers in opportunity-rich markets.

A common threat to renewal is not that managers will select bad projects, but that they will *not* select enough *good* projects. As one manager put it, "We can say no to projects and be right 90 percent of the time, but the other 10 percent that we never take on can kill our business."

Starving a company of strategic options is easy because the effects are not apparent early on. Opportunities decline slowly; the company's capitalization declines slowly. When a company runs out of options, it is only a question of the economic cycle time in which the company operates before remaining products move down the convergence curve to economic extinction. Just as it can take years to develop new capabilities, depriving a company of options is a failure in leadership that can take years to recognize.

Options-poor managing led to the abandonment of television production by U.S. manufacturers. Because it was no longer profitable to produce televisions, manufacturers left the business, in the process losing many of the competencies necessary to compete in consumer electronics markets that emerged later.

One solution to this problem can be found in an appreciation for the role of strategic options in the renewal process. Financial options, familiar to investors, increase the number of ways that long-term, uncertain investments can pay out benefits. They provide more alternatives—to accept or reject projects at specified points in time—than are provided for by traditional budgeting techniques. For product managers, options thinking applied to real projects provides a robust way to see the additional, hidden benefits of staying with or taking on projects.[2]

Consider Panasonic. The company makes a wide range of consumer electronics, as is well known. But they also make bicycles. Panasonic's bicycles were historically mass produced and were targeted to the low middle-priced buyer. Panasonic launched a line of bicycles in the late 1980s with individually sized frames, custom seats and handlebars, and special paint schemes. Since each bike was potentially unique, there could be no stock of finished products in the factory or the dealers' showrooms. Orders had to be processed individually, and each bike had to be built, painted, and shipped within a fixed window of time. This level of change, from mass production to a job shop, required a new manufacturing facility, a new class of workers, and new assembly techniques.

Custom bicycles were not particularly successful for Panasonic, but the project yielded other benefits. A better brand image was generated for Panasonic bicycles that helped sales of their low-end bikes. The process of taking orders for custom bicycles gave Panasonic managers insight into consumer preferences. This knowledge allowed low-end bike designs to be crafted more effectively. In this way, the value of the custom bicycle project was positive even though it was not possible to assign a reliable estimate directly to it.

Options-rich investments are often found in different types of organizational learning activities. Training programs can contribute to the development of new capabilities that only may be guessed at today. Or by staying in a market when returns are marginal, alternatives can be created to offer products that do not yet exist or to participate in a market upturn.

The challenge in justifying unorthodox, out-of-the-box projects such as Panasonic's lies in the messy, confused nature of risk. Traditional financial techniques use a single discount rate in evaluating a project. This often handicaps projects with unknown or changing risk. Often the largest portion of risk occurs during the first stage of a project, but then declines as time passes and progress is made. Using one discount rate for projects over their estimated life makes some projects appear less attractive than they are. Options thinking allows projects to be segmented into risk phases and valued sequentially. This way, options thinking helps renewal-based managers to reduce uncertainty.

The attractive feature of options is that the value of an option *increases* as the length of time to payback *increases* and as project uncertainty *rises*. (The details on this are complicated.) While these relationships may seem extraordinary, these attractive and theoretically sound features of strategic options give them a highly strategic quality in investment planning. In this way, options thinking fills in the important, strategic valuation mechanisms that can be missing in traditional financial analysis.

Segmenting the first, often more risky portion of projects and treating them as options provides an effective way to evaluate investments with changing risk. Rather than face a take it or leave it scenario, management can make incremental investments, taking on the first segment of the project to acquire information. This creates the option to add or drop the remainder of the project later, as more information becomes available. The first stage of the project will have contributed to renewal in two ways: by reducing the risk that the larger project is rejected when it should be accepted, but also by granting the company another chance to make the investment later.

Managers are offered the option of whether or not to invest in the smaller, initial effort in order to acquire an asset—better information—and the option to make the follow-on investment. If the initial effort is undertaken, the amount of money at risk is confined to the initial stage. When it is necessary to make a decision about whether or not to fund the follow-on investment, by then the associated uncertainty and risk of the project will be better understood. If uncertainty has been reduced significantly, so that the risk structure of the project is known, traditional financial analysis can come into use.

Options-rich projects can be set up as a series of staged, incremental investments. Exit points can be defined along the stages. By segmenting the initial, higher risk portion of a project by treating it as an option, the evolution of the commitment through economic time is taken on sequentially. An options approach to large, risky projects provides managers with a way to stage the analysis, develop its arguments, and assess its benefits. Funds for the initial stage are more likely to be committed, rather than held back until the risk or uncertainty, and the window of opportunity, has gone away. In this way, use of strategic options can keep managers especially concerned about risk from waiting until it is too late to commit to a project. It can also offer a compromise to managers who might take an investment stance that is too aggressive.

Limits of Options

One limitation of options thinking is that it can become complicated to communicate through the organization. Options estimates are often difficult to generate, especially for intricate, dynamic investments. They require more attention to be put on understanding the staging of commitments, how entry and exit options arise chronologically. This is where considerations of economic time can be helpful. Economic time distinguishes investment opportunities by their dynamic characteristics, thereby making questions of staging and sequential commitments more understandable.

Options can be used to justify almost any type of project, be it good or bad. Options managing is most justifiable when a project has benefits and risks that are long run in nature and poorly known. This, of course, is the realm where many renewal decisions should be made. Also justifiable are cases where investments can be made sequentially, are reversible, and where they will increase the quality of knowledge about the value of the project. By contrast, projects in mature markets, with little chance of creating spin-offs and building new corporate capabilities, are least likely to be justified on the basis of options.

Options-rich thinking makes it easier to persuade managers to forget and thus to eat their children. Options managing reduces the atmosphere of failure often associated with backing away from a project. Options-rich evaluation methods provide managers with an opportunity to evaluate projects in discrete stages, thus encouraging more candid assessments with limited knowledge. Well-specified exit points (option expiration dates) make it easier to shut down a losing project after it is initially accepted. Options thinking complements selection skills discussed earlier, making it easier to "know when to hold 'em and when to fold 'em."

One new drug packaging and distribution plant, under consideration by Merck, could not be justified by cost savings alone. Thinking in terms of options, Merck's management judged that there were benefits to be had in undertaking the project from a learning perspective, although those benefits were not yet well understood or quantifiable. Rather than using traditional techniques, the project was justified as acquiring an option on future automation. Subsequent results from the project clarified the benefits to the point that managers expanded automation to other company operations.

As you develop options, and these are understood by investors, you move up the renewal line. Your assets become more highly capitalized. The price/earnings ratio of your company will rise. Investors will expect that a greater fraction of your advantage will come through future profits, from projects that do not exist today but are possible. The pressure on you to maintain current profits will decline. To be sure, short-term profits will remain important, but the attention of your managers, your investors, and your customers will turn toward how you intend to create the future.

Options-rich thinking helps to institutionalize renewal cycles. Options encourage managers to treat uncertainty and risk associated with investments as a normal part of managing. Knowledge, acquired through the process, is a central benefit in itself. Options encourage managers to invest for the future, to operate in the 70 percent zone, to create new skills and new knowledge necessary for renewal.

Keeping your organization rich with options and exercising them at the right time works alongside traditional thinking. Ask yourself: Do we encourage or discourage options thinking in our business? Are options available for doing things differently, if only we would look for them?

Still, nothing lasts forever. Even companies that were once options rich can age to the point where renewal is not possible. When this happens, economic time—the dynamic creation of value—stops for the organization.

WHEN ECONOMIC TIME STOPS

Economic time can stop for the best managed of companies. Renewal cycles don't keep pace with industry change. Existing products continue down the convergence curve, perhaps at an accelerated pace, until current profits, as well as the expectation for future profits, disappear. Financial distress, also associated with less extreme changes in economic time, does not always result in a complete cessation of operations. Bankruptcy or near-bankruptcy is a temporary condition where a discrete opportunity exists to change control over the use of the company's assets and improve cash flows toward the goal of ultimately renewing operations.

Although the process associated with reorganization, or workout, differs by company and by industry, there are common elements that can be organized by economic time. It is not surprising that economic time provides guidelines to workout when questions of timing and expediency are at issue. While the focus here is on the legal ramifications of reorganization, the prescriptions should be useful as well for companies facing organizational disruptions short of bankruptcy.

Consider the extreme case of a company that has just filed for bankruptcy. Management is being retained, for now at least, with the goal of developing two strategies, one for the short term, which concerns how to get out of bankruptcy, and a second strategy which addresses how to position the company for long-term renewal. The questions sharpened through economic time center on the tradeoffs of how the company regroups in the short term while recasting its opportunities for the long term.

Slow-Cycle Workout

Begin with a hypothetical slow-cycle company. Assume that managers have gained ownership of some market factor and have captured a class of customers through lock-in. As in most reorganizations, creditors will press slow-cycle managers to cut costs to improve cash flows. But cost reduction in slow-cycle companies is inherently difficult. Particularly problematic is the risk of cutting at activities that maintain dynamic lock-in with customers.

This was the experience of one European elevator company. Efforts at cost reductions reduced product attractiveness and caused a significant loss of customers because elevator customers demanded and were willing to pay for custom installations. Because few slow-cycle companies face price competition, a better route to improving cash flow may be to raise prices carefully, perhaps by bundling features and services to products and expanding the scope of services based on relationships.

Keeping the company operating during reorganization should be in everyone's interest. At the extreme, customers can be called in to testify in court as to their inability to find other suppliers for the product or service on short notice. An example of this would be the government's support of Chrysler prior to bankruptcy, as only Chrysler could make the Army's highly engineered M-1 tank. Army personnel were called as witnesses for Chrysler to argue the benefits of continuing operations.

The relative predictability of cash flows of a slow-cycle company should be attractive to creditors. Management can use predictability to bolster arguments for proposing low-risk payout schedules for creditors. A lower level of debt for the company may be possible, in service of relatively high-confidence forecasts of sources and uses of cash. Still, in developing a long-term debt repayment schedule, be aware that it may take a while to renew cash flows. Debt levels should be renegotiated to a level of outflows that can be met based on the profits available from current customers. Managers in the slow-cycle company should be conservative in estimating the level of cash flows that can be dedicated to repaying debt.

The predictability of cash flows also suggests that there may be minimal leverage to negotiate an equity-for-debt swap with creditors, at least to the extent that they see few unanticipated future profit gains. The central negotiating advantage for the equity holders is that they have time; the business should be relatively resistant to damage from delays in workout.

Recall also that the organization structure in slow-cycle companies can be subordinated to superstar individuals. Creditors should make special efforts to identify and cater to those individuals whose special knowledge or customer relationships bolster the company's capabilities. Since good employees are likely to be tempted by outside offers when the company faces financial distress, it can be useful to offer them equity participation during the reorganization process. In light of the equity constraints discussed above, participation may need to be relatively large or combined with increased authority.

Management should be particularly cautious about pressures to sell slow-cycle trophy assets for quick cash. Competitors and creditors may or may not be able to identify trophy advantages as they come up for sale. Because these isolating mechanisms cannot be easily duplicated and are at the center of the functioning of some aspect of a market, it makes good sense for the competitor to offer a high price for them. At the same time, given the bias of bankruptcy law toward continuation of the company, it should be relatively easy to prove to creditors the value of holding on to trophy assets during reorganization. Special attention should be given to the need to distinguish trophy properties and key individuals from other, less essential assets during the workout process.

Since reputation can be important to slow-cycle companies, managers may wish to consider retaining distinguished law companies or high-profile reorganization specialists. Prestigious names will add to customers' confidence, consistent with close relationships. Extra time could be spent explaining to customers the internal details of reorganization, publishing articles, or doing industry association speeches to sustain the image of the company.

Standard-Cycle Workout

For standard-cycle managers, orchestration of volume growth, product design, process improvements, and organizational learning are the drivers of success. If a distressed company has small market share, and to the extent that antitrust restrictions will be eased to accommodate the distressed company, bankruptcy may be a good time to consider merging with another company in the same industry.

At the same time, managers should be cautious about their ability to absorb operations that are distressed. As discussed in Chapter 2, orchestration is a complex organizational task, requiring extensive methods and controls, as well as good working relationships between functional areas. To the extent that a lack of orchestration capability may be the cause of financial distress in the first place, the acquired organization may not blend well with existing operations.

Managers can go beyond traditional arguments about the advantages of reducing overlapping functions and look deeper, to the quality of the candidate's scale symphony. Ford, for example, found that its acquisition of Jaguar required twice as much management attention as expected.

Even without merger, workout can enhance a standard-cycle company's efforts to renew itself. The management at Chrysler Automotive found its employees and creditors more willing to work toward needed changes during workout. If management effectively sells the reorganization plan to workers, getting their cooperation, workout offers the chance to improve teamwork and unity. In a crisis situation, people are more likely to cooperate, so workout can be the best time to improve labor-management relations.

Workout can encourage overdue deliberations about rationalizing product lines (saying no to customers). It sharpens choices between what to buy and what to make. Workout gives management a window of opportunity to drive toward greater efficiencies, to make overdue process improvements, and to prune previously sacred products. As in the case of Chrysler Corporation, standard-cycle workout can provide a temporary advantage not available to competitors.

Fast-Cycle Workout

The uncontrollable pace of new products and services in fast-cycle markets presents special workout problems for managers. Managers will face extraordinary time pressures as they try to influence their employees and their creditors while pursuing new products and customers, all of whom should be brought into the company's rapid decision-making process.

In traditional workout situations, often the first area that debt holders seek to cut is research and development. This is consistent with increasing short-term cash flows to service debt. In fast-cycle companies, however, cuts in R&D may go directly to the heart of the company's renewal opportunities, leaving managers with few options for renewal. Cutting R&D and other market development efforts in attempts to reorganize a fast-cycle company can be little different from taking a fast-cycle company directly to liquidation.

Creditors, thinking that money can still be made with old products, may veto any plan that involves introducing innovative new products that make old products obsolete. Rapid price reductions and fast inventory sell-off may be viewed incorrectly by creditors as an attempt to defraud them of profits. To maintain credibility and convince debtholders of the legitimacy of rapid price and inventory reductions, managers should mount a strong defense of the dynamics of fast-cycle markets.

If the fast-cycle organization is properly set up, it should already have rapid decision-making ability. Creditors must understand the role and style of fast-paced decision processes and not let their own relatively slower-paced decision styles interfere with operations. One publishing house in bankruptcy never made it out of reorganization because creditors kept delaying the introduction of new books. Creditors who are accustomed to workouts in standard or slow-cycle markets may not understand the time compression aspects of the market situation faced by managers in a fast-cycle company, and so should be educated about the importance of maintaining a quicker pace of product introduction.

Without aggressive and effective renewal efforts the fast-cycle value creation process soon ends. Thus, delays in the workout process can destroy a fast-cycle company. Closely held creditors will be easier to educate than a large group of creditors and this translates into speed of workout. In this sense a fast-cycle company with a closely held debt structure may have an advantage during the workout process.

Sensing a turn away from innovation, fast-cycle employees, who tend to be among the most mobile in the work force, are likely to have little difficulty finding work elsewhere. While some selective pruning of product development activities may be necessary, convincing debtholders that market development is key to renewal is in their long-run interest.

RECAP: ALIGNING STRATEGY WITH INVESTORS

For advantage to be sustained, products must ultimately generate value greater than their cost of capital. This is true regardless of how you measure yourself. Managers who don't succeed in this way are removed from positions of strategic responsibility as they see their companies restructured or liquidated. In this way the laws of renewal provide a way to map the strategy choices required by managers to the criteria required by investors. Managers wishing to keep an investor orientation in their strategies can keep the following points in mind.

REMEMBER YOUR TENNIS GAME

Advantage is relative. You are only as strong as your competitors are weak. You can get stronger or weaker in a market entirely through the actions of others, as your competitors enter and leave your markets. The point is that capabilities cannot be defined in isolation. They should always be evaluated in a relative, competitive context, compared to the capabilities of whoever else is competing for the same customers. This obvious and simple idea is often forgotten by managers in markets undergoing change.

Consider doing things that do not necessarily come naturally, to stretch toward new competitive styles that regenerate the value in your aging capabilities. Like athletes in training, you should practice stretching continually, as you take your company into competition for new customers.

Continual testing of your business model is helpful, even when change is not immediately necessary. The goal is to build within your company higher-level capabilities of transformation, to encourage the cultural readiness to set aside the old for the new so that your managers are ready for change when change comes. Be particularly sensitive to the emergence of unnatural competitors, companies that can redefine the rules of the game in your markets to the point where your historical business model no longer works.

Organizational effectiveness can be aided by a broad knowledge of the various business models that are emerging in alternative markets. Expose your managers to the different management styles that may be available to you in changing market opportunities.

LOOK FOR RENEWABLE SUCCESS FACTORS

Monitor the most important success factors at work for each product. Pay attention to the degree and extent to which renewable success factors are being degraded to the status of necessary success factors, where they no longer provide a basis of profits. Attempt to forecast those emerging success factors that may become critical in the future. Estimate how they may require the company to operate differently than in the past.

Consider the extent to which success factors reflect mixed economic time at work in a market. How do success factors reinforce each other? Or do success factors work against each other, requiring different organizational approaches for each?

LOOK FOR HIGH-ENERGY MARKETS

The central question addressed by high-energy markets is the degree to which some watershed event may radically alter how value is capitalized. The purpose of thinking in terms of high-energy markets is to direct managers' attention away from day-to-day concerns and toward a major change or paradigm shift. To the extent that market energy levels are high, you can anticipate the entry of new competitors and altered competitive strategies. High energy levels in markets often signal a change in how business is managed.

High-energy markets give early warning that the capitalized value of capabilities is on the verge of changing. Attention to energy levels provides a way to orient your managers beyond short-term concerns to the long-run viability of your company's business model.

SEEK OPTIONS-RICH PROJECTS

Systematically orient your managers to how first-stage business opportunities lead to second-stage business opportunities. Options have a built-in logic that assigns value to those projects that can create a string of competitive advantages, far into the future. Another attractive feature of options thinking is to provide a way to surface the judgments often needed in forward planning. The dynamic, future-oriented considerations of options provide a counterbalance to traditional capital budgeting techniques, as well as to traditional thinking generally, that can bias decisions toward low-risk, short-term outcomes.

Options thinking makes it easier to stage the benefits and costs of strategic commitments. This capability is particularly useful when combined with considerations of economic time, which highlights the sequential aspects of competition. Combining economic time with options thinking yields a sharper analysis of strategic projects as they unfold, making it easier for managers to take on forward-based projects and to change their commitment to them as needed.

The ultimate test of options thinking is your organization's long-run viability. Companies with options-rich investments often have a higher price/earnings ratio, reflecting their richer opportunities, farther up the renewal curve.

GUIDE WORKOUT EFFORTS THROUGH ECONOMIC TIME

Slow-cycle managers can focus their workout efforts around the special valuation characteristics of one-of-a-kind, trophy assets. Standard-cycle managers can use the urgency of workout to tighten controls over their scale orchestra: to rationalize their product offerings, seek greater process refinement, and redouble their efforts at organizational learning. Fast-cycle managers and their creditors should know that delays in market development budgets, as well as changes to budgeted projects under development, will go to the heart of the prospects for the fast-cycle company to renew itself.

Next we focus on managing across the different cycles of economic time. These situations arise in multiproduct companies, where complex products are exposed to elaborate customer requirements. Common among what follows is a focus on the opportunities and difficulties available from operating across multiple competitive cycles. This focus is consistent with our belief that managers will benefit from operating among multiple business approaches and from moving between them on a routine basis.

CHAPTER 7

MULTICYCLE MANAGEMENT

In the present day, it is common to see a company operate across different markets. Before its voluntary reorganization, AT&T had a variety of products and services ranging from personal computers, credit card services, and cellular phones, to long-distance phone service. It had electronic consumer products businesses in fast-cycle, long-distance service in standard-cycle, and network systems in slow-cycle markets. As economic time cycles become aggregated within organizations like AT&T, they become more complex. The interwoven business operations of these kinds of mixed-cycle organizations increase the degree of management complexity enormously, and pose a challenge for managers.

Multicycle management is complicated because competition is a multispeed process. Hence, one of the dangers associated with managing multicycle companies is to underestimate the dynamic dependencies among the different cycles of economic time. When setting a strategy, a multicycle manager should first recognize the full extent of the differences between and among business cycles, and then select a strategy targeted not only at each specific cycle but also at the consequences of inter-cycle effects.

The way to understand multicycle management is to start at the point of sale for each product or service. This is the front line at which economic time operates, the most simple or homogeneous level at which to measure economic time. At its simplest level, economic time reflects the duration of company-customer relationships. Based on the strength or weakness of isolating mechanisms, economic time can move as slow-cycle, standard-cycle, or fast-cycle, reflecting a product's half-life, which can range from ten years or more to less than a year. Then, as economic time cycles become aggregated within organizations, company-wide product half-life cycles become more complex. See Figure 7.1.

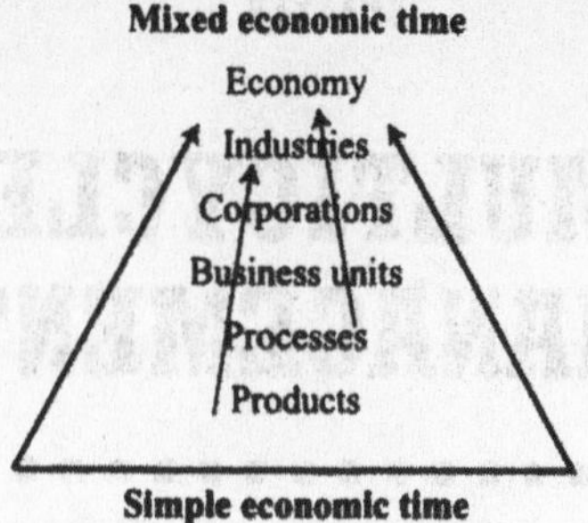

Figure 7.1. The Layers of Economic Time

Economic time is linked to the isolating mechanisms of the company. These range widely, from close personal relationships, as in the case of McKinsey, economies of scale for Starbucks, or easily copied innovation, as in the case of the many fashions of Liz Claiborne. The business units of a company are made up of these various processes, as well as consideration of the needs of customer segments, which may overlap in economic time. To the extent that this is true, mixed economic time effects will show up within a business unit, opening up the potential for conflicts in management styles.

Grumman Aerospace, a slow-cycle company, decided to diversify into the mass transit bus business, where economies of scale are critical. At issue were the challenges of transferring Grumman's one-of-a-kind, artisan orientation to a successful mass production situation. Subsequently, more than one hundred Grumman buses had to be recalled by the New York City Port Authority because their aluminum frames were cracking under the strain of traversing New York city streets. Grumman had overengineered the buses by designing them with light metal frames, similar to those used in their F-14s, thus creating a product that had to be manufactured almost as carefully as an F-14 airframe, but which could not withstand pothole stress. In recalling the company's experience, a Grumman manager concluded to us, "I guess we can't build buses like we build F-14s."

Managers faced with multiple product cycles need a careful balance of top-down authority, to reconcile potential cycle-time conflicts, and decentralized responsibility, so that each business remains aligned closely with the needs of its own customers. The speed with which Microsoft was able to respond to the Internet challenge shows that organizations facing this splitting effect benefit from strong managers with cross-business authority who understand the strains of multiple economic time and act quickly. At the same time, the sometimes conflicting needs of economic time cycles make centralized, uniform management difficult.

Now let us overlay the layers of economic time onto the organizational structure of the multicycle company, highlighting areas where potential cycle-time complementarities or conflicts may arise. Of special interest are companies that embrace widely different management styles successfully, across economic time cycles. In this regard we look at Johnson & Johnson, which has developed a track record of operating in highly diverse businesses.

MULTICYCLE ORGANIZATIONS

Gezinus Hidding, an expert on high-level decision making in strategic settings, looked at a wide range of variables that indicate differences across economic time. He found that strategy recommendations based on economic time orient managers effectively toward action. In particular, managers found such recommendations easier to translate into action than recommendations based on traditional analysis of industry structure.[1] Why is this?

When carefully reflected in an organization's structure, economic time dictates how the organization is set up to respond to market events. It reflects how an organization manages its activities to satisfy the demands of its customers, by mapping the character and sequencing of activities within the company to maintain profitable alignment.

An organization's cycle-time structure reflects relationships with customers and suppliers that have been shown to work best, how one functional area affects another, and the different styles of management that have withstood the test of time. It reflects also the incentives for managers, and the measurements used to determine success and failure. A corporation can be organized across a range of economic time cycles as represented in Figure 7.2.

Cycle-time structure highlights the systems and processes that bring the various business functions together. If processes are out of sync, events are out of pace with one another and what happens in one process does not reinforce what is needed for success in another function or supporting area. For example, research could be too fast or too slow to support a product's manufacturing or marketing. In these situations, research and manufacturing can work at cross purposes, as if half a football team were moving on a play while the other half stood still. Or if half of a football team and half of a hockey team got together to play the same game. When

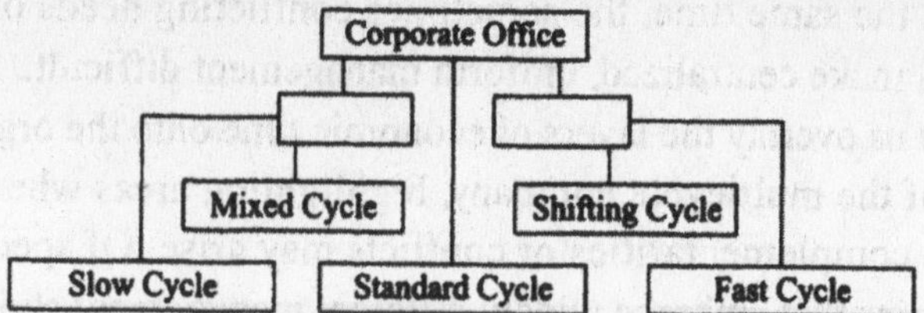

Figure 7.2. Organizing by Economic Time

actions are not synchronized, each process shortchanges the effectiveness of the overall organization.

Particularly important in a multicycle organization is the willingness to set highly diverse productivity goals, so as to reinforce the customer alignment requirements of each economic time cycle. For example, cost improvement is difficult in slow-cycle markets because these organizations do not benefit much from economies of scale. This contrasts with organizations operating at the other extreme of economic time, where supernormal productivity is common due, in part, to weak isolating mechanisms. Therefore, fast-cycle businesses should be benchmarked accordingly, against aggressive productivity and cost reduction goals.

Quality management programs originated and proved their value in standard-cycle settings, where high-volume repeatability is key. Total Quality Management, as another example, when applied across economic time without regard to the different needs of different businesses can turn otherwise good businesses into underperformers. Slow-cycle businesses are less likely to benefit from traditional quality management practices where products are one of a kind, where success is based on product or relationship complexity, or where products are made and supported through the high skills and talents of individuals. Quality programs in fast-cycle businesses may need to be rethought as well, if they unduly slow down the organization's ability to get product to market before price erosion sets in.

Functional Synchronization

We know, of course, that many processes of an organization, such as research and development, purchasing, manufacturing, marketing, pricing, distribution, and customer service, should be coordinated with one another. If we imagine these activities passing along product responsibility to each other along a value chain, we can imagine that they are linked by cycle-time dependencies. That is, the speed at which economic time operates in one activity, the forces of convergence, alignment, and renewal, is affected by the speed of economic time at work in upstream and downstream activities.

In some cases, activities operating differently upstream or downstream in economic time can reinforce advantage, as when a patent-protected product benefits importantly from economies of scale. An example is the twenty-year success of Polaroid. Or fast-moving products are distributed by an organization that benefits from buyer bargaining power, as in the case of Radio Shack.

In other cases, where different economic time cycles are dependent upon one another but operate at different speeds, managers should look for the possibility that activities within the corporation may operate at cross purposes. Operating styles may be incompatible, as in one case we know of where products on the same shop floor were customized alongside products that were standardized for high volume. Another example would be where products sold into a fast-cycle market are produced in a standard-cycle business culture, as was true for IBM in the early days of the personal computer industry. Many such cases of process-cycle mismatch are apparent. Thus, the multicycle manager should make special efforts to identify the potential for cycle-time mismatch, early in the management process.

Toward this end, next we describe some conflicts that can arise within a multicycle organization due to cycle-time mismatch. For the sake of brevity, we look at a few synchronization issues that can arise between standard- and fast-cycle processes. Synchronization issues can arise between these and slow-cycle functions as well. Synchronization issues also arise when managers are attempting cycle-shifting change, as discussed in the next chapter.

Research and Development

In the research and development departments of most standard-cycle organizations, research is focused on a balance of bringing new products to market and improving existing products, along with improving overall organizational productivity. The pace of research and development is dictated by the ongoing need to increase efficiency, reduce variability, and standardize processes across a range of products. R&D is part of the focus on efficiency and capital utilization. In fast-cycle research and development organizations, by contrast, fast development, selection efficiency, knowing how to shut down projects often, and rapid introduction of products take center stage. Although these differences can be overstated, they are likely to reflect styles of management that may be difficult to combine.

It is common that research and development are centralized at the stage of pure research, before commercial applications are apparent. Then, as the research effort moves closer to product development, research is decentralized, closer to the different management styles that distinguish commercial applications. What economic time reminds us of is that the speed of decentralization, or movement out of centralized R&D, varies by economic time. Thus, these structural differences may work against centralizing some research and development functions, or at the very least, argue for a watchful effort to keep the research and development cycles aligned with their different market needs.

Another implication is that the research and development budget in standard-cycle markets could be reduced temporarily during economic downturns without destroying the company's prospects. Within a fast-cycle company, the research and development budget should be maintained during economic downturns to sustain the viability of the enterprise.

Purchasing

Standard-cycle managers are understandably price-sensitive about raw material costs. At the same time, quality is paramount because the business's success depends on long-term relationships with its customers. Concern for costs and quality leads standard-cycle companies to buy in large quantities, seeking advantage of volume discounts, and to enter into long-term contracts that commit both parties to the relationship.

Since product requirements change rapidly in fast-cycle companies, the traditional bargaining power of the purchasing function is often reduced. Speed of delivery and flexibility to react to changing requirements become as important as price. Also characteristic of fast-cycle purchasing is the tendency to buy supplies at the last minute, as needed to meet revised sales forecasts. Purchasing supplies in large volumes can save money but also result in obsolete inventory if the market shifts unexpectedly. Due to the different purchasing needs of standard- and fast-cycle businesses, different management styles and incentives, as well as special organizational considerations and even different information systems, are needed to insure the effectiveness of each purchasing function.

Operations/Manufacturing

Because standard-cycle manufacturing is dominated by the need for economies of scale, zero defects, and repeatability over long production runs, the focus is on continually improving operational efficiencies to gain and hold market share. We also know that the manufacturing goal in fast-cycle markets is to bring capacity on line quickly, as well as to take capacity off line quickly to make room for newer products. Thus the ability to ramp up and ramp down production volume becomes more important than cost reduction. Similarly, capacity utilization gives way to flexibility and time reduction. In this sense, managers operating in mixed-cycle conditions should organize their production facilities so that different manufacturing strategies can be employed for these two manufacturing cycles without interfering with each other.

Marketing

Standard-cycle marketers seek precise descriptions of target customers. Once target market segments are identified, repeat purchase behavior is encouraged through reinforcing a constant image. Brand management has the responsibility of developing long-term product loyalty.

Standard-cycle marketing is likely to be organized along stable, product-oriented organization lines. Since standard-cycle marketing requires the greatest degree of orchestration of the cycles of economic time, the marketing function is closely coordinated with the other parts of the scale symphony. Teamwork and image control are common, insuring that the brand does not stray too far from its roots.

In contrast, the marketing function for fast-cycle products should be capable of initiating and responding to rapidly changing prices, expanding and contracting demand, and temporary brand awareness. Fast-cycle marketers should be able to transfer knowledge about customers from older to newer products, and should excel at originating demand for new products. Since the economic half-life of fast-cycle products is short, marketers cannot rely on extensive past customer knowledge, traditional market research, or brand loyalty. Fast-cycle marketing operates in an environment of fast learning and fast forgetting.

Fast-cycle marketers must learn to be disloyal as products age, and must be willing to eat their own children, thereby encouraging abandonment of existing products and spurring on the new product development process. As old products are abandoned, teams reorganize around new products, so that the marketing team composition changes often, along with product offerings.

The different requirements of marketing in standard- and fast-cycle settings suggests that these functions should be distinct from one another, or at least coordinated with a deep appreciation of how they operate differently in economic time.

Capital Budgeting

A question we hear from managers working across economic time is: "Which economic time zone is better?" Long product cycles, while they appear attractive, are not necessarily better than short product cycles in this regard. This is because the total amount of cash flows and the speed at which they are received represent a tradeoff between the stability associated with longer profit cycles and the speed of payback associated with shorter profit cycles. Thus, economic time cycles create opportunities—but the speed and means by which cash flows from different economic time cycles create value are highly differentiating.

In slow-cycle settings, cash flows can behave like annuities. Slow-cycle products have stable, relatively certain payback periods. Then, as products are positioned further up in economic time, the velocity and uncertainty of cash flows associated with them increase. Similarly, investments, in R&D, manufacturing, inventory, and marketing depreciate faster. The expected return from projects becomes less certain.

The capital budgeting process for a standard-cycle company is managed through a hierarchy. Budget approval can require long journeys with reviews at many levels. Consensus over several years is needed to sustain large commitments. In contrast, capital requests for the development of fast-cycle projects should be drafted, reviewed, and responded to quickly. Market opportunities, and the cash flow projections associated with them, change rapidly—even during the process of fast-cycle project evaluation itself.

There are many kinds of risk. Central among these is systematic risk, the risk that cannot be diversified away by investors. In a simple study of risk differences, we looked for systematic risk patterns among economic time cycles. Table 7.1 shows estimates of the cost of capital for the various groupings.

We caution against the generality of a simple study like this. The sample is small and risk estimation is a delicate matter. Still, the results are sug-

Table 7.1. Risk in Economic Time

ECONOMIC TIME	SLOW	STANDARD	FAST	MIXED	SHIFTING
Sample Size	43	34	4	13	10
Cost of Capital	12.4%	12.0%	13.7%	13.1%	14.1%
Standard Deviation	1.7%	1.3%	2.6%	2.1%	1.6%

SOURCE: Analysis of 104 different industry segments was based on information in Value Line's 1992 Industry Analysis manual. Each industry had its own average tax rate and debt-to-value ratio, which was taken into account in the calculation of the cost of capital. We unlevered the beta for each industry, and then, using a risk-free rate of 5% and a market risk premium of 8.6%, estimated the industry cost of capital. See "Wall Street Loves Standard Cycle Companies," Austin Miller and Sean O'Malley, 45-888 Report, Carnegie-Mellon University Graduate School of Industrial Administration, Spring 1996.

gestive. Standard-cycle businesses had the lowest cost of capital and the smallest standard deviation. The cost of capital associated with slow-cycle businesses was a close second. Industries with mixed business cycles came in higher, as these estimates are a mix of different businesses. Although the differences are small, both fast-cycle and shifting cycle industries had the highest capital costs, suggesting, with all the appropriate cautions, that these two classes of businesses are seen as most risky by investors.

It is little surprise that analysts like companies with stable cash flows and predictable, stable product life cycles. We know what to expect from standard-cycle industries. Standard-cycle businesses operate within carefully planned and structured investments. Cash flow momentum is high. Slow-cycle investments are shielded from competition, but they are idiosyncratic, difficult to control, and can face cash flow growth constraints beyond their original source of success.

The high risk for cycle-shifting businesses likely reflects expectations of framebreaking changes in how economic time operates; that new action-reaction cycles, untested capabilities, and unfamiliar management styles are emerging. These situations are highly enigmatic, so uncertain that risk can not be estimated with reliability. We would expect to discount future returns from these situations more highly. This kind of temporary risk premium may be an unavoidable cost of business restructuring.

Consider the divestiture of AT&T. After the Bell System breakup, AT&T and the seven regional operating companies, the Baby Bells, went in different directions. At the time observers thought that AT&T had received the better part of the deal; it would finally have the freedom to

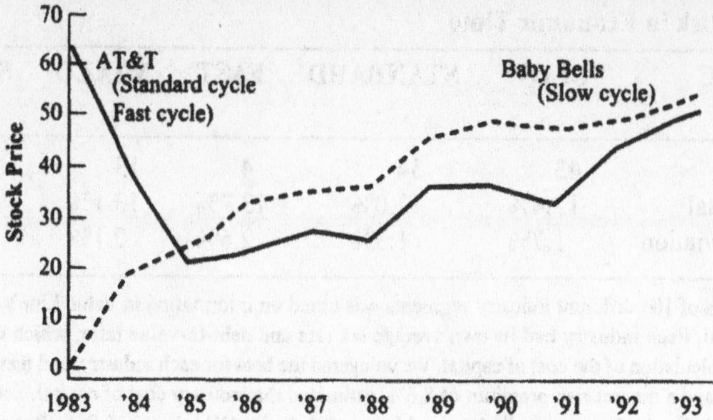

Figure 7.3. The Bell System Breakup in Economic Time

move into new, growing markets. However, AT&T's profits suffered compared to the profits of the Baby Bells. The regulatory monopoly granted the Baby Bells shielded them from competitive pressures, while AT&T was forced to undertake massive restructuring in its businesses. See Figure 7.3.

Which group got the better part of the deal? Compared to AT&T, which faced new competitors and the need to change its style of management, the Baby Bells saw relatively little competition, limited pressure for management change, and relatively stable cash flows. Even later in 1992, the Baby Bells boasted a 15 percent return on equity compared to a 10 percent return for the Business Week 1000 companies.

Consider the far end of economic time, where fast-cycle investments are capable of generating large cash flows quickly. Even with short product cycles, high risk, and the need for continual renewal, unprecedented wealth can be generated within a relatively brief period. An example is Compaq Computer, which holds the record for the fastest growing company in history; from startup to $10 billion in revenues in fifteen years.

Is the high risk of fast-cycle markets worth it? In four short years Adam Osborne grew his portable computer company from nothing to $100 million, only to face bankruptcy in year five. Should we regard Osborne, who created jobs and wealth, then faded, a success or a failure?

Our experience has been that any number of capable and seasoned managers will answer the question of which economic time cycle is better differently, based on his or her intrinsic business interests and personal values. While these differences are normal and reflect the diversity of the new economy, they point us back toward the importance of recognizing how economic time affects managers. As we see in Chapter 9, the challenge of competing in the new economy is that of recognizing this diversity and the range of attitudes toward risk that reflect each manager's professional and personal values. When managers are placed where they are best aligned in economic time, they are more likely to be productive and enjoy their jobs.

Compensation

Differences in risk in economic time should be reflected in compensation policies. A compensation package that is likely to attract, motivate, and retain employees in a fast-cycle company will be different than a compensation package with similar goals for employees in a standard- or slow-cycle company. While generalities like these are subject to limits, employees in a fast-cycle company will be more comfortable in a higher-risk, rapidly changing environment and should expect to be compensated accordingly. Fast-cycle compensation could include lower-than-average base pay with the potential for high levels of incentive compensation, through profit sharing, gain sharing, stock options, or performance bonuses. The compensation package, though not guaranteed, would have the potential to be higher than average and would be based on successes of project teams, rather than the company as a whole.

Employees within a standard-cycle company would respond to a more traditional compensation package: a more stable, hierarchical, internally equitable compensation structure focusing on base pay and leaving less compensation at risk. Rewards based on annual merit, cost-of-living, or across-the-board salary increases should be close to peer averages.

All kinds of mixed-cycle compensation arrangements are possible. Consider the problem of compensation services for employees at a hypothetical investment bank. When a new associate joins the slow-cycle advisory services group, his or her independent contribution, in terms of getting new business, is minimal. The new hire has long-term potential, but in the short term he is using the firm's reputation in attracting new clients and is focused on servicing existing client accounts. The new associate is not independent; he is intimately tied to the firm's existing clients. Initially, the new associate needs the organization more than the organization needs him. Under these conditions, compensation for the new associate could be based on a straight salary with a low bonus potential. As the associate progresses, he can be elected a partner, at which point he shares in the fortunes of the firm.

Notice that in the case of a trader at our hypothetical bank the scenario is different. A trader can be viewed as an independent contractor working under the purview of the bank. The trader uses the bank's capital, makes bets with it, and then either makes or loses money depending on how well the bets fare. Thus, compensation can be on a commission basis with a small base salary. In a given year, if a trader makes above-average profits, she keeps the excess. However, if she suffers losses, she has to pay the bank her cost of capital and the bank's margin. While there are limits to this kind of scheme, the important point is to compensate the trader for the quality of her ideas, recognizing that the trader's product line needs to be refreshed frequently—the essence of fast-cycle behavior.

MULTICYCLE CORE COMPETENCIES

Organizational issues such as culture, values, and performance measurement in economic time are many. In a single-cycle organization, like McDonald's or Starbucks, achieving harmony and uniformity of goals is a challenge in itself. But for other companies, managing cross-cycle boundaries adds another level of complexity. Clashes arising between the various cycles of economic time can lead to problems. These, if not understood, can drain the energy out of the organization and harm the multicycle company's ability to renew itself.

We can draw some lessons from companies that effectively manage across cycles of economic time. Johnson & Johnson competes in pharmaceuticals, consumer products, and professional products. Typical of products within each group are slow-cycle Sporanox, an antifungal prescription drug, standard-cycle Band-Aids adhesive bandages, and the fast-cycle Palmaz-Schatz stent, an innovative device used in the treatment of heart disease.

With what we know about the diversity of economic time, it is unlikely that J&J manages these businesses with the same strategies and uniform management styles. Some J&J businesses are centralized whereas others are decentralized, even where decentralization adds additional expense in the number of duplicated functions. There are common ties to various degrees between businesses and across economic time cycles. How does J&J make it work?

The Credo as Unifying Agent

Johnson & Johnson typifies a continually evolving multicycle company. Operating units are regularly split apart and recreated, and decentralization is negotiable. Because of the diverse nature of multicycle economic time, it is not easy to imagine how centralized control could be as successful as when J&J's businesses are run as independent units. Is J&J just a holding company, which might be better structured as separately owned companies? We know that investors can diversify much of the risk of individual businesses on their own; they don't need managers to do it for them. Further, isn't J&J always at risk of losing focus when far-flung operations get too large or too diverse for headquarters to understand?

One answer to these multicycle challenges for J&J and other successful multicycle companies is culture. The corporate glue that holds J&J together is a strong, common set of renewing values. The J&J Credo was written by General Robert Wood Johnson while he ran the company in the 1930s. The Credo states that the company's responsibility is first to its customers, second to its employees, third to the communities in which it operates, and lastly, to the stockholders. This Credo, simple to the point of appearing ordinary, is remarkable for its endurance.

Johnson & Johnson is one of those companies whose corporate culture is so strong that it transcends individual businesses. In this way, the J&J Credo is in the same class as the HP Way, the meritocracy at Intel, the embrace and extend philosophy of Microsoft, the quality orientation at Toyota, the dedication to customer service at Nordstrom, and the engineering mind-set at DaimlerChrysler.

Another cross-cycle capability is the capacity to attract and retain exceptional people. J&J's track record of hiring and retaining star performers is well known among pharmaceutical researchers. *Working Mother* magazine has also ranked the company as one of the "10 Best" for working mothers. A company store, good benefits, in-house athletic facilities, and deep-seated respect for people help J&J keep the best and the brightest, people who would otherwise be lured away by competitors and by entrepreneurial activities.

Does putting stockholders last in the Credo mean that investors don't count? Customers, employees, and community are the means to the end; they *should* come first. Companies like Johnson & Johnson likely would be worth less, not more, if broken apart.

This is not true for other highly decentralized, multicycle companies; witness the rise of AT&T's stock when AT&T announced that it would split itself into different companies: fast-cycle NCR, standard-cycle long distance, and slow-cycle Network Systems, later named Lucent Technologies.

Slow-Cycle Pharmaceuticals. Research on J&J (and the pharmaceutical industry in general) yields little mention of quality or cost savings. TQM, reengineering, and productivity gains are not drivers in pharmaceuticals. The sources of productive research are creative researchers and scientists; J&J employs seven thousand-plus research professionals of this kind, a large organization by industry standards, as research laboratories, rather than benefiting from economies of scale, tend to suffer from internal conflict as they get bigger. CEO Ralph Larsen sees the business as an artisan community, "The way we look at ourselves, we are not in the product business. We are in the knowledge business." All J&J employees enjoy mobility, but, in the pharmaceutical business, employees are particularly free to move from project to project as their interests dictate, like artisans, unhindered by job classifications. J&J gets high marks for its slow-cycle business.

Standard-Cycle Consumer Products. The Consumer Products group works to boost productivity and improve quality. The installation of a product release system in J&J's distribution centers turned a labor-intensive product release process into an easy-to-operate computerized tracking system, and coincided with the goal of reducing inventory from ninety days to fifty days. The Johnson & Johnson Signature of Quality program encourages managers to benchmark their performance in key areas relative to competitors, typical of standard-cycle companies. These initiatives are driven by a desire to achieve high volume, no surprises, and low costs.

Consumer Products managers wrestle with other four-hundred-pound gorillas. An example is the company's foray into the diaper business in the 1970s. J&J had a strong baby image, so why not diapers? Yet in the end J&J could not compete with the scale economies of Kimberly-Clark and Procter & Gamble. After losing hundreds of millions of dollars, J&J pulled back from the business.

J&J Consumer Products has one of the strongest brand names in the United States. The company logo is synonymous with motherhood, babies, and no-surprises, wholesome images. This was seen during the effective handling of the Tylenol scare in the 1980s. The expense of the nationwide recall was more than compensated for by the good will that it created. Through continual defense of the brand, Tylenol remains the leading analgesic in the United States, even though generic substitutes are sold alongside Tylenol at a fraction of the price. Other strong J&J brand names include Band-Aid, Reach toothbrushes, Stayfree, and Johnson & Johnson Baby Products. Large advertising budgets help to maintain these brands in a continual process of renewal.

The creation of the Sales and Logistics Company, a centralized function; the centralization of the worldwide tampon business within J&J's German subsidiary; and the relocation of the personal products staffs to a centralized location in New Jersey typify the command and control orientation of J&J's Consumer Products group. So in standard-cycle businesses J&J gets high marks, too.

Fast-Cycle Professional Products. In August 1994, Johnson & Johnson introduced the Palmaz-Schatz stent, which offered a solution to the tendency of arteries to reclose or reclog after being opened by traditional balloon angioplasty surgery. (Thirty percent of 400,000 U.S. angioplasties were failing for this reason.) A tiny metal-mesh tube no thicker than a pencil lead, crimped onto a tiny balloon that is threaded into the heart's arteries, the stent is inflated at a blockage site to create a permanent scaffold, like a ballpoint-pen spring, to keep vessels open. In just 37 months, J&J gained more than $1 billion of stent sales and 90 percent of the stent market. A huge success, with profit margins of 80 percent, the infant stent business accounted for 4 percent of J&J's corporate-wide sales and 8 percent of profits.[2]

Then, in the fall of 1997, Guidant Corporation launched a competing stent in the U.S., a stent that was more flexible, more narrow, in different lengths, at lower prices. Within 45 days Guidant gained an estimated 70 percent market share of this fast-growing market, most of it at J&J's expense. Discounts for what was perceived as inferior technology wouldn't work for J&J, and doctors weren't interested in J&J's argument that the Palmaz-Schatz stent had a proven track record. J&J's market share fell to near 10 percent over the next year—prompting *The Wall Street Journal* to cite the upheaval in stent market share as "the most dramatic transfer of wealth between two companies in medical-device history."

How could this happen to such a well-managed company? Upon reflection, J&J managers "didn't anticipate the temperament of the marketplace" (as one doctor put it), or as we would put it, misread where they were operating in economic time: (1) Although they had pioneered the fast-cycle stent market, J&J managers overestimated brand loyalty to J&J stents, (2) managers did not anticipate how easily the strong patent position of the J&J stent could be circumvented by fast-cycle innovators, and (3) the company maintained a rigid pricing policy for the $1,595 device as fast-cycle demand accelerated.

Acquisition of Cordis, an angioplasty balloon maker, through a hostile takeover, and subsequent overcontrol by the J&J hierarchy (Cordis's view) slowed down the ability of both groups to get new products to market quickly. The small J&J unit that developed the stent was so focused on getting it to market, and meeting enormous demand, that it devoted little time to quickly emerging, next-generation products. (Toward the end of this period, in the face of growing competition, J&J responded to these problems with innovative products in clinical trials, seeking to regain J&J's leadership.)

The lesson? Even for companies boasting the best of corporate cultures and personnel practices, multicycle companies like Johnson & Johnson, 3M, Hewlett-Packard, Bosch, Ericsson, and Asea Brown Boveri (ABB) can benefit by knowing how economic time is expanding the risks and opportunities of business, as well as the vital role played by new management styles.

RECAP: MANAGING MULTIPLE CYCLES

Mixed-cycle organizations operate across economic time, whereby the styles of management needed for different economic time cycles coexist with one another. Depending on their synchronous or time dependency on each other, multiple cycles can strengthen or weaken the overall organization. Thus, setting strategy effectively across a multicycle organization requires knowledge of (1) whether you are focusing on critical (or secondary) elements of the problem within each business; (2) how the cycle-time drivers of each business require different management styles; and (3) which cycle-time drivers are compatible and which are incompatible within and between businesses.

FUNCTIONAL SYNCHRONIZATION

Companies operating in multiple economic time cycles benefit from a balance of top-down authority, to reconcile cycle-time incompatibilities, and decentralized responsibility, so that the cycle drivers of key business functions stay aligned with each other and with the needs of customers. The following examples illustrate this for standard- and fast-cycle business functions:

RESEARCH AND DEVELOPMENT

Exploratory research can be centralized, as it is separate from the day-to-day operating styles of the various businesses. As research moves toward prod-uct introduction, cycle-time differences will increasingly distinguish how and how fast research is commercialized. The key here is to know how these pressures will grow to separate and decentralize the research activities, so that you can complement the innovation operating in each business.

PURCHASING

Relatively predictable demand allows standard-cycle companies to enter into long negotiations to earn favorable terms for raw materials. They can buy in large quantities, taking advantage of volume discounts, and can enter into long-term contracts whereby suppliers become integrated with extended commitments to products.

In fast-cycle organizations, speed of delivery is initially more important than price. Later, price will become unstable as competitors enter the market. Also characteristic of fast-cycle purchasing is the tendency to buy supplies only as needed and to revise commitments frequently. In these ways, the standard- and fast-cycle purchasing activities require different approaches to be effective.

OPERATIONS/MANUFACTURING

As a production process shifts from standard to fast cycle, capacity management becomes more important than efficiency. Production facilities are judged less on their efficiency and more on their ability to adapt quickly to changing market conditions. Standardized production and cost reduction are replaced by flexibility and time reduction.

It is difficult to satisfy these conflicting cycle-time drivers within one facility. Therefore, consider that companies producing effectively in mixed-cycle environments should organize and manage cross-cycle production facilities separately.

MARKETING

In standard-cycle marketing organizations, brand management is central to the marketing effort, with the goal of maintaining product loyalty and customer relationships through market research, mass market advertising, and selective market segmentation.

Fast-cycle marketing relies more on event marketing and less on long-term image support. Important also is the ability to manage rapidly changing prices and shifting distributor relationships in the face of quickly changing demand.

DISTRIBUTION

Standard-cycle distribution should reflect on cost minimization, scale economies, and no-surprises customer experiences. Fast-cycle distribution should reflect time reduction, minimizing of inventory, rapid changes in product volumes, and rapid market penetration.

SERVICE

Standard-cycle customer service is oriented to maintaining long-lasting customer relationships. Customer service is sold as an integral part of the product's extended value. Service quality is carefully coordinated, orchestrated, and renewed through tie-ins with backroom processes.

Often, fast-cycle service support is limited to disseminating information quickly and replacing defective products, functions that can be performed at a central location removed from customers. Since fast-cycle products change frequently, requirements for service support of older products can work against the fast forgetting needed to shift support to service new customers.

CAPITAL BUDGETING

No region of economic time appears inherently better than another in terms of its ability to create economic value. The total amount of cash flows, and the speed at which they are received, represents a tradeoff between the stability associated with longer cycles and the faster speed of payback associated with shorter cycles.

In slow-cycle settings, cash flows can be like annuities, with relatively certain payback. As a company positions itself further up in economic time, first the commitment to scale, then the velocity and uncertainty of cash flows, increases. Capital budgeting shifts toward accelerated depreciation, high-risk, high-return projects, and fast payback. Projects become more like options, where opportunities come and go quickly.

Standard-cycle industries may be seen as among the least risky from the investor's point of view. Fast-, shifting-, and mixed-cycle businesses may operate in less certain budgeting environments because isolating mechanisms are changing, or are unknown, and may be expected to continue to change with uncertain outcomes. Temporary risk premiums may be part of the cost of corporate restructuring.

The capital budgeting system for a standard-cycle company operates within a command and control structure. Budget approval processes require reviews at many levels in the corporate hierarchy. The capital budgeting system for a fast-cycle business should be responsive to the dynamics of fast-changing investment expectations. Capital requests should be drafted, reviewed, and responded to quickly, as delays will render their assumptions obsolete.

Our experience has been that any number of capable and seasoned managers will answer the question of which economic time cycle is better based on his or her personal values. Thus, part of the challenge of competing in multiple-cycle economic time is recognizing the attitudes toward risk that reflect each manager's personality and capabilities. Initially, managers should be placed where their risk preferences match the risk patterns of their products. Career development programs for high-potential managers can include training in the various management styles of economic time.

COMPENSATION

Secure, hierarchical, internally equitable compensation structures, focusing on base pay and leaving little compensation at risk, would be expected in standard-cycle organizations. Employees can be rewarded with annual merit, cost-of-living, or across-the-board salary increases.

The resulting total compensation levels can be close to competitor averages.

Managers in higher-risk, uncertain environments can be set up to receive lower-than-average base pay, with the potential for high levels of bonus compensation, such as through profit sharing, stock options, or performance plans. The total compensation package would be based on the success of product groups that come and go.

MULTICYCLE CORE COMPETENCIES

Certain corporate-wide attitudes and values can unify managers, enhancing effectiveness throughout a multicycle company. Universal, multicycle corporate values allow centralized command and control to coexist along with gardener- and creatively destructive-style management.

Another universal, cross-cycle source of excellence is the ability to attract and retain exceptional people. Successful multicycle companies embrace—actually celebrate—the diversity in management styles needed for different businesses. They provide working environments where people are renewed by what they do, by putting more energy into the business than the resources they take out, regardless of where they operate in economic time.

Most of the changes that occur across economic time, in multicycle as well as single-cycle companies, are incremental. The renewal of capabilities and the refinement of strategies take place at a pace that gives managers a chance to adapt. However, when the organization faces major regulatory, technological, or organizational disruptions, the speed and styles by which managers operate change so quickly that adaptation becomes difficult.

In the next chapter we look at cycle shifts in economic time. Here, change is so extreme that the laws of convergence, alignment, and renewal operate so differently as to bring on paradigm shifts. Shocks to how economic time operates are nearly always framebreaking and transformational. When economic time shifts, major restructuring efforts, the creation of new capabilities, and the adoption of new strategies are required to allow organizations to renew themselves. The leadership challenge becomes that of saving the organization—altering organizational DNA, as we term it—in hopes of bringing the organization back into alignment with what customers and investors want.

CHAPTER 8

MANAGING CYCLE SHIFTS

The thirty-five-year veteran of AT&T put it this way: "I have eight years of experience in the telecommunications industry—one year before 1984 (the year of the phone system breakup) and seven years after." The need for managing cycle shifts arises when economic time is transformed and markets begin to operate through different action-reaction cycles. Managers in cycle-shifting markets are seeking to alter historical capabilities and strategies, to realign the organization, to create wholly different relationships with customers.

Cycle-shifting managers work within environments where the very relevance of an organization—its business model—has come under question. An organization's competitive operating system, its time-honored practices and procedures, are being reshaped or cast aside to make way for a style of management that is genuinely new.

Cycle-shifting skills—the ability to lead through more than one style of management—are increasingly important. Deregulation forced unprecedented change upon managers in the airline, telecommunications, and financial services industries. Technological shocks redirected long-established patterns of convergence, alignment, and renewal for automotive, health care, and electronics companies. Cycle-shifting managers transformed economic time for banking and information services. For managers facing transformed economic time, historical relationships among capabilities, strategies, and markets were altered to the point where they became artifacts of the past. When economic time shifts, the rules of the game change, to be sure. But it goes deeper than that. Your business self-identity changes as well.

Look at the effects of shifting economic time in Figure 8.1. When the U.S. airline industry deregulated, the shielded, smaller, slow-cycle local carriers were able to maintain their operating styles and their profits. The

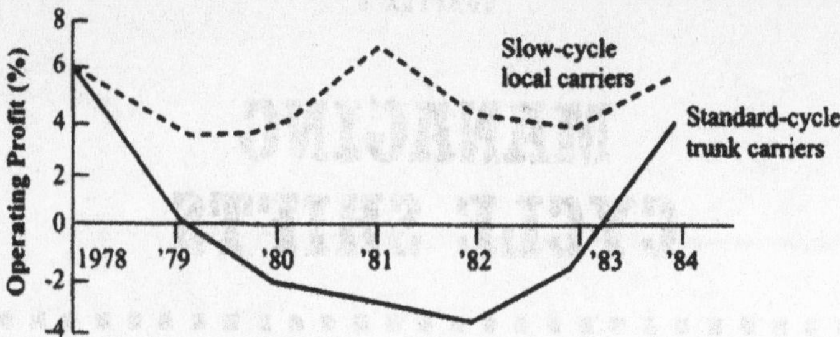

Figure 8.1. Airline Deregulation in Economic Time

large, standard-cycle carriers were affected the most.[1] They experienced losses as they made frameshifting changes in their management styles.

In these, the most difficult kind of strategy-setting environments, transformations in economic time raise the possibility that even the best managers will make costly mistakes. The first mistake is an error of omission: not understanding the new situation for what it is, thus orienting people in the company to the wrong problem. Analytical models and estimation procedures based on historical assumptions can easily fail to see or identify new competitive forces. Changing relationships between your company and your market render time-honored ways of doing things obsolete—and you don't even know it.

The second mistake is an error of commission: implementing your new strategy badly. Shifts in economic time alter the isolating mechanisms of your company, the ways that you create value through time. Once-strong isolating mechanisms may no longer block competitive entry. You face new competitors, with new skills and unfamiliar competitive styles. No matter how earnestly you apply historical approaches to the business, you begin to fall behind competitors in delivering effective solutions.

With transformations in economic time, you should be able to work across markets, understanding and managing by more than one set of rules; to think out of the box, quickly and effectively, as to whether long-held views about why your company exists are still valid.

In this chapter we look at ways to predict and react to cycle shifts or transformations in economic time. This work, based on studies of managers facing slow-, standard-, and fast-cycle transformations, is designed to forecast and minimize organizational disruptions caused by change. The goal is to build into your company a proactive way of thinking about change, an adaptive capability, where transformation in how your company creates value is managed effectively on a recurring basis, as a more normal way of doing business.

Forecasting Shifts in Economic Time

The discovery of new materials or innovative production processes can transform a company's productivity, increasing the speed of innovation and the expected rate of cost reduction. A new design can alter customers' perceptions of a product, modifying historical patterns of demand and resulting in shorter or longer replacement cycles. R&D breakthroughs may create substitutes for a product that shorten its economic half-life. A change in process technology from custom to mass assembly, increasing the importance of economies of scale, can force a product out of slow-cycle into standard- or fast-cycle economic time.

Changes in government policy, antitrust rulings, and tighter or looser environmental laws can change economic time. Deregulation can encourage innovation and open a market to new competitors. Environmental protection policies can set high entry barriers for competitors and cause cycle time to slow down. But regulation also can encourage a uniform, freely available standard, speeding up economic time.

Corporate strategy can proactively shift a product's economic cycle time. By changing the focus of how a company's resources are directed, a new strategy can realign competition and, in turn, bring on new market forces. Intel management encouraged the personal computer industry to speed up the rate of innovation because through increased innovation they could stimulate demand for newer and newer versions of microprocessor-based products.

Toyota management, in contrast, slowed down its pace of new product introduction, finding that the benefits of introducing new cars every thirty months were less than the organizational and political costs of fast development times.

Technology shocks, government policy changes, and revisions in corporate strategy do not work their changes on a market independent of one another. Instead, the cycle-shifting forces are often interlinked. Thus, often a shift in a product's economic time is not caused by one particular force alone but by a combination or particular sequence of changes. Understanding how transformational forces combine to cause shocks in economic time can be aided by gauging external market measures, like pricing and the rate of product introduction. Also useful are internal yardsticks, such as the extent of standardization and changes in the rate of productivity gains. These are discussed next.

Shift in the Rate of Innovation

Shifts in the rate of innovation can be a direct sign of a change in economic time. Innovation can work against the isolating mechanisms that sustain slower-cycle advantage. As innovation slows down, the focus of competition shifts from innovation to more stable activities like distribution and service, for example. As we will see, a slowdown in the rate of innovation can encourage slower-moving companies to dominate smaller, once innovative companies.

Shift in the Role of Standardization

Standardization can increase the extent to which products and their associated manufacturing processes are likely to come under pressure from competitors. Standardization brings on challengers, often on a global basis, that have the ability to serve a broad base of customers with similar, fixed-cost facilities. On the other hand, to the degree that standardization remains low, or decreases, economic time often operates more slowly, reflecting the prevalence of stronger isolating mechanisms.

Thus, if you are considering adopting tactics to increase or to decrease the rate of standardization, you may wish to consider whether your company is prepared to face a new set of competitors. Your success may bring managers in your company face to face with competitors with well-practiced management styles that are new to you.

Shift in the Rate of Change of Prices and Profit Cycles

Changes in price dynamics, or rate of price change, signal oncoming shocks in economic time. Shifts in the speed of a product's price reduction provide clues about changes in the speed of convergence, or how fast products are displaced. Another, related test of changes in economic time is the degree to which the profit cycles of a business are changing. Is the amount of time during which profits can be made becoming shorter or longer? While all businesses undergo some instability in this regard, look for big, systemic changes that appear to be imminent. These changes go beyond the traditional question of whether you are facing more or less price competition; they likely foretell the emergence of new styles of management and new patterns of cash flows.

Shift in Sustainability of Scale Economies

What is the historical relationship of your products to volume? How is competitive advantage strengthened by scale, or made stronger by an ever-increasing volume of product produced within the same fixed cost structure? As technological change becomes more rapid, fixed-cost investments age faster economically. The result is that the amount of time over which scale economies can be sustained is shortened. This reduces the importance of scale economies in an industry overall.

Shift in Productivity Gains

A productivity measurement related to scale economies is the expected per-unit cost reduction to be had by doubling volume. Shifts in technology can upset historical experience curve relationships, causing productivity gains to increase. Often this increase is passed along to customers in the form of lower prices and faster product introductions. Thus it can be helpful to monitor an industry's price dynamics for clues to changes in the productivity of competitors. More generally, as productivity gains increase, economic time moves faster, as seen in the semiconductor industry.

Shift in the Fraction of Orders Based on Price

As customers see a product more and more as a commodity, the fraction of orders based on price increases. In fast-cycle markets, products are initially price insensitive, but then become more price sensitive as they move from first-mover to fast-follower status. In slower-cycle markets the shift to commodity status occurs more slowly, or in the case of some slow-cycle products like Disney's character properties (Mickey Mouse, Sleeping Beauty), not at all.

Shift in Dynamic Value Chain Drivers

As the amount of value contributed by different activities within the organization changes, a product's overall economic time cycle can shift. An example is the watch industry, which in the 1970s saw new competitors and the onset of market turbulence, brought on by the displacement of mechanical watch movements. Faster-cycle, solid state electronic components altered economic time for competitors in the industry even as the rest of the watch (bands, displays), and slower-cycle watch companies like Rolex, remained unaffected.

Another clue to cycle shifts is that economic time transformations are most strongly felt when the affected activities account for a high fraction of value added. Thus, as we discuss next, being able to pinpoint changes deep within a product in the stability of different stages of value added can be an effective tool to analyze the effects of cycle-shifting changes.

DYNAMIC VALUE CHAIN ANALYSIS

The dynamic value chain encourages managers to think in terms of how products are made as a sequence of activities. By adding a dynamic view to traditional value chain thinking, dynamic value chain analysis accounts for products that may operate in different cycles of economic time. The analysis is dynamic because it distinguishes the relative price-cost stability at each stage and the extent to which individual stages are synchronously dependent on each other. Value chain activities operating in slow-cycle economic time show stable and sometimes rising prices and costs. Standard-cycle value chain activities show a gradual rate of decline and renewal, on the order of five years, in keeping with standard-cycle economic time. In contrast, prices and costs in fast-cycle value chain stages are dynamic, rising and falling at cycles of one to two years, in keeping with the short product half-life of fast-cycle activities. Figure 8.2 shows a dynamic value chain. Each stage of the value chain can reflect its own action-reaction cycles and distinct management styles.

For a typical product or service, any combination and sequence of cycle

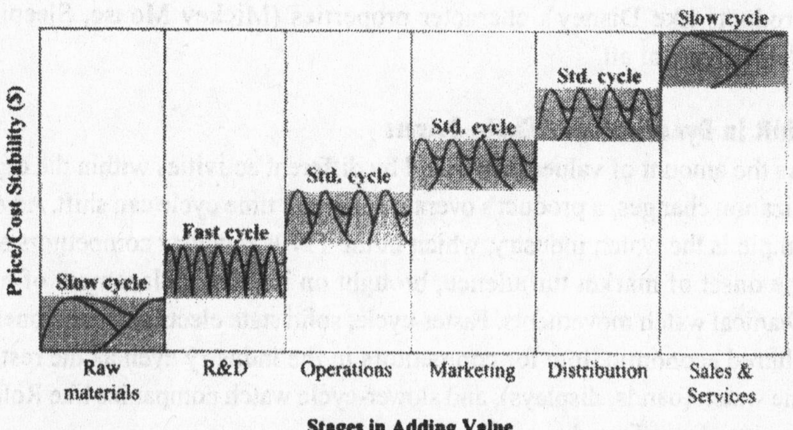

Figure 8.2. Dynamic Value Chain Analysis

time drivers may be at work in the process of adding value. Where economic time operates slowly, that value chain stage will show long profit cycles. Where economic time moves more quickly, that value chain stage will have shorter profit cycles. Accordingly, faster rates of renewal, associated with faster-cycle management styles, will be required.

By distinguishing renewal opportunities at distinct value chain stages, dynamic value chain analysis can help managers understand the sequencing of activities that operate differently in economic time When economic time operates differently at different stages, managers need to be alert to where the associated styles of management at each stage complement or conflict with one another.

Consider the alliance between the Windows operating system and Intel microprocessors. On one hand the Wintel alliance is highly complementary; the increasingly complex code structure of Windows operating systems requires increasingly powerful Intel microprocessors (Windows NT 4.0, for example, has 26 million lines of code). This co-dependence creates complementary demand for both products.

On the other hand, the slow pace of innovation characteristic of software operating systems works against the faster rate of performance increases possible in fast-cycle microprocessors. In the sense of economic time, there is a productivity mismatch between these two value chain elements in the personal computer industry. The result is like what would happen if you bought a Ferrari capable of speeds of 200 miles per hour and were required to drive on city streets at 35 miles per hour. In this way, managers operating in multiple cycle stages should pay particular attention to how the different rates of change in different stages will affect the overall performance of the company's products.

Dynamic value chain analysis can also help with the analysis of shifting economic time. Typically, when a market shifts in economic time, some value chain stages are affected more than others. The change at one stage may be minor, while at another it may signal the onset of framebreaking change, as for the advent of electronics in the mechanical movement stage of the watch industry.

In the next section we look at cases of cycle shifts in economic time. We look at three scenarios, drawn from the automotive, investment banking, and health care industries, spanning the spectrum of standard-, fast-, and slow-cycle competition. In each case, economic time cycle shifts affect some value chain stages in each industry more than others. We recap each scenario with a list of indicators that can be helpful in gauging cycle shifts in economic time.

STANDARD TO FAST CYCLE

Historically the automobile industry has typified a classic, standard-cycle market. A typical car has about 12,000 parts; each must be manufactured and assembled efficiently with a minimum of variation. Global auto producers manufacture millions of cars a year through carefully orchestrated design and production. Producers typically overhaul their models every five years or so, consistent with economic time in standard-cycle markets.

The heart of technology in automobiles for decades has been the engine, and to this day mechanical innovation in this area is controlled. Engines are carefully designed for relatively stable mass markets and to fit several models of car (GM's Northstar engine is an example). Other mechanical items such as carburetors, lights, and seatbelts are standardized across the industry and present controlled opportunities for innovation.

Increasingly, however, underneath the hoods of the Fords, Hondas, and BMWs are increasingly valued, technologically dynamic components. Many of these components operate in fast-cycle economic time. There are several reasons for this, a review of which illustrates the broad analysis that should be done to predict the onset of cycle shifts.

Regulatory Change. When the U.S. government issued regulations concerning auto emissions, they were unattainable using standard, mechanically controlled engines based on the carburetor. Computers designed to improve the performance of the carburetor first used simple transistors that evolved into the complex microprocessors of the modern automotive control system. The typical onboard engine control unit of an automobile is the size of a small book and has the power of an early mainframe computer. (You know the analogy: If engineers of the 1950s had built a vacuum tube computer of the same computing capacity it would have been the size of two bedrooms.)

Technological Innovation. Physical factors within an automobile's environment influence performance of an engine, such as humidity level and barometric pressure. Engineers continually redesign computers and peripherals that will read these factors and perform accordingly. As environmental issues gain importance, new government mandates are expected to put more pressure on automakers to improve automotive technology. In California, for example, a law took effect in 1996 that requires all new cars to have an onboard diagnostic system that immediately shows when emission controls have failed. This system is typically built into the engine control unit.

Antilock braking systems (ABS) were demonstrated on automobiles in the late 1960s but harsh environmental conditions faced by automobiles disrupted operation of transistors within the devices. In the late 1970s the Bosch Company of Germany was able to develop electronics that could be used reliably as an ABS computer. When BMW and Mercedes built Bosch ABS into their cars they proved attractive to all automobile segments. As other automakers demanded ABS, competitive suppliers entered and the ABS market converged. The price that Bosch charged for an ABS system declined from 750 to 100 German marks in the ten-year period ending in 1997.

Increasingly, electronic engine control units that replaced carburetors, antilock braking systems that displaced traditional braking mechanisms, and airbag systems that supplement seatbelts are taking on a greater fraction of a car's market value. Automobile manufacturers continually seek ways to make these electronic components smaller, lighter, more reliable, and less expensive. Automakers advertise them as important, differentiating features in an automobile purchase.

It is estimated that the growth rate of automotive electronics will continue at 10 to 15 percent per year, faster than for other automotive components. Increasingly smart systems will control functions like navigational aids, and be produced by nontraditional automotive suppliers like Hughes Electronics. By 2005, 33 percent of a typical car's components will be electrical and electronic based.

Product development for Ford has typically averaged sixty months. It is estimated that Ford will have reduced cycle time for electronics to twenty-four months by the turn of the century. If trends continue, Ford's average overall vehicle age would decrease to 2.3 years by 2004.

In the year of introduction, the profit margins on electronic components are high, typically 300 percent or more. Car manufacturers implement their newest innovations on luxury and sports cars, where the customer segment is less price sensitive. Ford introduced its electronic engine control (1980), ABS (1985), and passenger-side airbags (1989) in its luxury Lincoln models. Then within one or two years, the ideas were copied and new products began to converge rapidly. Shortly thereafter, these products became, in effect, commodities, at which point they were offered as optional equipment in lower-end models at greatly reduced prices or as standard equipment.

Standard- to Fast-Cycle Signals

Imagine yourself as a manager of a well-established automotive components supplier, in a meeting, discussing some of the problems you are facing. The following hypothetical discussion gives an overview of some early warning signs that can be expected in a market changing from standard- to fast-cycle economic time.

Industry Evolution. "We position ourselves to compete for extended periods and all of a sudden we have new competitors, products, and markets to contend with."

Product Life Cycles. "About the time we get a product or process just right it is outdated."

Value Chain Relationships. "We spend a lot of time maintaining upstream and downstream relationships. Now, any advantage we might try to gain through our positioning disappears before we can capitalize on it. The supplier with the hot item gets the profits no matter where they are in the value chain."

Price Competition. "Price has always been important to keeping competitors out, but now it often does not help. Customers want either the latest, greatest, or the cheapest. They are willing to pay a lot more for a little improvement. We spend a lot of effort getting ourselves down the learning curve so we can offer a better price but then the demand for that product shifts elsewhere before we can recapture our investment."

"When we use prices to try to discipline competitors to establish some sort of reasonable margins the competitors don't understand. They either drop their prices to match, drop out of the market, bring some new product out, or a combination of all of the above. There is no reasonable competition. Everything seems out of control with cutthroats in old products and monopolists in new products."

Economies of Scale. "We go for volume but it doesn't provide sustainable advantage. We get all geared up and then can't change course with the market. Our size sometimes seems to be more of a hindrance than a help."

Organizational Structure. "We have a structured organization that is highly efficient. Commands are given, taken, and carried out to the 'T.' But the structure is so rigid that it takes us too long to react to shifts in the market. By the time market information traverses our company, and everybody has the opportunity to propose his or her response, we are way behind the competition."

Switching Costs. "We get geared up to make a product or distribute a service but cannot exit existing commitments without big expenses. Our competitors chop and change quickly, offering something for a limited time then offering something else. We cannot recover our sunk costs before competitors are offering new improved products that ruin demand for our products. Competitors and customers seem to be able to switch easily, and do so."

Profitability. "Products don't maintain their profitability as they used to. As the product matures we get better at making it so the profit margins should be steady, but they aren't. Profit margins decline rapidly and we start losing money on products just as we get really efficient at making them."

Growth. "We strategize to grow in a market but the market grows faster than we can keep up. Then, no sooner than we catch up with the market, the market shifts to another product. Competitors rise up to take huge shares of the market for that product then stop making it just as we get good at making it."

Market Structure. "We think we know who our competitors are, and we get positioned to compete with them. Then out of the blue somebody new comes in and the whole market is in turmoil. We are used to competing with a few competitors for our customers but now there are lots of companies shifting around satisfying different needs for different customers."

Barriers to Entry. "Companies come in and go out of the market in a seemingly random manner and we can't seem to keep them out. Size, patents, cost, and knowledge are irrelevant to these competitors. Nothing we do remains distinctive for long. New ideas get around everything we do to stake out a market."

Standardization. "Standardization of the product and process does not provide a lasting advantage. We pride ourselves on our ability to standardize products and processes and have worked very hard to drive defects out of products, but the customers are not loyal. They want different things all the time and move continually from one standard to another."

Globalization. "Market boundaries are moving faster than we can keep up with them. Products introduced in this market today are launched overseas next year, and vice versa. We are expanding globally but not fast enough. There are many global competitors who rise, fall, and rise again as products change. There seem to be few barriers to the global competitors coming or going into and out of our markets."

Service. "We are structured to provide great service—and we do—but customers don't care anymore. Competitors merely support a product until it is outdated by the second or third generation of the new, improved model."

Bargaining Power. "Whatever bargaining power we used to have is swept away by innovation."

SLOW TO FAST CYCLE

By 1915, investment-banking houses were well established. The commonly accepted houses had large corporate clients who needed capital and wealthy investors looking for investment opportunities. Often the corporate clients were the same companies that the investment bank had helped fund when they were fledgling companies. Corporate clients had loyalty to their investment banks and the banks had strong ties with the corporations. Relationships were so strong that corporations generally used the same bank for all their financial needs and rarely switched. Customers who had profited from their bank's advice generally continued to do business with that bank.

Stable Industry Structure. Investment banking was based on relationships and trust, which take time to develop. A good reputation brought in new business, but developing a solid reputation could only be achieved with repeated success over years. Marcus Goldman started a business of buying note receivables in New York around 1869. After approximately two decades, he brought in his first partner, his son-in-law Samuel Sachs, and established the partnership Goldman Sachs. It took Goldman Sachs one hundred years to grow to a level of around 160 partners. Similarly, most modern-day investment banks trace their origins back a century.

Long Product Life Cycles. The products of investment banks remained unchanged over the century. Stock and bond underwriting and brokering (buying and selling stocks for clients) were little changed from the time of the founding of these companies.

Little Price Competition. Ties between a bank and its corporate client were strong and corporations did not switch banks on the basis of price. There was little price competition on the corporate clients' side. On the investor side, commissions on client trades were fixed by the exchange at 1.5 percent of the dollar value of the deal. All banks adhered to the same rate.

Limited Economies of Scale. Securities underwriting issues were different in terms of size, price, nature, and quality of the company. Business was done on a deal-by-deal basis. On the investor side, client trades had different customer preferences, risk-bearing characteristics, and personal judgments. Standardization and associated economies of scale were rare.

Organization Subordinated to Individuals. Investment banks were conservative businesses with time-honored rules and cultures, and they looked for recruits who fit their culture. There were "Goldman Sachs types" and "Salomon Brothers types." Recruits came from Ivy League schools like Harvard and Yale, and brought with them personal relationships from their years in college. Classmates who attained positions in business and industry turned to their college acquaintances, the investment bankers, when they needed financial advice. The distinction between social and business relations blurred. Developed over decades, these relationships were difficult for a prospective competitor to imitate.

Reputation of Organization and Individuals. Deals were sealed with a handshake, and a common phrase on Wall Street was "a man's word is his bond." Privately held Goldman Sachs's 160 partners owned the majority of the firm's capital of approximately $5 billion. Million-dollar bonuses were not rare.

Constrained Growth. Because the personal touch was so important, U.S. investment banks tended to be domestic businesses. Successful banks were located in New York City, the historical center of American industrial activity. By locating close to their clients, New York investment banks were better able to service them.

Through the 1960s investment banks profited from these strong isolating mechanisms. Slow economic time made for long-lived, stable business relationships, relaxed pricing, and long product life cycles. By the 1970s, however, shifts were taking place in the industry that altered these isolating mechanisms.

Rise of the Institutional Investor. This period saw changes in tax laws. Employees could include pension benefits in collective bargaining agreements. Pension contributions by taxpayers were made tax deductible. An employee paid capital gains tax on pension investments only when he or she cashed out, and thus employees no longer had to pay capital gains tax every year. The result was that institutional investors, pension funds, and mutual funds grew to immense proportions and all but displaced the individual investor. Institutional investors began to exercise power over brokerages. The market changed from one with a large number of small investors, over whom the investment banks had power, to a small number of large institutional investors exercising control over the banks. Big funds began to extract some of the profits that investment banks had earned previously.

Because institutional accounts were huge, competition among rival banks became fierce. Commissions were still fixed by the exchange, so banks started competing on nonprice attributes, by providing research advice, for example. As these services increased, the banks' ability to control the relationship with investors, based on their superior knowledge, decreased.

Negotiated Commissions. The Securities and Exchange Commission made commissions fully negotiable in 1975, largely due to the lobbying influence of institutional investors. Commissions plunged from 50 cents a share to 2 cents a share on large blocks.

Loss of Relationships. By the 1970s, many corporate founders had retired and had been succeeded by professional managers who were responsible to their shareholders. They lacked the founders' strong personal relationships with and loyalty to investment bankers, which made them more inclined to jump banks if they got a better deal. This put increased margin pressure on the banks and affected their profitability.

Expanded Powers of Banking. In January 1989, commercial banks were allowed to underwrite corporate securities. (The Glass-Steagall Banking Act of 1933 had made it unlawful for banks to engage in investment banking while performing normal functions such as receiving savings deposits.) Because Glass-Steagall did not prevent them from trading, big money-center banks like Bankers Trust, Citibank, Chase, Chemical, and J.P. Morgan developed sizable trading divisions. Insurance companies made forays into this business, as did oil companies like Enron, for example, that started gas futures trading divisions.

After this change commercial banks gained substantially. *The Wall Street Journal* reported that J.P. Morgan, a traditional commercial bank, edged out Salomon Brothers, the investment banking powerhouse, as the sixth-largest underwriter of corporate bonds in 1995.

Technological Innovation. Investment banks, faced with steady erosion of profits, found a profitable way to respond: proprietary trading. The competitive advantage in this business comes from developing highly sophisticated financial instruments and then executing arbitrage trades in those instruments. This business originally focused on stock and bond options, treasury strips, and calls and warrants. But, as indicated earlier, the development of powerful computer workstations led to the innovation of new, derivative securities.

The attractive feature of these new products was that they were difficult to value when first introduced. The firms that introduced them developed a good understanding of their cash flows under various economic conditions and so could value them accurately. But clients and rival investment banks lacked that knowledge.

With time, however, rival firms and clients developed their own in-house technology to develop and value derivative securities, and the markets for them became more competitive. As competitors developed their own products and imitated each other's products, spreads declined and profits fell. Relationships gave way to the need to develop still newer products quickly. The recruiting emphasis shifted to hiring smart, young traders to make fast money on short-lived products.

Rapid Product Obsolescence. Clients' exposure to economic factors changed and their requirements shifted, fueling the development of new products as well as a high rate of product obsolescence. Mortgage-backed securities that were the darlings of the big banks in the late 1980s become commodities a decade later. Citibank, once a big player in the market, closed its MBS business in 1997.

Persistent, Uncontrollable Price Reductions. Innovative derivatives trade at spreads as large as 500 basis points. If the instrument proves to be popular, spreads are driven down to 50 basis points in months.

High-Risk/High-Return Orientation. Of the countless securities that come out of the Street, most come and disappear quickly. Although uncertain at first, a single successful product can produce significant profits. Kidder Peabody, one of the originators of mortgage-backed securities, made hefty profits; later, Kidder's decline coincided with the demise of the mortgage-backed securities market.

In response to these changes, investment banks retained their traditional lines of underwriting and retail brokerage but added separate groups for proprietary trading and new product development. Goldman Sachs, Salomon Brothers, Lehman Brothers, CS First Boston, and Merrill Lynch became, in effect, mixed-cycle companies, by organizing fast-cycle proprietary trading and slow-cycle advisory services separately. Each of the businesses got its own management style, business processes, and compensation plans.

Slow- to Fast-Cycle Signals

Industry Evolution. "We no longer know what is going on in our industry. Every move we make seems to be too little, too late, before we have even finished making the move. The entire industry is chaotic with things coming in and going out before we can react, and we can never get ahead of the curve."

Product Life Cycles. "We have solid, stable, reliable products that are out of date the day we commercialize them. We can never match supply with demand. Either demand way outstrips our ability to produce or later, when we are ramped up, we have to dump product at prices way below cost."

Value Chain Relationships. "We are used to stable relationships; now things change erratically. The upstream and downstream relationships in our industry used to be tightly linked. Now they are easily pulled apart and fluid, with a lot of strange, new competitors."

Price Competition. "Pricing is scary. If we price high we sell for a while, then competition comes in and ruins our profit margins and we don't recover our investment. If we price low, we take the market but suffer stockouts and lost profits. Either way, the market dies before we can recover our investment. We used to change our price to meet our needs, now we seem to change our price to chase the market. Pricing is like in a spot, or auction market. This is upsetting our relationship-driven marketing people"

Organizational Structure. "We used to look to our veteran salespeople to solve our problems with customers, to look for the right person to reestablish a close relationship. Now, these old soldiers can no longer keep our key customers. We know our customers and how their needs relate to the product better than anyone else, but it doesn't help anymore."

Company Reputation. "Even though we attach our name to our products and advertise that connection heavily, it doesn't help. Customers just don't seem to be making the important connections to our key people. They don't seem to understand the importance of having these people involved in the chain. Current price and current performance is all that counts and it doesn't count for long."

Switching Costs. "Our old customers used to develop long-term relationships with us and stay with us for years. We knew the ins and outs of their business and developed customized solutions for them that kept us together for years. These new customers though, they don't value loyalty. They switch whenever a new idea comes along. They switch easily and fast."

Profitability. "We had stable profits but now we are all over the place, huge profits one month when we are up and then horrible profits the next month when we are down."

Growth. "The good news is that we have lots of opportunities to grow. New customers are willing to buy from us without the long process of selling and relationship building. Used to be we couldn't get to new customers easily, but now we have so many opportunities, if only we can get into new markets and sell new products quickly."

Market Structure. "We are used to having a stable group of competitors, each with its customers staked out. Now there are competitors moving in and out of the market all the time. We just can't count on customers or segments to be stable or reliable."

Barriers to Entry. "Barriers used to be stable and predictable, now they are changing rapidly, to the point where there are different products within the same product lines. We had an easily protected market. Our 'castle walls' kept us in and others out. Now barriers rise and dissolve so quickly we can hardly understand them before they change."

Competition for Profits. "We are used to a stable pricing and steady profit structure. Now everybody seems to be cutthroat, to the customers and to the competitors. Our innovators in our industry charge an outrageous price, taking away our business with the slightest change. When they have the slightest competition, they drop the price like a rock and kill everybody's profits."

Service. "We have a great service philosophy but it just doesn't work for us. We emphasize our historical ability to be there for the customer, but the customer doesn't care. These new products don't need much service anyway. It's no wonder customers shy away from the thought that we would emphasize long-term service tailored to their needs and just want some sort of low value added, quick service."

Bargaining Power. "We had a stable power relationship; the customers needed us. We always worked things out as problems arose. Now we have power on some products, but on others the customers dictate the terms. Actually, come to think of it, our bargaining power may be inversely proportional to the age of our product."

FAST TO STANDARD CYCLE

Richard Grimm, CEO of Technicare, explained his company's entrance into the CT scanner market. "We decided to manufacture medical equipment because we saw it as an innovative, high-growth industry. More important, it was a fragmented industry with lots of small, specialized markets. Right at the beginning, we didn't want to be up against the monsters who would give us more competition than we could handle." Technicare's potential competition came from large, established medical equipment suppliers: EMI, General Electric, Siemens, Philips, and Toshiba. Until the entrance of Technicare in 1974, only EMI had the capability to produce the CT scanner.

When Technicare began making its CT scanner, the company outsourced the components and assembled them at its production facility. To respond quickly to customers, Technicare produced scanners in small lots. While this approach limited economies of scale, it provided flexibility and responsiveness. Technicare management worked within a compressed OODA loop. They would observe what the customer wanted, orient their product designs to meet those customer needs, decide on the best way to move forward with product development, and then act on those plans in a time span of eighteen months, faster than competitors.

Compressed Product Life Cycles. Technicare outpaced its slower-cycle competitors that took between five and nine years to develop products. Due to continual change, Technicare managers were able to standardize only a few of their processes or components. Demand for innovation drove everything in the company. Technicare held 90 percent market share of a fast-growing industry. Revenues had increased 20,000 percent in five years.

Uncontrollable Innovation. Each year Technicare came out with a better, faster CT scanner that made previous models obsolete. Technicare's CT4000 scanner offered an eighteen-second scanning capability. This made the sixteen-month-old CT2200, with its two-minute scanning capability, antiquated. The pace of new products continued with the introduction of a two-second scanner in 1978, the CT5000. All told, there were four major developments in three years that made prior CT scanning devices obsolete.

One of the reasons for the fast pace of innovation was an inability to patent new ideas. Technological developments were considered to be evolutionary since they were based on the widespread principle of sending X rays through the body to a receptor on the other side. Improvements were based more on scanning speed rather than on new scanning technology, processes that were difficult to patent.

Yet, because they were first, Technicare demanded and won high prices from customers. The CT2200, Technicare's slowest scanner, was priced at $200,000 when it entered the market in 1975. Four years later, the CT5000, the two-second machine, sold for $1,000,000.

High-Risk/High-Return Orientation. Managers at Technicare were given free reign to make decisions as long as they submitted a general market plan. A manager's personal success depended on making changes to gain new customers. Most of the top managers were top athletes in college and were strongly competitive, creating an environment with a work atmosphere and esprit de corps that was difficult for competitors to copy.

Demand Creation. Technicare prided itself on its ability to create scanner demand. Technicare's engineers incorporated the latest technology into products before the competition knew the technology existed and, in some cases, before customers knew what they wanted. By the time competitors introduced their new model, Technicare was ready to introduce a new model that changed the focus of customer buying decisions.

Capacity Ramping. Technicare complemented its new scanner technologies with an ability to ramp up production quickly. By quickly increasing production, and just as quickly ramping down production as demand waned, Technicare was able to direct its limited supply network to the most profitable segment of the industry. Technological innovations often were based on changing the arrangement of purchased parts, an approach that allowed flexibility but would prove easy for competitors to copy. Assemblers were well trained to adapt to new product designs.

But by 1979, the rules of the game began to change. CT scanner technology had been largely proven, at least to the levels where customers no longer desired large performance improvements. Instead, the aging base of installed scanners needed service. Advantage began to shift to competitors better able to offer reliable, cost effective service and distribution. Customers demanded extended service capabilities for scanners; the typical scanner purchaser now budgeted up to 25 percent of original price on service, to be spread over three years of normal use.

Scale Orchestration. GE had a large network of four hundred service centers, which it had developed over decades to service its conventional X-ray machines. Technicare had only six regional service centers.

Government Regulation. There was a need to work within an increasingly regulated hospital environment. Certificate of need legislation required community approval of hospital expenditures on equipment priced over $100,000. Since CT scanners were now priced at $1 million, health care providers had to go through a lengthy ordering process to gain purchase approval. The lack of effective innovation combined with the bureaucracy of legislation gave GE more time to align organization with the maturing scanner market. GE had more time to emphasize its extensive service network and more experience with regulation.

At first, Technicare stuck to its fast-cycle strategy, turning its efforts to developing nanosecond CT scanner technology. But as the cost of innovation grew, and as the pace slowed at which innovation could be turned into much-needed cash flows, it became evident that Technicare's successful business model was aging. Technicare's market share had dropped to 35 percent, for the first time equal to GE's share, which was growing.

An assessment concluded that in service capabilities it would take years to duplicate GE's distribution strengths. Yet the scanner market was quickly becoming competitive in distribution and service. Technicare's renewal cycle would not be fast enough. As time went on these assessments were proven true. The situation worsened.

The shift in economic time was epitomized by CEO Grimm: "Pride and fun . . . those are our two key words. Pride in doing a successful job and the fun to be had in the process. That philosophy was written up in the company when we started and that is still management policy number one. If we ever get too big, or lose the sense of fun, then we will do something different. We'll get out or break up the business."

Technicare management worked with First Boston to contact companies as potential suitors. Johnson & Johnson expressed interest. Technicare's management was impressed with J&J's strong reputation. The sale of Technicare to Johnson & Johnson was made in 1979.

Fast- to Standard-Cycle Signals

Industry Evolution. "We plan for continual change, structure our strategy for the anticipated changes and then the change happens slowly. The industry seems stagnant by our standards. It doesn't have the entry possibilities that we have been accustomed to. Companies get locked in and have a hard time entering or exiting. The relationships, structures, and competitive advantages evolve slowly, which cramps our fast-moving style."

Product Life Cycles. "We devote a lot of effort to developing new offerings but a lot of it seems a waste. New products don't sway customers like they used to. They give us very little sales boost, until we can get their price to a level that is competitive with older products. We offer new and improved products but the market doesn't respond. Increasingly, customers don't even seriously consider our new products. They want better service with old products rather than new products with new advantages. What happened to our customer?"

Value Chain Relationships. "We no longer work hard to predict what is going to happen in the future. Now we need to fine tune what is happening now. Alliances are more important and enduring than what we looked for in the past. Suppliers and customers are becoming linked. Instead of getting what we need fast at any price, we must now nurture relationships up and down the chain and help each other be more efficient."

Price Competition. "We have always excelled at making good margins on new products. Now we have to find a way to cut costs so we can price-compete on old products. Creative energy that should be going into new product development is spent trying to save a nickel on a dollar everywhere. It's no fun anymore."

Economies of Scale. "We hate to say it, but bigger is better. This is like a gorilla cage. We will have to get big to get that next increment of cost savings so we can cut prices to make margin. This 'three yards and a cloud of dust' is not our cup of tea."

Organizational Structure. "We have always prided ourselves in being able to outmaneuver our rigid and bureaucratic competitors. We should be able to beat them but we cannot. We have teams looking at a number of alternative approaches—we need staying power. Everything points toward discipline and control."

Company Reputation. "We are used to selling the performance of our products; now we are going to have to develop a reputation for our overall enterprise, at many levels. Customers like our products but seem more interested in our commitment. They want to deal with a firm with a big name and established reputation."

Profitability. "We used to get a nice margin on product introduction, now we need to get all the elements into balance, get the volumes up, and get the price down."

Growth. "The market used to come to us. Now we have to cut prices to gain share. New or improved offerings don't get us much unless the price is right. Gaining share is only accomplished by increasing investment and scale. We want to use our innovative ability and flexibility to provide better products, but the numbers say focus on better processes."

Market Structure. "We are used to having the market to ourselves, at least for a time. Now we have competitors after us all constantly, and they are four-hundred-pound gorillas. Our guerilla tactics don't work anymore. Now we are competing with a few companies that scrutinize each other—and us—for every yard of turf."

Barriers to Entry. "We are used to getting into markets easily with our new products. Barriers used to be everybody else's problem. The barriers we now face are enormous relative to that situation. Size seems to be imperative. We now spend less time worrying about what might be coming from left field and a lot of time worrying about what the companies already in the market are going to do to us because of their bargaining power."

Competition for Profits. "Competition is fierce but in a different way than we are used to. Competitors are willing to spend anything to defend their share. Change prices and everybody responds, keep them the same and nobody notices. After a while, we realized that you just don't mess around with price."

Globalization. "Competitors are going global by tying into entrenched networks. We get into a new market and do well for a while but when our competitors get into that market they wear us down with their established distribution and service."

Service. "Service is more important than in the past. We always provided the service that was needed for our product by just giving the customer another complete product. We cannot afford to do that anymore. Now customers want consistent, long-term service arrangements that are reliable and resilient. The service infrastructure needs to be large and efficiently run, something we are not good at."

Bargaining Power. "It used to be that we had the market power because we had the new ideas. For the first time we are feeling small and weak compared to the four-hundred-pound gorillas that chase after us. Customers don't care about our new ideas anymore"

The automotive, investment banking, and Technicare scenarios illustrate the scope of competitive transformations that managers operating in the new economy can face. A diagnosis of impending cycle shifts based on early warning signs, an analysis of the changes possible, and a complete mapping of the competitive responses that your organization may employ requires a comprehensive understanding of how economic time operates for you. As these examples suggest, transformation in economic time may occur slowly or quickly, and may or may not be readily apparent early on. As also should be evident, cycle shocks are accompanied by the need to respond to the very basic question, "What kind of a company do we want to be?"

RECAP: MANAGING CYCLE SHIFTS

When economic time shifts, the rules of the game can change so much that you may need to question the competitive purpose of your company. In setting strategy under these difficult circumstances, economic time helps you to minimize errors of omission (failing to consider some important factor) and to lower errors of commission (recognizing some important factor but making a wrong choice about what should be done about it).

Cycle-shifting managers should turn toward far-reaching ways to understand the new situation. Economic time can help to identify, with precision, the competitive solutions possible, and the risks, opportunities and scope of change possible. Be prepared to compete on a wholly different basis, the most important challenge a leader faces. In thinking through the possibility that a market may be undergoing such a shift, you can follow these general steps:

BE ALERT FOR PARADIGM-SHIFTING CHANGES IN ECONOMIC TIME

Shocks in economic time arise when regulatory, technological, and managerial changes combine to redefine an industry's action-reaction cycles. In these situations, it can be helpful to monitor transformations in economic time by acquiring information on:

- rates of innovation
- degrees of standardization
- rate of change of prices
- sustainability of scale economies
- historical productivity gains
- fraction of orders based on price

ESTIMATE DYNAMIC VALUE CHAIN SHIFTS

Shifts in technology, regulation, and management strategy may affect a large or a small part of your business, leaving the other value chain drivers of your business unaffected. To the extent that value chain drivers are affected to a greater degree or are more strategic, cycle transformations in economic time will have a greater effect and will be more difficult to manage. In response to this, pay particular attention to how anticipated changes affect the different value chain stages of your organization, relative to those of your current and potential competitors.

MONITOR SIGNALS FOR CHANGES IN ECONOMIC TIME

Changes in the following indicators can give early warning signs as to the extent and direction of change of economic time:

- Industry evolution
- Product life cycles
- Value chain relationships
- Price competition
- Economies of scale
- Organizational structure
- Company reputation
- Switching costs
- Profitability
- Growth
- Market structure
- Barriers to entry
- Competition for profits
- Product standardization
- Globalization
- Service
- Bargaining power

Monitor these indicators for signals that the action and reaction cycles in your markets are changing. Small changes are normal, of course, and reflect variations that can always be expected. Remember also the 80 percent rule; look for signs from several indicators that markets are changing in the same direction of economic time. Indicators that point uniformly to changes in one direction of economic time provide reliable warnings of the transformation of a market to new competitive opportunities, new cash flow investment patterns, and new styles of management.

Effective management of cycle shifts in a business requires leadership. Managers become entrepreneurs, but also analytical problem solvers—innovating new management processes, organizations, and procedures through a process of guided discovery. In the next chapter we compare styles of innovation. We see how innovation and economic time complement each other. We then turn to the question of personal renewal.

CHAPTER 9

INNOVATION: THE ORIGIN OF RENEWAL

In the 1980s, Campbell Soup Company managers embarked upon a major change in corporate strategy. They stepped up the pace of innovation, as part of a well-intentioned plan to introduce three hundred new products within a five-year period. But how well did customers value Campbell's "new product boutique atmosphere," as it was described by one company executive? A few products, like LeMenu and Great Starts, were successful, but overall, resources were shifted away from time-honored, mainstay products. Division chiefs were pulled in many directions. Profits fell.

Campbell's customers did not perceive enough value in the stream of new products to pay for them. The company's bold, innovative strategy created misalignment between itself and its customers. Campbell CEO David Johnson stressed, "We simply backed too many ideas." In correcting the problem, he added, paradoxically, that he had to "fight the motherhood of innovation," the view that having more new products was always better than having fewer. In the end, Campbell adopted a controlled pace of innovation, renewing its commitment to mainstay product lines through cost reduction, quality enhancements, and advertising. The result? Profits improved.

Innovation is good. Then more innovation must be better, yes? Not exactly. The right speed and style of innovation depends on where your organization operates in economic time, just as the renewal cycles for organizations depend on economic time. When considering the speed of innovation, it is important to know whether innovation will change historical relationships with customers. This is where considerations of economic time can help. In this chapter we look at innovation associated with new products, organizational change, and the reshaping of professional careers. We find that these basic types of innovation can be managed by the same laws of renewal that are emphasized throughout this book.

INNOVATION PATTERNS

We know a few things about innovation. A study of 650 R&D executives found that patents are more important for product than process innovations. Patents were found to be less of a factor in innovative industries such as computers and other commercial equipment where the pace of innovation is fast. For slower-moving chemical products and basic mechanical inventions, patents can provide effective protection. For products that involve new configurations of existing components, or new manufacturing processes, patents are less effective; these kinds of innovations are easier to imitate. In extreme cases, for weakly isolated innovations, active patenting may actually facilitate competitive imitation by offering a clear target for imitation.

Thus, we advise managers to be sensitive to the relative benefits of patenting products and processes in the different economic time cycles. Generally, as economic time speeds up, patents are less effective.

One proven innovation strategy calls for moving faster than your competitors through a stream of small innovations. This strategy takes place over time, involving a series of best-in-class incremental innovations. The idea is to gradually accelerate your innovation efforts while hollowing out the capability-building efforts of your competitors. Successful fast-cycle companies, like Sony, do this by developing advantages in component markets first that become platforms for short-lived product extensions. These companies have been able to parlay their success into greater share in end products in some cases, and to dictate the evolution of applications in other cases.

Sony's market share in CD mechanisms, lasers, and CD sensors runs at 60 percent, 65 percent, and 60 percent, respectively. Its component position in compact audio disk-related core products, data drives, and lasers has allowed the company to influence the evolution of standards in computer peripheral businesses based on optical media storage. Although the products of successful fast-cycle companies are short-lived, the platform of innovations on which they are based can be longer lasting, providing a more stable base from which to conduct product and market planning.

We also know that companies become world-class innovators as a defensive tactic. Gillette dominated the straight razor market for a half-century, with a market share of 70 percent, until 1962. Then, Wilkinson Sword of Britain introduced a stainless steel blade that lasted three times longer than Gillette's carbon steel blade. Gillette's share fell to 50 percent in a year. Notably, Gillette had known of the new stainless steel technology, as Wilkinson Sword had licensed some of this technology from Gillette, which held the patents.

The Wilkinson Sword galvanized Gillette management into cannibalizing its own, established products. Gillette introduced the Trac II twin-blade razor in 1972, and saw its older brands yield to the twin-blade technology. Then, while Trac II was still in its prime, Gillette introduced Atra pivoting-head razors in 1977, knowing that this product would cannibalize Trac II sales. Still later, threatened by the imminent entry of the Bic disposable razor, Gillette introduced the innovative Good News twin-blade disposable razor, even though the cheaper disposable cut into immediate profits.

All of these actions were expensive in the short run, but were rewarded in the long run, as Gillette retained dominance in its market and eventually expanded its market share. In 1989, Gillette introduced the Sensor, a razor with twin blades that moved independently. This innovation resulted in such a good shave that its higher price began to reverse losses in revenue from less profitable disposables.

Process innovations accompanied each new blade. Because razors were sold in huge volumes, the emphasis was on efficiency and consistency. Successive process innovations would build on previous experience as the company tailored the knowledge needed for the next innovation. In this way, process innovations followed product innovations, to be followed again by product innovations, as is often the pattern for standard-cycle innovations.

There is also a general consensus that strategies to stymie technological innovation for fear of cannibalizing established products are not sustainable. Gillette delayed its introduction of the stainless steel blade rather than cannibalize its carbon steel blade technology, which opened an opportunity for Wilkinson. Or take IBM, which rather than develop minicomputer and workstation designs, chose to protect its lucrative mainframe market, even as sales were declining. And there is Ampex, the technological pioneer of video recorders, which failed to commit to large-scale investment and lost millions of dollars of later sales to Sony, JVC, and Matsushita.

However, as important as these insights are—and there are many others—they don't tell us enough about how to manage innovation. Why? Because traditional thinking has no way to predict how fast and by what means different innovations will unfold.

INNOVATION IN ECONOMIC TIME

Innovation is not sustainable, merely renewable. Yet, the innovative companies in our database originate new products and reduce costs through technological innovation year after year, beating their competitors to the market with new ideas that reshape markets. Examples range from Hewlett-Packard's laser jet printers, Chrysler's Cab Forward design, Sony's data Discman, Hitachi's maglev train, Intel's Pentium chip, Norfolk Southern's just-in-time boxcar deliveries, 3M's Post-it Notes, Kao's line of perfumes, to Rubbermaid's plastic storage shed.

The commercialization of innovation, often studied as a technological phenomenon, takes place through the same laws of competitive evolution that affect other business activities. That is why, as David Teece points out, when considering your ability to innovate, you should pay as much attention to your *appropriability regimes*—your ability to capture profits from

Table 9.1. Appropriability Regimes in Economic Time

ECONOMIC TIME	APPROPRIABILITY REGIME	EXAMPLES
Slow cycle	• Innovations are gardener-style, create winner-take-all markets • Isolating mechanisms strong, enduring, idiosyncratic	Disney, Merck, Microsoft, Intuit, USAirways, McKinsey, Lockheed Martin
Standard cycle	• Innovations orchestrated for extended, high volume • Innovations balanced with product and process improvements	Starbucks, UPS, Toyota, Wal-Mart, Andersen Consulting, Southwest Airlines
Fast cycle	• Innovations freestanding, idea driven, organizationally simple • Isolating mechanisms weak, convergence pressures intense	Sony, US Robotics, Intel, Hewlett-Packard, Liz Claiborne, Sharper Image

innovation—as you do to the innovation itself.[1] Why? Because, ultimately, so will your customers.

Table 9.1 compares appropriability regimes for the different economic time cycles. It shows that innovations can be profitable anywhere in economic time. Strong isolating mechanisms help a company prolong the advantages of innovation by making products difficult to displace. As isolating mechanisms become weaker, the speed of displacement of innovation increases and the payback period from innovation becomes shorter.

But—and this is noteworthy—*attractive profits can be gained for innovations of any length or duration.* This can be true when an organization is set up to manage innovations according to the dynamics of economic time in which it operates.

As the examples in the table show, weak isolating mechanisms are not necessarily bad for innovators. Even when innovations are copied quickly, they can generate high profits, as they do for Intel.

More generally, economic time emphasizes that the goal of managing innovation does not have to be that of sustainability. Instead, the policies and capabilities needed to support innovation can be tied to a range of management styles and organizational capabilities, depending on the action-reaction cycles that maximize discounted cash flows in economic time.

Suppose that, rather than committing to an innovation, you were picking a team for an athletic event. If it were a pick-up basketball game, your strategy might be to choose the tallest people. However, if the event switched to a power-lifting contest, your hiring strategy would fail. Similarly, good ideas for new products often fail when they are matched with the wrong commercialization capabilities. Next, we overlay the styles of innovation onto each of the economic time cycles.

Winner-Take-All Innovation

Innovation can be a "narrow trail through a thick forest" where obtaining the needed capabilities in a gardener environment is a circumscribed, extended process, not easily accelerated by management. Where innovators enjoy strong geographical or regulatory ties, complex company-customer relationships, or specialized human capital, their resources and capabilities become embedded in relationships with customers.

Guild-like custom engineering skills, found in defense contractors like

Lockheed Martin, support innovation through long-term, exclusive relationships with clients. Modern technological progress implies a constant flow of unsolved technical problems for companies like this, many of them requiring one-of-a-kind problem-solving approaches. These provide strong isolating mechanisms that discourage imitation.

Polaroid's leadership in instant photography is protected by a platform of complementary assets: the technology embodied in the camera and film, the brand name, the manufacturing facilities, and Polaroid's position in distribution channels. Patent protection helps, but it is aided by a range of market-ownership strengths throughout the company.

As for many slow-cycle products, slow-cycle innovations can be so sticky as to create mobility barriers for companies attempting to grow beyond their initial success. Recall that in spite of its considerable efforts and talents, Lotus was not able to expand beyond Lotus 123 until later, when its innovative Lotus Notes software was introduced, followed by IBM's acquisition of the company.

In pharmaceuticals, the returns to R&D do not depend only on being the first company to successfully complete the patent process. Important also is an evaluation of which competitors have access to the complementary activities required to best commercialize a patent. Expenditures on R&D, where they are long, drawn out, and combined with significant investment, should be accompanied by careful analysis of whether other companies are pursuing similar research avenues and, if so, what complementary assets those companies have.

Innovation can also be blocked by standards setting. Sony learned that lesson from its inability to establish a VCR standard for the technologically superior Beta format. Beta technology was more compact and produced a better picture than VHS technology, but Beta was overcome in the marketplace because of tipping to the VHS standard. In the information economy, competition for technology standards is increasingly part of the innovation process. Companies currently compete for standards in digital audio-visual media (Sony vs. Philips) and the high-density laserdisc format (Toshiba and Time Warner vs. Philips and Sony).

Managers considering committing to a string of innovations should pay particular attention to the emergence of standards battles. Standards outcomes influence the speed and shape of innovation, the profitability of innovation, and which companies succeed and fail. Moreover, as discussed earlier, if the standard in question is the proprietary property of one company, the potential exists for creating lost-lasting profits.

Scale Orchestrated Innovation

Customers do not always want a faster pace of innovation. As the Toyota and Campbell Soup Company examples show, important also is assurance that innovations will be harmonized with past experiences and expectations. In standard-cycle markets, above all, innovation should be balanced with consistency and repeatability of experience.

Companies in standard-cycle industries have less powerful isolating mechanisms. They serve mass markets, have less specialized resources, and their innovations face direct competition for extended periods. It is precisely the extended rivalry in these industries and the limited opportunities for overturning established advantage that make complementary assets like process innovation, marketing, distribution, brand loyalty, and customer service so important to the success of a standard-cycle innovation.

First-mover status is often sacrificed for low cost and reliability. Dominant competitors like IBM and AT&T, for example, are often not the first to introduce innovations. Innovation under extended rivalry requires vision and persistence. Often against the odds, and in a climate of skepticism, managers make substantial commitments to change. This requires leadership, especially when costs initially will exceed revenues, and when market acceptance is uncertain during the period of development and early market growth. Recall our principle that demand is not "out there," it is often created through leadership.

As innovations become established, standard-cycle managers focus their efforts on a stream of incremental improvements, building upon the company's position within existing markets. Development priorities shift from novelty and towards dependability, design modification, and cost efficiency. Steel, textiles, food processing, insurance, automobiles, fast food, and hotel services are industries where the pace of innovation is controlled and balanced.

Standard-cycle innovations reflect the refinement and recombination of features and components developed earlier. Innovations in the automobile industry during the postwar era involved the refinement of existing technologies and gradual applications of microelectronics and new materials, plastics, and ceramics. The basic car concept, and the platform of technologies needed to make the car, changed slowly.

Once product designs or new technical standards become dominant, product innovation becomes orchestrated with process improvements, which gradually leads to increased productivity and lower product costs. Product innovation is incremental rather than radical. Process innovation is continual.

Innovations require forward planning, procedural orchestration, and system-wide compromises. Because standard-cycle companies have considerable momentum, they have both the resources and the time to explore the implications of technological discontinuities. While isolating mechanisms give these organizations time to prepare for change, they can make standard-cycle organizations complacent, as discussed earlier. Chronically noninnovative practices can persist for years before the organization faces market-driven demands for change. By that time, the momentum of standard-cycle innovations can make renewal a long, particularly costly process of catch-up.

Creatively Destructive Innovation

Innovations in fast-cycle markets are freestanding and offer only temporary advantages. They can be easily imitated through replication because they do not benefit from strong isolating mechanisms. Complementary assets that would slow down imitation in standard or slow-cycle markets are few or nonexistent. Reverse engineering, for example, can be done quickly, allowing competitors to gain sufficient knowledge of new products to copy or improve upon them within months of their introduction. Technology for fast-cycle innovation is diffused throughout an industry more quickly than in slower-cycle markets because of the organizationally simple structure of fast-cycle organizations.

Still, complementary assets can help fast-cycle organizations immensely. Much of Hewlett-Packard's innovation in consumer products comes from complementary capabilities that it has built into its product development, ordering, scheduling, and production processes. By translating customer needs into finished, delivered products faster than the competition can, HP reaches many time-sensitive buyers quickly. A variety of fresh products, coupled with ways to get lots of new products to customers swiftly, enables HP's managers to stay current with, and ahead of, the changing needs of customers.

Where customers have volatile preferences, careful monitoring of market trends is crucial. Identifying lead users, whose present needs will eventually become general market trends, is another common skill for successful fast-cycle innovators. Lead-customer ideas trigger many of the innovative products introduced by companies like Hewlett-Packard, 3M, and Sony. Lead market teams allow these companies to modify design and entry strategies in real time. Dewey & Almy, a supplier of technical specialties to OEMs, uses technical sales networks to uncover customer needs quickly. These companies have flexible, applied technology groups working close to the marketplace.

The important point is that like so many fast-cycle companies, HP's fast-cycle capabilities are *not designed to sustain product advantage.* Their purpose is to speed innovation to market before competitors do, at high volumes to capture profits, coupled with timely product withdrawal as innovations age. Complementary assets in fast-cycle markets don't slow down imitation. Instead they allow organizations to capture the full technological, organizational learning, and financial benefits from innovations that age rapidly.

Innovative Management Styles

Companies like GE, Xerox, Motorola, IKEA, and Toyota have become world renowned for their innovative management. IKEA innovated the customer's role in the manufacturing process by making the customer a participant in furniture manufacturing and sales, thereby cutting costs and enlarging the do-it-yourself home improvement segment. GE created the workout process, a participative, employee-focused problem-solving retreat, as its version of reengineering. The workout process has led to significant cost reductions and increased responsiveness within many companies. Xerox and Motorola adopted Total Quality Management, an organizational innovation that reshaped whole industries. They got the idea of TQM from companies like Toyota, which pioneered many of the management innovations that shook automotive markets in the 1980s.

We have been asked, "Are some management styles better than others? Are some styles of innovation universal to these companies?" What management styles, attitudes, and cultural norms can be shared across organizations regardless of the economic time cycle in which they operate? To find out, we looked at company brochures, annual reports, and recruiting literature of the innovative companies in our database. We looked for references to innovation that spanned economic time cycles. Table 9.2 shows what we found.

Table 9.2. Innovative Management Styles

ATTITUDES TOWARD	EXPRESSED VALUES	COMPANY	ECONOMIC TIME
Risk	"Freedom to try new things"	Intel	Fast cycle
	"Acceptance of mistakes"	J.P. Morgan	Slow cycle
	"Challenge the status quo"	Air Products	Standard cycle
	"Positive attitude about change"	Silicon Graphics	Fast cycle
Change	"Ideas are valued"	Kodak	Standard cycle
	"Top management support"	Johnson & Johnson	Standard cycle
	"Celebrate accomplishments"	American Airlines	Standard cycle
	"Respect for new ideas"	Eli Lilly	Slow cycle
Openness	"Open communication"	IBM	Fast cycle
	"Share information"	Deloitte & Touche	Slow cycle
	"Bright people"	Siemens	Standard cycle
	"Gain a customer perspective"	Xerox	Standard cycle
Autonomy	"Decisions at lower levels"	Nordstrom	Standard cycle
	"Decentralized procedures"	Hewlett-Packard	Fast cycle
	"Expectation of action"	Ford Motor Company	Standard cycle
	"Quick, flexible decisions"	Digital Equipment	Fast cycle

The list speaks for itself. Its insights can be found in other studies of innovation that treat change as normal, that assume that nothing lasts forever, and that celebrate the innovative nature of the human spirit. But as important, they show that innovation may not be successful without consideration for where in economic time the organization operates. What attitudes toward innovation reflect *your* organization? What innovative management styles describe *you?*

Our study of innovation now brings us to our last, and most personal, aspect of renewal. It is managing your *own* career when nothing lasts—including your job. We would like to begin with a story told to us by a student familiar with the ideas of economic time.

PERSONAL RENEWAL—YOUR CAREER

"I was about six years old at the time, when I found myself standing in the middle of a grass field surrounded by other children my age. My parents had just signed me up to participate in a local baseball league and this was my first practice. I remember three coaches who were patiently trying to teach us the fundamentals of baseball—the rules of the game. The coaches had us spread out within the infield and one of them began hitting the ball into the air. The ball seemed to almost disappear, as it made its way toward the sky.

"When the ball descended, it fell in between two children who were trying to avoid getting hit by this fast-moving object. The coach reminded us that we needed to catch the ball before it landed on the ground. The next ball he hit seemed to go higher than all the previous ones. I stood and admired its flight, when all of a sudden I realized that it was headed in my direction.

"Nervously, I reached out my hand and snatched the ball out of the air. I was amazed that I had caught it and remained there for a while extremely proud of my accomplishment. One of the coaches yelled out, 'Nice catch Phil, but next time use your glove—that is what it was made for.' This was my first experience at crafting strategy."

My Competitive Advantage

"As I participated in leagues designed for specific age groups, I realized that I was taller and more developed than the rest of my competitors. Throughout my childhood I seemed to grow at a faster rate than others who were in my age group. In addition, my arm was stronger, which allowed me to throw the ball harder and more accurately than the others could.

"The coaches, realizing my core competencies, assigned me to become a pitcher. My strategy was simple—stand up on the pitcher's mound and throw as hard as I could. The opposing batters usually had never experienced trying to hit a fastball with so much velocity. I would normally win these battles with just one critical success factor, my arm strength. This strategy worked well and provided a good fit with my capabilities, strategy, and market. I was operating in a slow-cycle environment because other competitors could not copy my endowments. I had a virtual monopoly on the market, standing at the very top of the convergence line."

Economic Time Kicks In

"When I reached high school, my competitive advantage had disappeared. I was now competing with players who were as much as four years older and possessed the same arm strength along with the new capabilities of hitting a high-velocity fastball. All of a sudden I was free falling down that convergence line with little chance of sustaining advantage. My environment had instantly switched from noncompetitive to competitive. In order to sustain my advantage, I had to search for a renewal mechanism that would place me higher on the convergence line.

"With assistance from several coaches, I developed a curveball and learned how to strategically pitch to batters. These newly developed skills allowed me once again to obtain a competitive advantage. However, as time went on, even these skills could not be sustained for long.

"During my high school period, I did well enough to allow my baseball career to continue. As I had discovered once before, the move into a different market quickly readjusted my position further down the convergence line. Now, I was competing with players who had developed strong competitive advantages. Being in this position once before, I realized that I had to search for renewal. I developed a third pitch, a slider. In addition, I improved my stamina by lifting weights and running more often. These new skills, combined with my previous skills, allowed me to extend myself into a new role as a relief pitcher. My stamina and wide selection of pitches provided me with a competitive advantage over others. I could pitch a couple of innings a day and easily bounce right back, ready to pitch again the next day.

"This was a valuable asset to a college team that played sixty games in a three-month period. My new core capabilities allowed me to augment my previous skills to succeed. However, I had to segment the market to remain competitive. Brand loyalty and switching costs were low; discipline, repeatability, and no surprises were important, as if I had shifted to a standard-cycle market."

The Paradigm Shift

"The niche that I had found in college provided a route into a still more competitive market, professional baseball. In June of 1991, I was drafted in the thirty-first round by the Cincinnati Reds organization. There I quickly made the switch from standard cycle to fast cycle.

"In this type of environment, you had to quickly deliver 'product' or be forced out of the market. Change was a constant in this environment, where players quickly came and went. It was very difficult to establish any type of competitive advantage because, with the large numbers of players in these organizations, there was always someone who had successfully developed the same skills that you possessed. Sustainable advantage—except for the few superstars around us—was almost nonexistent.

"My skill set was no different from that of my competitors. As I continued my career journey, I felt myself very close to the end of the convergence line. Renewal was becoming more difficult because I was getting older and my capabilities were starting to become depleted. My body was not completely renewable.

"The 160 games during the summer were starting to take a toll on my skill set. My arm was simply saying 'enough already.' My career in professional baseball lasted for two and a half years before I made a dramatic renewal move: a paradigm shift into the business world.

"Here, I extracted some of the capabilities from my baseball career and used them to develop a competitive advantage in the corporate world. These capabilities included physical endurance (working long hours), the ability to react quickly to change, and the capacity to work in a team environment. These skills, coupled with an MBA education, will—I hope—allow me to renew myself again."

And so the story ends. While our friend may have taken poetic license with ideas of economic time (as we have been known to do), his eloquent story applies to any career. Railroad engineer; canal operator; candle maker—all once prized occupations. Or take steel making, which evolved from a highly paid craft to a world commodity. Tomorrow? Software engineers will be as ubiquitous as plumbers are today. Nothing lasts forever, including the influence and profitability of professions.

Andy Grove, a prototype of the new economy's manager, puts it this way: "It is not Intel's responsibility to provide employment for you—it is your responsibility to remain employable, and we can help you."

So can a knowledge of economic time.

Strategic Career Management

Your career is like a business. Just as businesses develop strategies to increase corporate value, managers should manage their careers in order to maximize their long-term earning potential. While we use the familiar term "income" to describe the medium of exchange, compensation includes job status, the ability to influence and help others, the opportunity to make a lasting contribution to society, and deep, personal or spiritual fulfillment.

Regardless of how you measure income, the same laws of competition that affect companies can help you manage your career. As for products, developing a career strategy begins with assessing your capabilities, evaluating markets for your skills, and developing a specific renewal plan to bridge short- and long-run behavior. And, just like for businesses, you will end up thinking about your career half-life and renewal cycles of careers.

Career Capabilities

Like products, careers move from noncompetitive to competitive status over time. The reason for this is that, as in business, high income (analogous to high profits) attracts competition. Jobs garnering high profits for individuals will attract high-level competition. And as with products, the speed and means by which this happens can be predicted by how career skills are complemented by isolating mechanisms. In this way, economic time can help you forecast how quickly and by what means you need renew your career skills to sustain your earning power.

Ask yourself: How fast do various career skills become commodities? Do your job skills move in slow-, standard-, or fast-cycle economic time? How long will the career market value your particular capability or skill set? How easily and by what means can your skills be renewed?

Job skills and human endowments may reinforce each other. Professional athletes, for example, undergo rigorous physical training in order to keep their endowments—such as running ability, strength, and agility—at full capacity. And, as we saw in the case of our baseball player, endowments are normally renewable only up to a certain point, at which time they can become limiting capabilities, as is the case for companies.

Having high-level capabilities increases earning potential. Still, it is not enough. Many, too many, talented and ambitious people don't attain their career goals. A number of factors may contribute to this failure, but the factor over which you have most control is your strategy for exchanging your skills and abilities for income (30 percent of the game) and then for renewal (the 70 percent zone). How the game is played, and how you can systematically renew your skills, are more complex and dynamic than simple job-skill matching. In fact, the strategy employed in your career is as important as, maybe more so than, the capabilities you begin with.

From childhood, we are told that we are unique. However, the career market by nature tends toward a commodity market. The world labor pool is so large and mobile that it is relatively easy to find people with a needed skill. Moreover, as in organizations, competition in career markets has the effect of nullifying advantages. At one time, a college education was a guarantee of a high-paying job. Now, so many people have attained undergraduate degrees that people without them often are at a disadvantage. Thus, in the language of renewal, a college degree has become downgraded from a renewable success factor to a necessary success factor, or a price of entry to professional careers.

Capabilities are reinforced in many ways, One is by an inborn passion to know more about a particular subject, to discover, or to make a contribution. Merely possessing an endowment, an innate ability such as physical strength or height, is worth little without interest. In order for career capabilities to unfold you need the drive to use your capabilities; you need *passion.* You have to *want* it so much that your energy is perpetual and self-renewing from within. What, if anything in business, gives you *passion*?

Career Strategy

Your career strategy should align what you do well with what the career market values. Just as for organizations, there will be short-term and long-term aspects to this strategy. In the short run, unless you are financially independent, this strategy likely will be reactive. You will align yourself with what the market currently values, just as do organizations. But, over the long run, as for organizations, you will evolve new capabilities to re-align yourself with evolving market opportunities.

When you couple your interests with your capabilities, you generate energy for renewal. We gravitate toward our interests and seek knowledge accordingly, reinforcing what we do well. This is why we so often advise that the job that provides the highest amount of satisfaction also provides the greatest value to society—and is the job that you would most enjoy doing for free.

If you are particularly fortunate, or have reshaped your capabilities and interests accordingly, your career capabilities and career passion are in perfect alignment to generate high income. When your capabilities and career passions are aligned, when you are asked what you have to offer, your answer is, "Myself."

Artisans. Experts are artisans who have defined their field through individual accomplishment. The marketplace recognizes them as experts because of their knowledge and skills. The field in which they operate and they are inseparable. An example would be the legal profession, where experts exist as top trial lawyers or legal scholars. The field of law may undergo change, but new systems or theories of law are rarely discovered to replace existing systems. Innovations are made on top of a stable base of understanding.

By being at the pinnacle of their profession and understanding the system, experts maintain their position by leading and controlling changes to the system. The evolution of legal thinking is like a renewal staircase, where additions are made by the artisans on top of an existing body of knowledge. As in the medical, academic, and scientific communities, these experts exert gate control over new ideas. Experts set the price for their innovations. It comes naturally. It's in their style of play.

Orchestrators. Here we find salaried wage earners who compete in large, common skill pools. They are the orchestrators and players in an arena where they perform a range of carefully segmented tasks assigned to a particular field. They perform or craft standardized activities based on unskilled, skilled, or professional labor. Orchestrators could be engineers, technicians, accountants, clerks, and managers. They pursue brand loyalty through their professional reputations as viewed by employers and trade associations.

Advancement is measured through improvements in work output. Productivity is measured by the value of output over wages and is easily quantified and compared. Orchestrators recognize that competitive markets for supply and demand determine their value, and so they expect wages similar to those in their peer group. Their resume is a codifiable measure of their value. Often, as in oligopolistic competition, a few career orchestrators come to dominate based on their ability to manage large groups of people. They are called organization leaders.

Children Eaters. Managers who spawn and eat their innovations can be accomplished professionals or rank amateurs. However, ease of movement from one opportunity to the next is common among them. They rely heavily on their own innate capabilities, often believing that their superior knowledge and capability will see them through. They have a low affinity for established rules and cumbersome committee processes.

Often they are either new to the game or have little investment in the status quo.

Innovators look for opportunities with high payoff, enjoy intense feedback, and find risks to be stimulating. They enjoy out-of-the-box problems and become bored when situations stabilize. As Apple Computer chairman Steve Jobs put it when asked about success in Silicon Valley, "All that matters is that you have to be smart."

The implication? With these growing differences in management styles, career counselors and management books should focus more on how economic time and professional skills reinforce each other. Thus, traditional interviews would determine if the following characteristics are present: Does Jen know programming language? Will she show up for work on a regular basis? Will she get along with the other programmers? Many questions should be answered, but no one has paid attention to the fact that Jen is a fast-cycle kind of person.

Jen likes to learn new languages and new technologies. She likes fast, intense feedback. She likes to be creative. She likes to take risk and be rewarded for success. She wants to be held accountable and be able to hold others accountable. The programming job she is applying for won't change much. Bonuses will be based upon seniority. Jen may take the job out of necessity or lack of understanding, but if she doesn't realize where her career passion lies, chances are good that she will eventually leave or, worse, meander through life, never fulfilling her potential.

If this happens to Jen, she becomes an undervalued asset. Remember undervalued assets? An inability to understand what one does best (capabilities *and* passion) and what career markets value most, can result in a person chronically suppressing his or her own career value. The mechanisms analogous to capital market restructuring are lost promotion opportunities, dead-end jobs, and layoffs. Nobody but you can be ultimately responsible for how the laws of competition direct your career.

Career Renewal

The purpose of career renewal is to recapitalize your aging job skills and rekindle your passion for work. Just as organizations pursue economic renewal, we can pursue career renewal through education, innovative thinking, and restructuring of core competencies.

And, just as companies can struggle when they aspire to do everything, we need to come back to something we know: that achieving success in one career hardly ensures success in another—even *with* intense interest and determination. Just as for companies, our history matters. A mismatch of skills, even for highly skilled individuals, often leads to misalignment. Michael Jordan is one of the greatest players in the history of basketball. In 1993, Jordan decided that he wanted to play baseball, reasoning that his interest in the game and his natural athletic ability would be enough to enable him to succeed.

We applaud Jordan's personal integrity, his willingness to take risks and to explore new opportunities. But Jordan's career strategy failed. Many of the skills needed to be successful in basketball do not carry over to baseball, and conversely.

Baseball is a static game where hand-eye coordination is critical. Basketball, on the other hand, is a fluid sport, requiring players to recognize offensive and defensive patterns, excel at man-to-man defense, and be able to read the eyes of opposing players. A sport with characteristics like basketball is football. While it is unlikely that Jordan would be an excellent football player, perhaps due to lack of interest, he might be a better football player than a baseball player. The sporting world has stories of athletes who play basketball as well as football. Florida State University Heisman Trophy winner Charlie Ward is one example.

The Jordan example shows that experimentation is important. Even without immediate benefits, experimentation helps us to understand what is possible and what is not; experimentation slows down aging. Experimentation reshapes intrinsic interests. Experimentation changes organizations, and it changes you. The key, as in the Jordan story, is to avoid commitments where choices can become particularly costly or irreversible. This advice benefits you and your employer.

Ask yourself: Which of my job skills are more renewable than others? Is career sustainability even a goal? Job stability is fine, of course. But career goals go beyond stability, to include job excitement, the chance to help others, an opportunity to make a lasting contribution or to gain deep, spiritual fulfillment, as well as the chance to make a fortune and shape economic history. Few of us achieve these goals. Most of us are fortunate to achieve one of these goals in a lifetime. But, as for organizations, attention to how the laws of competition operate on careers will help you decide what is possible and how to change direction as you age.

A relative of one of our students graduated from high school in the early 1970s. He was good in math and English, and developed a fondness for computers. While discussing his career choices with his guidance counselor, the counselor told him, "Computers are a fad. They won't be around for long. Why go to college when your earnings as a computer programmer will be the same as the guys now are earning in the mills. Do yourself a favor, get a job in the mills." Because he chose a nonrenewable career strategy, our friend later struggled to make ends meet after he was laid off in the mills.

Your chances of working for the same company throughout your lifetime are like the chances that any given company will keep its product line unchanged for the next fifty years. Like products, careers come and go. But the laws of renewal can always point you to true north.

Career innovators ask: What are my skills and endowments? What gives me a distinctive advantage over others in the work force? I am only "tall" if others are "short"—what *are* these dimensions? What gives me passion, elicits energy, and promotes creativity from within me? How fast are my various career skills aging and which ones can be renewed? Revisiting these questions on a regular basis establishes the foundation for a dynamic, robust, enjoyable career. What is necessary is that you remember that nothing lasts forever.

Sound familiar? These questions are similar to what many of us ask when thinking about our careers. This said, we wonder how many highly capable, hardworking people ignore them, or stumble in applying these simple, universal laws of competition that can enrich their lives.

RECAP: INNOVATION—THE ORIGIN OF RENEWAL

There are cycle-specific and universal management styles for managing innovation. These management styles can help to renew products, organizations, and individual, professional careers.

INNOVATIONS IN ECONOMIC TIME

When considering your ability to innovate, pay as much attention to how you will capture profits from innovation in economic time as you do to the innovation itself. Look for the emergence of standards battles where the outcome will set the dominant design paradigm and long-term advantage.

Remember that customers do not always want a faster pace of innovation. Look for where customers may want assurance that innovations will be harmonized with past experiences and expectations, consistency and repeatability of experience.

Know that, where innovating organizations are organizationally simple, innovations are likely to diffuse quickly throughout an industry.

Remember also that fast-cycle capabilities are not designed to sustain innovation. Their purpose is to capture the fullest profits possible in a short amount of time.

The important point is that rapidly imitated innovations can generate as much value as longer-lived innovations—if an organization is structured to operate appropriately, in economic time.

PERSONAL RENEWAL—YOUR CAREER

As with business organizations, your professional capabilities come from a mix of skills, education, experience, personality, and interests. Distinguish between limiting versus renewable career capabilities. Renewable capabilities allow you to adapt, as well as to know when you cannot adapt. Some career capabilities can be taught while other career capabilities, often based on endowments, cannot be learned or easily extended.

Consider how each of the economic time cycles affects the ebb and flow of job skills in your career market. Look for isolating mechanisms that can shield your career capabilities from imitation or obsolescence.

Dependability, dedication, and task orientation are found in standard-cycle managers. Creativity, passion, and the desire to take calculated risks are attributes of people in fast-cycle companies. Patient, pleasant problem solvers with a genuine interest in customer satisfaction fit well with slow-cycle companies. Some exceptional, especially gifted managers share these attributes.

Develop short-term strategies to achieve fit now with what you do well. Set long-term strategy to change your skill set, to realign yourself with opportunities that recapitalize your earning power and your career interests.

Career strategy should include short- and long-run objectives, a personal mission statement, and a plan for how you intend to renew yourself.

The laws of competition make the markets for products and services more robust, and they make the market for careers more efficient. The result is economic growth and a greater chance that the human spirit can be renewed through work. Steven Covey, one of the people who inspired this book, describes how personal mission statements can be crafted and renewed, in *The Seven Habits of Highly Effective People*.[2]

In the end, regardless of where you operate in economic time, renewal of innovative products and processes, organizational styles, and your own career is simply—and profoundly—good management.

Our goal for you? If you ever find a job that you like so much that you are willing to work for free, odds are that this is where you will contribute the most. It certainly will be the most important and lasting expression of your personal journey.

CHAPTER 10

CREATING YOUR FUTURE

Look at your company's mission statement. Does it call on your organization to be "the most profitable," "innovative," or "the leader"? While these goals are attractive, they can be limiting in renewal. The reason is that they reveal little about competitive evolution. Freeze-frame thinking sees the business world as a snapshot or, at best, a series of snapshots, rather than as a motion picture, with continually changing images.

Our surroundings do not change much from day to day, so we accept our environment as more or less unchanging. But the reality is that we exist in a stream of ever-changing images. A year from now, ten years from now, a century from now, what today seems unchanging will likely be different—even unrecognizable. Stability is the exception. Nothing lasts forever. Although we don't normally think in terms of change, evolution is normal.

Creating your future, gaining more control over business events, is what renewable advantage is about. It is about knowing how to evolve from what you are to what you might become. It is about knowing your limits. It is about moving from a focus on current results to the deeper, underlying processes of value creation. It is about being proactive in creating market opportunities, about taking steps today that help your organization tomorrow. It is about what you might do in the future, and about what you should not try to do, at least without an organizational transformation.

We have looked at the newer dynamic forces in the economy. We have also looked at familiar territory, even as it is changing. Against this backdrop we have pointed out that traditional strategy thinking can be upgraded to understand, contrast, and choose between these dynamic business opportunities.

In response to this we developed the idea of economic time. Through economic time, strategy is crafted by leveraging what your organization does well and by transforming you into what you can become. Economic time provides a strategic compass. It redirects your organization's priorities when faced with framebreaking change, and it keeps you on course when transformational change is not needed or not possible.

WHAT WE KNOW

Our forty-five-industry study led us to develop the idea of economic time, to help us distinguish how markets work and how organizations renew themselves differently. Our major findings are these.

Business Is Splitting Apart in Economic Time

Economic time is an organizing mechanism; a way to understand and contrast the increasingly dynamic management styles in the new economy. Economic time addresses the need for a universal, dynamic measure of competitive diversity. Economic time comprises multispeed competition, and it moves at different speeds for different kinds of businesses. This is true within companies, as well as within industries.

There are many measures of economic time. Each has roughly an 80 percent chance of being right in correctly identifying where your company is operating in economic time. This is why we settled on the 80 percent rule, a comparison of three or more descriptors for any business as a good overall test for determining where you are managing in economic time and where you are headed.

Much of traditional thinking is still important and useful. Economic time instills dynamic reasoning in traditional thinking, while expanding it to account for the newer business opportunities.

Gorillas Have Become Scale Orchestrators

The four-hundred-pound gorillas, our metaphor for companies that fit the mold of traditional business thinking, have evolved into scale orchestrators. A simple quest for economies of scale—size for the sake of size—has given way to the need to orchestrate technologies with product choices and organizational learning. The four sections of the scale orchestra are economies of scale, product design, process improvements, and organizational learning. Size and market share still matter. But also important is the ability to recraft products and services to maintain alignment with continually changing customer expectations. Process improvements should be ongoing, spread evenly throughout the enterprise. Organizational learning completes the scale orchestra, by improving the ability of your people to coordinate their actions with each other, with changing product designs, and with ongoing process improvements.

Are you good at scale orchestration? Do you:

- Build a no-surprises culture throughout your organization?
- Control innovation by harmonizing new ideas with your continually improving scale orchestra?
- Say no to customers, while making them like it?
- Defend your brands?
- Bring suppliers into your orchestra? (You don't have to vertically integrate to behave like an effectively integrated company.)
- Recalibrate the balance between cost leadership and differentiation, on a regular basis, for your evolving portfolio of products?

Above all, master a balance. Don't overemphasize one section of the scale orchestra at the expense of the other sections. As part of this, fight entropy. Complacency and indifference are common in standard-cycle organizations. Leadership is the ability to continually rejuvenate scale-orchestrated organizations, to instill an ongoing, enterprise-wide desire to improve.

Orchestrate well; master the balance; then you can grow. Organizations that take these steps in the reverse order run the risk of collapsing in on themselves when faced with better-run competitors. Ask yourself: Which of my markets are characterized by a high volume of gradually changing, competitively similar, no-surprises products and services, produced through harmonizing enterprise-wide, repeated activities?

Children Eaters Can Sustain Advantage

How is a Pentium chip like a Cabbage Patch doll? They both operate in fast-cycle economic time because both products lack isolating mechanisms or complementary assets that shield them from imitation and obsolescence. Fast-cycle products, and the organizations that make them, are simple, idea-based, and readily deconstructed. Economies of scale are important, but scale economies, because they can be copied quickly, convey only temporary advantage.

Fast-cycle products benefit from supernormal productivity gains, which are passed along in the form of rapid reductions in market prices.

The result is a type of competition thought unlikely years ago but increasingly prevalent today. Although product advantage is brief, the Schumpeterian gale of creative destruction offers unprecedented opportunities for companies that manage effectively. Do you operate, or are you headed into fast-cycle markets? Using the 80 percent rule, do you face:

- Rates of market hypergrowth of 30 percent or more?
- Escalating commitment, which requires large financial outlays that put strains on your financial structure?
- The problem of not having enough time to grow (if you are a small or start-up organization)?
- Price compression, in which prices are driven down at rates of 30 percent per year or more?
- Weak brand loyalty or, at best, strong brand awareness with only a brief time possible to capture profits from innovation?
- The need to create demand over and over again to keep market opportunities alive?

Now, look inward, and ask yourself if you are good at, or are capable of becoming good at:

- Dynamic pricing, the ability to lower price rapidly, but not too rapidly, so that your organization operates at capacity with no stockouts?
- Preplanning market exit on a repeated basis?
- Encouraging your managers to look for the options components of projects, and to seek market opportunities not obvious today?
- Selection efficiency, repeatedly choosing among many projects and deciding which to fund and which to shut down?
- Capacity ramping, building capacity up or down quickly in response to rapid swings in demand?

If your company is fast-cycle, you should encourage forgetting as a means to learning. Put aside established ways of doing things to make room for novel ideas, fresh practices, and new management styles. Reward smart mistakes when they help to expand your decision processes and competitive outlook. Ultimately, know that it can be OK to be disloyal to your products—in fact, it is necessary in order for you to survive.

New Artisans Are Building Mighty Fortresses

Against a backdrop of rapid change, it is still possible to create highly sustainable advantages. Slow-cycle markets provide stable pricing, require few cost reduction demands, and offer long-lived profits. These attractive features stand in contrast to notions that all advantages are becoming increasingly temporary.

Slow-cycle advantage reflects near-complete ownership of some factor necessary for the functioning of a market. Local monopolies arise from more than geography. They include ownership of software operating systems and products that become industry standards. They require high levels of human capital, idiosyncratic product designs, complicated customer relationships, brand ownership, as well as patents or copyrights, particularly for entertainment properties and information appliances that are valued worldwide.

Slow-cycle markets have a winner-take-all quality, which means that the size of your organization may not indicate much about where your advantage comes from. Slow-cycle organizations, from Disney to Merck to winemakers, large or small, reflect the size of their "garden" (or market), to use a metaphor, rather than the ability to grow as a result of economies of scale.

The growth opportunities of slow-cycle markets include the possibility of tipping, whereby market demand tips all the way toward one company. Tipping can happen when your product's share of a slow-cycle market approaches 70 percent, although threshold share varies among markets. Once a product has achieved tipping, market lock-in occurs and near ownership of that market results. Tipping does not occur in all slow-cycle markets. Thus, managers should be sensitive to whether or not tipping will occur, and if it does, how it will change market opportunities.

To understand the style of leadership in many slow-cycle organizations, think of a gardener, cultivating his field, tending and pruning, waiting to harvest the best that grows. Gardener-style management, because it relies on judgments and actions that can be difficult to codify, can make innovation difficult and, similarly, can make it problematic for the slow-cycle organization to grow beyond its original field of success.

Thus, in assessing the potential for profitability and growth, slow-cycle managers should estimate the amount of market growth remaining for current products. Beyond that, the approach is to think about how new or existing products can be used to build stairways to new markets.

Staircase strategies do not rely on economies of scale, but rather on the ability to provide an unbroken link, in the mind of the customer, between past and future products. Like a staircase, each new product is linked solidly to older products. In planning for growth, staircase strategies rely less on pricing and production efficiency and more on creating a series of unbroken steps, as well as strengthening the links between steps.

Slow-cycle managers can benefit from developing a robust understanding of the evolving idea of monopoly. As this concept evolves, slow-cycle markets, their products, and the managers in them will play a role in shaping antitrust policy. Considerable slow-cycle opportunities await those managers who can anticipate their emergence.

The renewal challenge for the slow-cycle artisan is to expand the fortress walls while keeping them high. Above all—don't lose sight of your source of market ownership.

The Three Laws of Renewal

The three laws of renewal are convergence, alignment, and renewal. They act together to determine how markets work, which companies succeed and fail, and how much companies are worth. The speed by which competitors attack your products, the quality of the relationship between you and your customers, and how you can recapitalize your aging investments are determined by where you operate in economic time.

Convergence. Thirty percent of a typical company's value is determined by its products' location and movement on the convergence curve. The position of a product on the curve influences its current profits. The speed at which a company's markets are becoming competitive shows up as the rate of movement along the curve, or the rate of convergence, or how fast profits are eroding, and the economic time cycle in which the product operates. The capitalized value of two businesses that have similar profits can be very different, depending on their convergence and renewal cycles.

Convergence is a universal law affecting all organizations. Convergence moves managers toward the transforming idea that all advantage will be lost unless it is renewed. Once managers become comfortable with the idea that, because of convergence, advantage is temporary, they are more likely to take on responsibility for creating their future.

Alignment. When the relationship between your company and your customers is as close as it can get, your organization is capturing the full profits possible for any product's location on the convergence curve, the degree of profitability in a market. You can be in an attractive market, but if you are poorly aligned with what your customers want, you won't be profitable. High profits require both good alignment *and* products that are positioned high up on the convergence curve.

Customers often don't know what they want until a company supplies it, and begins the company-customer learning experience. Thus, long-run strategy is a commitment to the future—to create demand and to craft capabilities that change how markets work.

Through strategy you react to market needs in the short run and initiate market changes in the long run. Make this distinction in your planning processes and assign responsibilities accordingly. Remember to distinguish between those capabilities that are renewable and those that will limit growth. The ability to renew based on skills accounts for about three-quarters of success. Endowment-based capabilities may have built-in growth barriers associated with them.

Be sensitive to the half-life of your different strategies. Like new products, new strategies convey advantage until they are copied or rendered obsolete. There are several implications of this:

- A change in strategy should not be seen as a sign of failure but as a source of renewal.
- Put procedures in place to encourage your managers to develop new strategies. Don't confine their innovative abilities to new products alone.
- Be willing to spend money and take calculated risks in order to learn from your environment. The ability to do this is a valuable skill.
- Monitor the speed at which critical success factors are degrading and being replaced.
- As with capabilities, distinguish between critical success factors that are renewable and those that are not.

Forecast those success factors that are likely to assume greater importance in the future. Note how new success factors will require your organization to operate differently than it did in the past.

Renewal. Seventy percent of a typical company's value is determined, not by current events, but by what is expected to happen in the future. This is where renewal operates. Renewal, which is approximated by a company's price/earnings ratio, recapitalizes aging products and services. It keeps your organization from sliding into the black hole of competitive markets. Economic time shows the different ways that asset recapitalization can occur.

Knowing where you are in economic time can help you judge the amount of time needed to complete your renewal cycle. The speed at which a market is converging provides estimates as to whether an aging business will have sufficient time to change, or whether it can acquire new capabilities in time to renew itself.

Aligning Investors with Strategy

Investors operate by the same laws as do managers. For investors, the laws of convergence, alignment, and renewal show up through a concern for the speed and duration of cash flows. In this way, the question for investors is the same as for managers: "Where is the business in economic time?" And, "Where is the business heading in economic time?" Several techniques can align managers with investors in crafting strategy:

The idea of renewable success factors is, in keeping with the ideas of this book, that nothing lasts forever. Like products, success factors that previously were the basis for success in an industry decline to the status of necessary success factors. At this point it still may be necessary to engage in the activity, but excellence in the activity will not likely generate attractive profits. When this happens, newer success factors must arise that can be the basis of renewal. Otherwise an industry will be characterized by few opportunities for profits. Thus, part of the manager's job is to monitor the evolution of success factors in the company's various markets, with an eye toward which new activities are likely to be the basis of distinction in the future.

Investors, like managers, can look for high-energy markets, where there is a significant chance that a change will occur in how the market capitalizes profits. In a high-energy market, payoffs are especially high to those who can identify which new success drivers have the potential to most radically recapitalize the value creation process.

Options thinking encourages managers to look for projects that can open opportunities in the future, even where they may not be obvious today. Investments that expand an organization's opportunities, even when they do not yield immediate returns, can be options rich and contribute to capitalized value (the 70 percent region). Many successful efforts at renewal can be traced to managers that encourage options-rich behavior throughout their organizations.

Focusing on renewable success factors, high-energy markets, and options-rich thinking, combined with considerations of economic time, provides a powerful way to search for new sources of value on an ongoing basis, as investors do.

Managing Multiple Cycles

The proliferation of management styles in the new economy makes it clear that, in setting strategy, you should ask whether you are focusing on the most important elements of the problem. And, you must determine how the answer differs by each business unit. Mixed cycle components within the same business can reinforce or weaken a business overall.

Particularly important in a multicycle organization is the willingness to set cycle-specific productivity and quality management goals, so as to reinforce the different ways in which productivity and quality add value in each economic time cycle.

Functional synchronization may become an issue in multicycle companies. The different management styles appropriate to each cycle may or may not reinforce each other along the value chain, moving from research and development to manufacturing, and then to marketing. Where cycle time dependencies are weak, a decentralized structure allows each business the freedom to align itself to customer needs. Where cycle time dependencies are strong, the efforts of top management will be needed to resolve conflicts in style, performance measures, and incentives.

No economic time cycle appears better than another in terms of its ability to create economic value. Long economic time cycles, while they appear attractive, are not necessarily better than shorter cycle times. Fast-cycle cash flows are relatively brief, but during this time the velocity of cash flow can be high, making fast-cycle markets attractive in spite of their potential risk.

Simple cost-of-capital estimates suggest that there may be systematic differences in risk among cycles. Risk may increase for businesses operating in shifting economic time. Thus for the manager, as for the investor, economic time distinctions can sharpen the assumptions needed for capital budgeting processes. Through economic time, the manager and the investor can both focus on the alignment of management styles to the risk, timing, and magnitude of cash flows associated with different projects.

Some companies appear able to operate effectively across the cycles of economic time. In these companies one common factor is culture, a set of values that transcends cycle time styles and provides for their growth. Values such as a concern for customers, employees, and community, when effectively diffused throughout a multicycle organization, can enhance business performance anywhere in economic time.

Managing Cycle Shifts

You may find your business shifting across economic time, moving to markets where action-reaction cycles operate differently than they have in the past. Economic time can be altered through regulatory change, technological innovations, or new management practices. Shifting economic time requires that managers decide if they are ready to change their management styles, to alter their time-honored practices and procedures to accommodate the new success factors at work.

Shifts in economic time can affect the individual value chain activities of a business differently. Some stages of a value chain may be altered significantly or disappear altogether. Other value chain activities may remain unaffected. Dynamic value chain analysis is a method that highlights how much value each of the individual activities adds to an organization, and how stable value contribution is. Doing a dynamic value chain analysis as part of the strategy-crafting process can pinpoint where economic time is changing and, thus where managers should focus the bulk of their renewal efforts.

Shifts in economic time affect a number of critical success factors. These include the rate of industry evolution, the duration of product life cycles, price dynamics, the importance and sustainability of economies of scale, profit margin compression, standardization, and the importance of service. Traditional factors are also affected, such as switching costs, market structure, barriers to entry, and bargaining power.

As economic time speeds up, and isolating mechanisms weaken, some measures become less stable while others grow or decline in importance. In building an early-warning capability for shifts in economic time, managers should establish procedures that monitor changes in success factors on a regular basis.

Economic time may stop for an organization. When this happens, workout efforts can benefit from a knowledge of how value is recapitalized in economic time. Slow-cycle managers can focus their workout efforts around the degree of market ownership remaining and the salvage value of one-of-a-kind, trophy assets. Standard-cycle managers can use the urgency of workout to improve control enterprise-wide, to restore balance throughout the scale orchestra, and to infuse a new sense of commitment. Fast-cycle managers will need to move quickly, to dispose of inventory, work with distributors, and make decisions as to which products merit further development.

Innovating in Economic Time

Innovation operates according to the same renewal principles that govern other business activities. While innovation is the ability to commercialize something new, the nature of innovation, how it is managed, how much it affects other activities, and how long it lasts, will be affected by the strength of an organization's isolating mechanisms.

Fast-cycle innovations are weakly isolated, and so will attract competition quickly. Success requires the ability to ramp up production quickly, absorb information on changing opportunities, and select when to accelerate or withdraw commitment. Just as important is the ability to turn away from rapidly aging fast-cycle innovations, to take capacity off the market quickly, and to forget. The only way a fast-cycle organization can free up resources for successive rounds of innovation is to cannibalize its products. In fast-cycle organizations, innovations must be destroyed in order to preserve their benefits.

Standard-cycle innovations are more strongly isolated against imitation and obsolescence. Success depends on how well innovations are orchestrated within the four sections of the scale orchestra. Consequently, innovation is controlled, and is part of a process of carefully segmenting markets and evolving customer expectations. Innovations should not unduly surprise the customer or confuse the process of defending brand loyalty. Differentiated cost leadership requires a balance between process innovation, to reduce cost on the one hand, and product innovation to permit higher prices on the other hand.

Slow-cycle innovations should have the objective of reinforcing or extending ownership of some factor necessary for the functioning of the organization's market. Innovation based on reinforcing market ownership can aid in gaining threshold share and market tipping. Innovations should be part of a carefully staged staircase of innovations, tied backward to the source of market ownership. It is particularly important that innovations be seen by the customer as a continuous series of meaningful experiences, unbroken steps leading up from the original sources of market ownership. With distinctions based on management practices in each cycle, economic time helps to organize the styles of innovation among multicycle businesses.

Yes, but. . . ?

Is anything really new here? Or is economic time another management fad, an idea that repackages old ideas? The ideas behind economic time won the Pacific Telesis Award for new thinking in management.[1] A universal gauge of competitive diversity, based on product economic half-life, is new. A general measure of dynamic diversity, based on the assumption that nothing lasts forever, is a transforming assumption. The promise, for the first time, is effectiveness in crafting and executing strategy across a range of multispeed markets.

Where does economic time work best? The methods of economic time are most effective in complex organizations, and in organizations facing change. Where is economic time least helpful? In organizations where there is little opportunity for renewal.

Do you have to throw out traditional thinking? No. Economic time is compatible with earlier strategy ideas and methods, by virtue of its reinterpretation of standard-cycle competition. What you get is a refreshed view of traditional thinking and an expanded roadmap of what is possible outside of traditional markets.

How do we know it works? We know because we have tested it. There is logic. It allows an audit trail of what went wrong and what can go right. We have used it. It changes behavior.

Once you have been exposed to the ideas of economic time, the way you think about business opportunities may unfold in ways that you could not have imagined.

Ultimately, the ideas in this book can be reduced to one enormously powerful and transforming question: *"Where in economic time does my business operate?"*

If you can get this question right—and can execute on it effectively—then you master the processes of renewable advantage.

OVERCOMING OBSTACLES: STARTING THE PROCESS

Early on, antitrust economists saw in business strategy the use of market power, large size, collusion, and signaling. These positioning behaviors are still with us, but they are not the focus of today's economic growth. If traditional thinking were still dominant, General Motors would still have 50 percent of the U.S. automobile market instead of 30 percent. The United States would still command 50 percent of the postwar global economy instead of 20 percent. According to traditional thinking, Microsoft should never have happened. In moving toward renewal, keep these points in mind.

Belief in zero-sum, I-win-you-lose competition, prevalent in some companies, treats innovation, creativity, and organizational transformation as an aberration. Change and learning don't count for much. Companies can be studied in business schools, and then managed as "black boxes," with little organizational character. But, in economic time, the individual, evolving life force of organizations matters enormously.

In economic time, innovation, organizational adaptation, and rate of progress are central. Organizations exist for customers and customers exist for organizations. They evolve together. Then they may split apart, and may or may not come together again. Joint alignment, how each shapes what is wanted from the other, is a continually evolving, reciprocal process guided by strategy.

Managers create demand. Supply is not fixed. It operates on a shifting network of technological and social change. Where does progress gain its direction? From the voice within the human mind that sees beyond the obvious and toward what is possible.

Through economic time, your managers will know why Intel, with an 85 percent share of the microprocessor market, faces more intense competitive pressures than smaller companies with less market share; and why Netscape goes public and on the first day creates $3 billion in value, only to see its value drop by half shortly after; and also why Disney can issue hundred-year bonds, a remarkable expression of sustainable advantage in the new economy.

You can know how traditional thinking can separate strategy from investors. As in the biblical tower of Babel, you can guard against fragmented ideas that cannot communicate with each other. Business complexity has left hardworking managers with insufficient understanding at a time when decentralized global knowledge is needed. Bright, committed people suffer from a lack of purpose and direction. They feel estranged from the organization, from each other, and from their own deep-felt needs for a sense of understanding about their place in business history.

Through economic time you find the conceptual glue that holds living companies together and provides for their growth. You get a language to track the new creatures roaming around, rich with options, dynamic insights, and opportunities. You gain a better knowledge of when change is possible and when it is not.

The legacy of traditional thinking is strong and for good reason. The blueprint of the industrial age has served managers well. Thus, your charge as a manager will be to preserve the best of traditional thinking while supplementing it with a dynamic road map of the new economy.

SEVEN STEPS TO RENEWABLE LEADERSHIP

Business leaders in the new economy will operate in one fundamental way differently from their predecessors—they will condition their organizations to systematically destroy and recreate themselves. The focus will be on the ebb and flow of advantage, the ways that success can develop, the forces that cause advantage to decline, and how success can be created over again. Crafting strategy will be a process of managing flows rather than stocks, of operating in the 70 percent region, the realm of renewal.

The central concept is the transforming assumption that nothing lasts forever. Rather than assume that advantages continue unless they are upset, know that advantages perish unless they are renewed. As you take the ideas of renewal through economic time forward, keep the following points in mind.

Encourage Guided Discovery

Organizations, like people, are shaped by their histories. Your organization's history has been defined by a series of renewal pathways, or competitive corridors through which you have evolved. In the process of serving customers you have helped to create markets. Your reputation, investments, customer relationships, organizational resources, and leadership styles have given your organization a distinct shape and character, a unique competitive personality.

Your renewal opportunities are unique, unlike those of any other organization. Your history says a lot about what can and cannot be accomplished—your successes, your mistakes, your opportunities taken and opportunities forgone.

Are you considering a merger or acquisition? Consider AT&T's purchase of NCR, a decision to merge telecommunications and computers that was initially lauded by investors but later proved to be unsuccessful because of mismatches in economic time. Or remember IBM's limited success at commercializing OS/2, General Motors' profitless attempts at automation, and Apple Computer's loss of leadership in computing. Keep these lessons in mind as you move beyond the bounds of proven behavior into new territory.

Recall that for companies once deeply in trouble, like Chrysler, Intel, and Disney, renewal was a purposeful process of guided discovery. These companies progressed step by step, yet remained flexible, guided by disciplined and creative processes of self examination and experimentation, informed guesses, mistakes, course changes, and trials by error, played out day by day against a backdrop of shifting opportunities, wavering customers, and changing competitors—all operating somewhere in economic time.

Economic time will guide your discovery process. You will come to regard change as normal, based on a knowledge of where you have come from and where your realistic opportunities lie. You won't have to do it alone; economic time can help you select managers who wish to take the journey with you and identify those that don't.

As the business terrain becomes uncertain and changing, you will see that some advantages will remain stable, while others will be fleeting. Confidence in the knowledge of your renewal pathways, the opportunities that can be opened and those that will remain closed, will give you a solid basis from which to operate as you seek to bridge your past successes to what you would like to become.

Plan for Obsolescence

Obsolescence is natural to all processes. So it is with businesses. Death is necessary to clear away obsolete forms. Resources are freed up to operate at higher levels of performance. Without death, species could not evolve. Older organisms would block higher-level functioning and restrict the chances that new forms could gain acceptance. While this is accepted in science, in business the central role of obsolescence in the shaping of advantage is just emerging.

Today, leadership means seeing organizations, no matter how successful, as temporary, with a finite life. Like biology, with its laws of evolution, the reproductive cycles of organizations have predictable patterns. Some of these patterns are knowable through economic time.

But unlike biological organisms, managers can purposefully change their organizations. Leadership willfully creates new skills and new rules of the game. Altering how organizations operate in economic time is difficult and risky, but the alternative can be economic extinction. Economic time encourages adaptation, a proactive approach to change, increasing the odds that organizations can transform themselves.

The best way to sustain your advantage is to build a culture that knows that you can always lose it.

Strategize Through Alignment

Renewal pathways are like avenues or corridors along which organizations operate. Within renewal pathways, framed as cycles of economic time, organizations are closely aligned with the needs of customers. Strategy is the means by which company/customer relationships are reinforced in the short run. In the long run, strategy crafts new renewal pathways, new relationships based on new capabilities and new customers.

The role of strategy in the short run is to match the existing resources of organizations with the current needs of customers. But in the long run this orientation changes completely. Strategy goes from being reactive to being proactive, shaping new resources and new customer expectations. Your job is to create new dependencies between your organization and its customers, to overcome the dynamic gap between where you are now and where you want to be in the future. Knowing how much and how fast to stretch organizations is aided by experimentation and a knowledge of what is possible in economic time.

No organization maintains ideal market alignment all the time. But organizations go out of existence when the mismatch between what they do well and what customers are willing to pay for becomes too great or persists for a long enough time. This is why the reshaping of alignment is the central expression of leadership, marking those organizations that evolve beyond their initial success.

Emphasize Movements

Renewable leadership is centered on flow-based reasoning. The focus is cause and effect, whereby one action leads to a reaction and then to another series of actions and reactions, and so on. Motion, activity, and the rate of progress are at the center of decisions. This systems orientation does not always focus on moving faster, but instead on the interdependence of dynamic movements possible. Innovation, progress, speed, search, momentum, acceleration, deceleration, growth, and decline make up the ecology in which twenty-first-century business decisions are made.

Actions taken in the past set the stage for what can be done in the future, what is possible and what is not. Ask yourself if you are taking some action today that may foreclose or hinder your ability to make progress tomorrow. In dynamic thinking, innovations do not arise in a haphazard way. Each new innovation benefits or suffers from the history created by prior innovations. Keep in mind how your company became successful and make sure that your people do the same. Then will you know how much you really need to change and whether you can.

Layer Intelligence

Renewable advantage is aided by the nurturing of intelligence within your organization at the points where responsibility and opportunity lie. Knowledge of renewal opportunities includes the priorities facing managers, the rationale for actions taken, actions forgone, and the milestones to be surmounted. Localized and layered, dynamic intelligence aids purposeful renewal. Decentralized global knowledge is self-generating, adaptive, and self-correcting. Layering of intelligence goes beyond traditional arguments for centralization or decentralization.

Data account for the elementary details available about markets, such as product characteristics and profitability. There is little organization to data, which has limited dynamic logic. At the next level of intelligence—information—data are organized into meaningful chunks and take on competitive meaning, such as market share and the number of competitors in your market. The third level of intelligence is more like knowledge, which represents a highly refined sorting of intelligence to the high-level strategic needs of your organization: knowledge of customer needs, competitor behavior, and organizational strengths. Most high-level decisions are made based on knowledge.

The highest level of intelligence is insight, global, dynamic knowledge. Insight is focused on asset recapitalization. Insight is the kind of intelligence that moves organizations into new markets, helps chart new courses of action, and changes the way markets work. Insight is the intelligence of the entrepreneur. Economic time can help to pull insight out of intelligence.

The language of economic time has the attractive property of being deep and wide; deep in the sense of providing detail on how specific markets work, but wide in that it can compare and contrast success factors in a range of markets, and specify change between markets with a useful degree of precision. Use your knowledge of economic time to help you acquire a deep and wide intelligence capability that fosters renewal at the many points of opportunity that arise throughout your organization.

Judge by Value, Not Size

In global capital markets, the ultimate test of management is the ability to create value. Economic time is designed so that the criteria needed for setting strategy are the same as the criteria used by investors in selecting investments.

Remember that there is a natural affinity between the laws of renewal and investors' interest in the capitalization of cash flows. Through renewal, you keep your organization focused on what is expected to happen beyond the current period. This forward-oriented behavior may require adjustments at first, but this style of management can transform how you do business and create value as never before.

Demand Action and Accountability

In one case we know of, managers used traditional methods to do an analysis of their construction equipment market. Nine months of study, involving a team of consultants and senior managers, resulted in eighteen recommendations for improving the business. After unsuccessful attempts to carry the process forward, the manager in charge confessed to us that none of the recommendations was actionable. The expensive and time-consuming analysis failed to identify the renewal pathways open to the organization. The fundamental questions left unanswered were what could be done and what should not be attempted.

The insights and stories in this book may be interesting. But to us they fall short unless they change actual day-to-day and, eventually, long-run strategic behavior. This is because when and how people act is the ultimate expression of renewal. We looked up "action" in the dictionary. We found: "accomplishment, conduct, deed, delivery, execution, performance, activity, animation, liveliness, movement, motion, to-do, operation, engagement, achievement, act, doing, exploit, feat, behavior, and maneuver." These words are the stuff of renewal. Understanding how they fit together, differently in different settings, is the responsibility of economic time.

Accountability requires an "if-then" logic. If we do this, then that will happen. Economic time, because it has a holistic cause-and-effect structure, helps to pinpoint responsibility. Decisions are characterized by precision, staging, and timing; these give early warning if an organization is off course and indicate what can be done to take corrective action.

Predictability and clarity *are* possible in the new economy. The ability to specify with precision what should be done, when, and by whom, is central to the staging of commitments in the evolution of advantage. Economic time provides a compass by which to turn your managers into avid, disciplined explorers. Economic time helps to discover how to replace "what is" with "what can be."

RECAP: OK, NOW IT'S MONDAY MORNING . . .

As you think about renewal, consider whether you:

ENCOURAGE GUIDED DISCOVERY

Do your managers know how your markets operate? Do they understand where your organization came from, your history, what has made you successful? In your forward thinking, do you encourage reasoning based on a strong sense of how markets operate and what you are, balanced against a creative sense of what you can become and the new rules of the game?

PLAN FOR OBSOLESCENCE

To what extent do your managers appreciate that every successful product and process in your organization is doomed to eventual failure? Failure is not bad; it is necessary for progress. Do you have a sense of how much time you have before your new advantages will need to be in place?

STRATEGIZE THROUGH ALIGNMENT

How effectively does your strategy lay out plans to transform what you do today into what your customers will likely want in the future? How much of a gap—a dynamic gap in economic time—is apparent in your forward thinking? Are your long-range actions seeking to fill this gap, through new skills or new customers, or are you spending too much time maintaining the status quo?

EMPHASIZE MOVEMENTS

Do you understand how key success factors unfold in your markets? Which key success factors today will become merely the price of entry tomorrow? Are you taking actions today that could foreclose your ability to do something tomorrow? To what extent has your organization internalized the simple and profound truth that renewal is accomplished by moving step-by-step in new directions, through disciplined creativity, one day at a time?

LAYER INTELLIGENCE

How well have you placed the knowledge required for organizational regeneration throughout your organization? Do the people responsible for carrying out renewal have the balance of local and global knowledge required to be responsible for renewal? Do they understand how their actions support the needs of others in your organization?

JUDGE BY VALUE

How do you measure success? Do your people equate long-lived products with success? While this is understandable, the increasingly vital question is how long your relationships with your customers create value. Do your people naturally seek out new opportunities while leaving aging products and practices behind? Strive for a healthy, life-giving balance between keeping aging customer relationships alive and charting newer, options-rich commercial opportunities.

DEMAND ACTION AND ACCOUNTABILITY

Make sure your people know the difference between a good and a bad decision beforehand. If you are not sure what to do, maybe you should just do *something*. Experiment. Take some carefully considered action, informed by economic time, that helps you learn what your organization is capable of, how much you can adapt, and whether the rules of the game in your markets are changing.

You will find that a knowledge of how markets work, and the ways that organizations can renew themselves—a knowledge of economic time—will increase the willingness of your people to operate outside the box and be held accountable for their actions. The human spirit is fueled by a need to know how things work and what is possible.

"Where am I in economic time?" It's a simple question. Yet it counts for so much. God speed you on your journey.

POSTSCRIPT

Standing at the front of the room, before practicing managers and soon-to-be MBAs, I sensed that they wanted me to encourage them. What did I give them? Lists of the "dos" and "don'ts" based on static thinking. I wondered whether their exposure to me would make things worse, if they would leave still not knowing where they had been or where they were going in the great scheme of things.

In the beginning, if they wanted a vision, I gave them boundaries. If they wanted a sense of excitement, I gave them measurements. If they wanted a deep sense of purpose, a way to see their own meaningful place within the vast dynamic forces at work, I had little to say.

A colleague once pointed out to me that most sciences have an enemy, an obstacle or central goal to overcome that gives a field its purpose. In health care it is disease, in thermal engineering it is entropy. What, he asked, is the enemy in business?

The enemy is whatever suppresses the human spirit. Power-based business relationships, the machine-like treatment of the human spirit, precision at the expense of vision, and the relentless pursuit of quarter-to-quarter profits at the expense of renewal. Bottom fishing in the sea of human potential. We were put here for more.

Wealth is important. It influences so much of our experiences. But we are spiritual creatures too. Traditional practices of management can treat the human spirit like a fool, a boisterous child who must be taught how to behave.

The practice of management has evolved into a highly refined method for creating wealth. We are better off. The problem is that the economic machine requires so much of our daily energy to understand and service that there is little time left over for renewal. Individuals remain free, of course, to pursue outside activities to restore themselves, but it is more difficult to find the time now as we devote more of our energy to a powerful, fascinating, sophisticated, ubiquitous economic machine.

For many, the corporation has become the central source of self-identity, self-expression, and personal growth, a house of worship where we live out our human potential. Yet the corporate house does not have a renewal-based language, one that encourages discovery and change.

Can color, joy, energy and action, discovery and vibrancy—and dynamic accountability—be brought to the mainstream of management? Three years ago I wondered, what kind of a book can I write? The answer became this book, based on the logic of discovery, search, learning, innovation, transformation, and pathfinding. A book on renewal.

In the new economy, transforming will be more important than acquiring. It won't seem like it on a day-to-day basis, but when we look back, that is what we will remember. At the core of our history will be the unorthodox actions that people take, full of hope and worry, full of life. The process will be one of trial and error, leadership, and guided discovery. Change will be normal; lack of change, the exception.

Renewal comes about when we are joyfully productive, when we are driven from within, when we have fun and share responsibility for what we do. Innovation is the key to energizing the human spirit and the economy. We now know that 70 percent of the value of a typical company is due to expectations about future opportunities. Renewal, creating the future through economic time, offers rich ground for creative behavior, development of special skills, talents, risk taking and, hopefully, human renewal. Renewal-based managing brings the life force back into business.

Nothing lasts forever, but the journeys we take to better ourselves and our surroundings will be our legacy. When the growth of the human spirit matches productive, wealth-creating work, we "till the field" better, in ways that make the human spirit and the business machine full of life.

NOTES

Preface

1. The industries in the Renewal Database were aerospace, airlines, automotive, baseball, beer, bicycles, biotechnology, computers (mainframe, servers), computers (personal hardware), computers (software), consulting, copiers, clothing, defense, electric utilities, electronics (consumer), electronics (semiconductors), entertainment (film making), entertainment (television), farming, fashion (women's clothing), fast food, financial services, health care, hotel, infant care, information systems, insurance, internet, investment banking, mail order, motorcycles, music, package delivery, pharmaceuticals, recreation, retailing, soft drinks, software, steelmaking, telecommunications (cellular phones), telecommunications (long distance), toys, wine making, and wristwatches. For a listing of the companies in the Renewal Database contact the author at jw0f@cyrus.andrew.cmu.edu.

Chapter 1. The Advent of Economic Time

1. These questions were the subject of a conference designed to get at the fundamental issues in strategy: its scope, its limitations, and how strategy theory best can make contributions to the practice of management. See *Fundamental Issues in Strategy: A Research Agenda,* Richard P. Rumelt, Dan E. Schendel, and David J. Teece, eds., Harvard Business School Press, Boston, 1994.

2. The roots of evolutionary, ecological thinking about organizations can be found in Michael T. Hannan and John Freeman, "The Population Ecology of Organizations," *American Journal of Sociology,* 82 (1977): 929–964, and Richard R. Nelson and Sidney G. Winter, *An Evolutionary Theory of Economic Change,* Harvard University Press, Boston, 1980.

3. We became aware of the OODA loop concept in Joseph Bower and Thomas Hout's "Fast-Cycle Capability for Competitive Power," *Harvard Business Review* 66, 6 (November-December 1988), 110.

4. The idea of isolating mechanisms is explained by Richard Rumelt in his article, "Theory, Strategy, and Entrepreneurship," in *The Competitive Challenge: Strategies for Industrial Innovation and Renewal,* David J. Teece ed., Ballinger, Cambridge, MA, 1987. Richard P. Rumelt is Professor of Business Policy at INSEAD, and at UCLA he holds the Elsa and Harry Canon Chair in Business and Society at the Anderson Graduate School of Management.

5. Schumpeter's most influential works are regarded to be *The Theory of Economic Development*, Harvard University Press, Cambridge, MA, 1934, and *Cap-*

italism, Socialism, and Democracy, 3rd ed., Harper, New York, 1950. In an interpretation of creative destruction for managers, Richard D'Aveni shows how hypercompetitive companies succeed by disrupting the status quo and creating a continuous series of temporary advantages. See Richard A. D'Aveni, *Hypercompetition*, Free Press, New York, 1994.

6. For a comprehensive overview of dynamic capabilities, see D. J. Teece, G. Pisano, and A. Shuen, "Dynamic Capabilities and Strategic Management," *Strategic Management Journal* 18, 7 (August 1997), 509–534. David Teece is Mitsubishi Bank Professor at the Haas School of Business, University of California, Berkeley.

Chapter 2. The Scale Orchestrators

1. James M. Utterback, *Mastering the Dynamics of Innovation*, Harvard Business School Press, Boston, 1994.

2. The Starbucks story is told by its founder in Howard Schultz and Dori Jones Yang, *Pour Your Heart Into It: How Starbucks Built a Company One Cup at a Time*, Hyperion, New York, 1997.

3. George Stalk, Jr. and Alan M. Webber, "The Dark Side of Time," *Harvard Business Review* 71, 4 (July-August 1993), 93–102.

4. For an overview of strategic aspects of manufacturing, see Robert H. Hayes, Kim B. Clark, and Steven C. Wheelwright, *Dynamic Manufacturing: Creating the Learning Organization*, Free Press, New York, 1988.

5. David A. Aaker, "Building a Brand: The Saturn Story," *California Management Review* 36, 2 (1994), 114–133. David Aaker is the E.T. Grether Professor of Marketing and Strategy at the Haas School of Business of the University of California at Berkeley.

6. Jeffrey H. Dyer, "How Chrysler Created an American Keiretsu," *Harvard Business Review* 74 (4) (July-August 1996), 42–61.

7. Michael E. Porter, *Competitive Strategy*, Free Press, New York, 1980.

8. William K. Hall, "Survival Strategies in a Hostile Environment," *Harvard Business Review* 58, 5 (September-October 1980), 75–85, and Aneel Karnani, "Generic Competitive Strategies: An Analytic Approach," *Strategic Management Journal* 5, 4 (October-December 1984), 367–380.

9. For more on the orchestration of Southwest, Herb Kelleher style, see Kevin L. Freiberg and Jacquelyn A. Freiberg, *Nuts: Southwest Airlines' Crazy Recipe for Business and Personal Success*, Bard Press, Austin, 1996.

Chapter 3. The Children Eaters

1. We extend our enthusiastic gratitude to Clark Jordan for authoring the study of the Pulse Delay Line as an outgrowth of his experience as vice president, Hybrid Products Division, of the Pulse Engineering Company.

2. George Stalk, Jr. and Thomas M. Hout, *Competing Against Time*, Free Press, New York, 1990.

3. These and other references to the innovative management style of Intel can be found in Andrew S. Grove, *Only the Paranoid Survive*, Doubleday, New York, 1996.

4. See Robert A. Burgelman, "Fading Memories: A Process Theory of Strategic Business Exit in Dynamic Environments," *Administrative Science Quarterly* 39, 1 (March 1994), 24; and R. A. Burgelman, "Intraorganizational Ecology of Strategy Making and Organizational Adaptation: Theory and Field Research," *Organization Science* 2, 3 (August 1991), 239–262. Robert Burgelman is a professor of management and director of the Stanford Executive Program at Stanford University's Graduate School of Business.

5. Andrew S. Grove, *Only the Paranoid Survive*, Doubleday, New York, 1996, p. 88.

6. Kathleen M. Eisenhardt, "Speed and Strategic Choice: How Managers Accelerate Decision Making," *California Management Review* 32, 3 (1990), 39–54.

Chapter 4. The New Artisans

1. See Glenn Carroll, "The Specialist Strategy," in G. Carroll and D. Vogel, eds., *Strategy and Organization: A West Coast Perspective*, Pitman, Marshfield, MA, 1984, and G. R. Carroll, "Concentration and Specialization," *American Journal of Sociology* 90 (1985), 1262–1283. See also G. R. Carroll and M. T. Hannan, eds., *Organizations in Industry: Strategy, Structure and Selection*, Oxford, New York, 1995, 215–221. Glenn Carroll is the Paul J. Cortese Professor of Management at the Haas School of Business of the University of California at Berkeley.

2. Tibor Scitovsky, "The Benefits of Asymmetric Markets," *Journal of Economic Perspectives* 4, 1 (1990), 135–148.

3. See W. Brian Arthur, *Increasing Returns and Path Dependence in the Economy*, University of Michigan Press, Ann Arbor, 1994; and "Increasing Returns and the New World of Business," *Harvard Business Review* 74, 4 (July-August 1996), 100–109. Brian Arthur is a professor of economics at Stanford University and at the Santa Fe Institute in New Mexico.

4. William R. Baber and Sok-Hyon Kang, "Estimates of Economic Rates of Return for the U.S. Pharmaceutical Industry, 1976–1987," *Journal of Accounting and Public Policy* 15, 4 (1996), 327–346.

Chapter 5. The Three Laws of Renewal

1. Krishna G. Palepu, Victor L. Bernard, and Paul M. Healy, *Business Analysis and Valuation: Using Financial Statements* (Texts and Cases), South-Western Publishing Company, Cincinnati, OH, 1996, Chapter 5, 5.5.

2. Steven A. Lippman and Richard P. Rumelt, "Uncertain Imitability: An Analysis of Interfirm Differences in Efficiency Under Competition," *Bell Journal of Economics* 13, 2 (Autumn 1982), 418–438.

Chapter 6. Aligning Strategy with Investors

1. For a comprehensive guide to thinking strategically about value see Alfred Rappaport, *Creating Shareholder Value: A Guide for Managers and Investors*, Free Press, New York, 1988, revised and updated, 1998. Alfred Rappaport is the

Leonard Spacek Professor Emeritus at the J. L. Kellogg Graduate School of Management at Northwestern University and the co-founder and former Chairman of the Board of the Alcar Group Inc.

2. Richard A. Brealey and Stewart C. Myers, *Principles of Corporate Finance*, McGraw Hill, New York, 1988.

Chapter 7. Multicycle Management

1. This chapter benefited from contributions by Gezinus J. Hidding, who statistically examined 25 variables that affect decision making in economic time. See Gezinus J. Hidding, "Strategy Decision Making: A Systems Approach," Ph.D. thesis, Carnegie-Mellon University Graduate School of Industrial Administration (Information Systems), May 1992; and Gezinus J. Hidding and Jeffrey R. Williams, "Sustainability Analysis for Competitive Intelligence: Success Factors for the New Economy," *Competitive Intelligence Review* 8, 1 (Spring 1997), 33–39. Gezinus Hidding is a professor at Loyola University in Chicago.

2. Ron Winslow, "How a Breakthrough Quickly Broke Down for Johnson & Johnson," *Wall Street Journal* (September 18, 1998), 1.

Chapter 8. Managing Cycle Shifts

1. An early analysis of economic time can be found in Elizabeth E. Bailey and Jeffrey R. Williams, "Sources of Economic Rent in the Deregulated Airline Industry," *Journal of Law and Economics* 31, 10 (April 1988), 173–202.

Chapter 9. Innovation: The Origin of Renewal

1. Complementary assets and appropriability regimes are discussed in David J. Teece, "Profiting from Technological Innovation: Implications for Integration, Collaboration, Licensing, and Public Policy," in *The Competitive Challenge: Strategies for Innovation and Renewal*, D. J. Teece, ed. Ballinger, Cambridge, MA, 1987.

2. Steven R. Covey, *The Seven Habits of Highly Effective People*, Simon & Schuster, New York, 1990.

Chapter 10. Creating Your Future

1. Jeffrey R. Williams, "How Sustainable Is Your Competitive Advantage?" *California Management Review* 34, 3 (1992), 29–51.

INDEX

ABOUT THE AUTHOR

Jeffrey R. Williams is professor of strategy at Carnegie-Mellon University Business School, where he is the school's highest-rated speaker and advisor to the school's executive programs. He has published some forty studies on strategy, including works for the National Science Foundation, the Federal Trade Commission, and the Sloan Foundation. His article "How Sustainable Is Your Competitive Advantage?" won *California Management Review*'s Pacific Telesis Award for improving the practice of management. His early training was in engineering and finance, which he applies to the study of how organizations age and renew themselves. His consulting clients include IBM, AT&T, National Semiconductor, Bristol-Myers Squibb, Mellon Bank, Holiday Corporation, and Robert Bosch GmbH. This book, including the original concept of economic time, centers on the management of complexity and change. He lives in Fox Chapel, a suburb of Pittsburgh, with his wife, Rebecca, and two children.